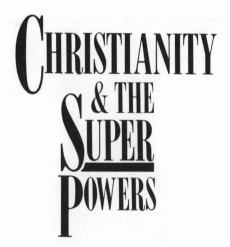

CHRISTIANITY
& THE
SUPER
POWERS

Alan Geyer

CHRISTIANITY & THE SUPER POWERS

Religion, Politics,
and History in
US-USSR Relations

ABINGDON PRESS,
Nashville, in cooperation with
THE CHURCHES CENTER FOR THEOLOGY
AND PUBLIC POLICY
Washington, D.C.

CHRISTIANITY AND THE SUPERPOWERS

Copyright © 1990 by Abingdon Press

This book is printed on acid-free paper.

Library of Congress Cataloging-in-Publication Data

Geyer, Alan F.
    Christianity and the superpowers : religion, politics, and history in US-USSR relations / Alan Geyer.
        p.   cm. — (Publications of the Churches' Center for Theology and Public Policy)
    Includes bibliographical references.
    ISBN 0-687-07694-3 (alk. paper)
    1. United States—Foreign relations—Soviet Union. 2. Soviet Union—Foreign relations—United States. 3. Christianity and international relations. I. Title. II. Series.
E183.8.S65G49   1990
947.084—dc20   89-78031
                                                                        CIP

Excerpts from *Russia and the West Under Stalin and Lenin* by George F. Kennan, © 1960, 1961 by James K. Hotchkiss, Trustee, used by permission of Little, Brown, and Company.

Excerpts from *Land of the Firebird: The Beauty of Old Russia* by Suzanne Massie, copyright © 1980 by Suzanne Massie, reprinted by permission of Simon & Schuster, Inc.

Excerpts from *The Russians and Their Church* by Nicolas Zernov, copyright © 1976, reprinted by permission of St. Vladimir's Seminary Press.

MANUFACTURED IN THE UNITED STATES OF AMERICA

To Barbara
Peacemaker Extraordinary

CONTENTS

Foreword... 9

Preface... 11

1. The Challenge of Sovietology............................ 15

2. The Russian Story..35

3. Between the Revolutions.................................61

4. Between the Wars..83

5. The Perpetual Post-War Non-Peace...................... 105

6. So Different, So Similar..................................135

7. The Largest Christian Country........................... 155

8. The Harsh Symphonia.................................... 169

9. Glasnost and the Millennium............................ 181

10. Ecumenism and the Superpowers...................... 193

A Theological Postscript....................................209

Notes.. 221

Index..233

FOREWORD

Alan Geyer's *Christianity and the Superpowers* is the first in a cooperative venture between the Churches' Center for Theology and Public Policy and Abingdon Press. Professor Geyer, the first Executive Director of the Center and now our Senior Scholar, has launched this series with style and power. The topic clearly is timely, and Dr. Geyer writes with an acute consciousness of the major changes underway in the Soviet Union. Yet, the book will remain relevant for emerging times, because it focuses on both historical interactions and the prospects for future reconciliation. When the Churches' Center offers our warmest thanks to Alan Geyer for his creative labors on our behalf, we are not muttering formalities; we are meeting a demand of justice. We are rendering to Professor Geyer a small portion of his due for a work that expresses both his commitment to the Churches' Center and his craft as a scholar.

The purpose of this series is essentially the same as the purpose of the Churches' Center itself: to interpret the implications of Christian theology and ethics for the formation and implementation of public policies, in order to strengthen the public vocation of churches and Christians. Negatively speaking, we hope to contribute through this series to the elimination of the standard disjunction between theology and advocacy. Positively, we hope to reinforce the vital linkage between theological-ethical reflection and Christian action on issues of "justice, peace, and the integrity of creation." Christian theology and ethics are the struggles to interpret the Vision which is the source of Christian identity and vitality. This Vision is also the compass for our integrity, helping to keep us on a course consistent with the Vision itself. Maintaining the connections between ultimate affirmations and public actions, therefore, is no light or optional task.

The Churches' Center for Theology and Public Policy is a national, ecumenical research center. It publishes the journal *Theology and Public Policy* and provides consultations and educational programs in the areas of peacemaking, urban policy, economic justice, poverty and hunger, racial-ethnic and women's rights, health care, and ecological integrity. The books in the Abingdon Press-Churches' Center series will focus on topics within these prime areas of concern.

An editorial committee will oversee this publishing project. Their names appear opposite the title page. Their responsibilities are to establish directions, propose authors and subjects, and evaluate future manuscripts. We are very grateful to these scholars for their commitments and cooperation.

We also would be derelict in our duties if we did not thank the academic editors and staff of Abingdon Press. They have been extravagant in their civility, cooperation, and even pastoral sensitivity. Our encounters with these virtues contribute to our sense of excitement about this series.

James A. Nash
Executive Director,
Churches' Center for Theology
and Public Policy

PREFACE

This book is indubitably an immodest attempt in one modest volume to offer a comprehensive grasp of what Americans most need to know if they would understand the Soviet Union and their relationships with that longtime "enemy" nation. While the book is aimed in some special ways at Christian readers, I hope that its approach might be instructive for others.

This is largely a work of Sovietology: a study of the peoples of the U.S.S.R., their history, culture, institutions, and policies. But it also offers some sketches of U.S. diplomatic history, cross-cultural images, ecumenical ventures, and theological perspectives. Every one of these subjects has been addressed in much greater depth and with much greater competence by other scholars. My concern as a sometime political scientist and Christian ethicist is to bring together those topics that are most crucial for ethical understanding and for policy analysis. My method is largely historical and cultural before it becomes ecclesial and theological. Yet it is impossible even to sketch Russian (or American) history in skimpiest outline without showing significant lines of religious influence. Indeed, one of the most salient truths about the superpowers is the parallelism of their religious origins and the continuing messianism of their self-images—not an altogether positive fact.

I bring to this work many years of teaching and writing about the Soviet Union, the experience of dozens of exchanges and encounters with Soviet citizens in their country and elsewhere, some unpleasant adventures at the hands of Soviet authorities, some special responsibilities in U.S.-U.S.S.R. ecumenical relations, some precious friendships with Russians, an ever-growing attraction to the treasures of Russian artistry and spirituality, and an unending commitment to political action for more peaceable relations between our two nations.

My greatest debts to particular scholars will be readily apparent in these pages—above all, to George Kennan, a personal inspiration for more than thirty years. I must also mention Trevor Beeson, John C. Bennett, James Billington, Herbert Butterfield, Stephen F. Cohen, Robert V. Daniels, Raymond Garthoff, Suzanne Massie, Reinhold Niebuhr, V. Bruce Rigdon, and Timothy (Kallistos) Ware. There are Russian friends whose contributions should not be identified with my own judgments and misjudgments herein. Many of the historical, ideological, and ecumenical issues addressed have been illuminated by my finest teacher, Walter G. Muelder, who has always nurtured the rigors of comprehensive scholarship. And I am sure that there is a very radiant place in the Communion of Saints where precious truth continues to beam forth from Nicholas Berdyaev. The diversity of vocations among these mentors testifies to the cross-professional, cross-disciplinary style a study such as this requires.

Throughout this writing, I have been made almost breathlessly aware of the daily ups and downs of the struggle for liberalization in the Soviet Union and Eastern Europe, as well as the contradictory prophecies of U.S. officials and pundits. This is either a very bad or a very good time for such a book. On the good side, there have been substantial encounters with both Soviet citizens and U.S. policy-makers in the late stages of writing—no guarantee, of course, of any permanent worth to this study.

A word about nomenclature: For the most part, I have used "Soviet" and "Russian" interchangeably, except where the specifics of ethnicity are at stake. Neither label is without sensitivities and other difficulties, whether ideological, ethnic, or religious.

I am especially grateful to those who have read the manuscript and offered suggestions for its redemption (alas, without wholly succeeding): Vladimir Berzonsky, for more than a decade my amiable bond with the realm of Russian Orthodoxy; Mark S. Burrows, Wesley Seminary's historian of early Christianity; Harold P. Ford, former head of the National Intelligence Council of the Central Intelligence Agency; Bishop James K. Mathews, ecumenical statesman and minister to the World Parish; James Nash, my successor as executive director of the Churches' Center for Theology and Public Policy; Don Nead, founder of Purdue University's Conner Center for U.S.-U.S.S.R. Reconciliation; V. Bruce Rigdon, my longtime colleague in ecumenical doings concerning the U.S.S.R.; J. Philip Wogaman, my colleague in Christian ethics at Wesley Seminary; and Barbara G. Green, my colleague in ministry in both East and West—as well as in homemaking.

Finally, I want to record my deep appreciation of the editors at Abingdon Press who, with this volume, have launched a series of works to be co-published with the Churches' Center for Theology and Public Policy. It is indeed an honor to be first up in this series that will continue to mix religion and politics—faithfully, we trust.

—Alan Geyer

CHAPTER 1

THE CHALLENGE OF SOVIETOLOGY

In both Soviet and American thinking there is a strong strain of puritanism which tends to turn opponents into enemies, enemies into devils, and devils into ugly monsters.
—Harold J. Berman
"The Devil and Soviet Russia"[1]

In a cold-war environment, everything moves on the level of a cheap western. You have a concrete enemy who is the source of all evil. You have a crystal-clear goal—to bring this enemy down. . . . You find yourself in a two-dimensional world of black and white, and quite importantly, you can describe your political platform in one minute of television prime time.
—Georgi Arbatov
The Soviet Viewpoint[2]

As Ronald Reagan's secretary of state, George Shultz usually presented a great stone face to the public. His laconic utterances were seldom graced with a smile or creased by a frown. But on January 17, 1989, addressing a diplomatic gathering in Vienna at the end of his tenure, he warmed the occasion with generous rays of sentiment. It was the closing session of a twenty-six-month-long meeting of the Conference on Security and Cooperation in Europe

15

(CSCE), following up the Helsinki Final Act of 1975. Secretary Shultz indulged in particular sentiment toward Soviet Foreign Minister Eduard Shevardnadze, recalling their first acquaintance three years before. He added:

> My wife and I decided we must get to know the Shevardnadzses as human beings, whatever our political differences might be. They must have taken the same view. We have done so, and each have met the other's children and grandchildren—in other words, our common future. This human contact is in many respects the very essence of the CSCE process.[3]

This book is written at a moment when many Americans and many Russians seem suddenly to have discovered each other as human beings and glimpsed the possibility of a common future. Some observers have even announced the end of the Cold War. This is partly because of Ronald Reagan's change of mind and rhetoric, an INF (Intermediate Nuclear Forces) Treaty, and four theatrical summit meetings with Mikhail Gorbachev. In large part, it is due to the stunning personality of Mikhail Gorbachev himself, along with his *glasnost, perestroika,* "new thinking" in foreign policy, and relentless diplomatic initiatives. And it is immeasurably due to the fact that many thousands of American Christians have gone to the Soviet Union on ecumenical exchanges during the 1980s and met many thousands of Soviet Christians, while growing numbers of Soviet citizens have come to the United States.

This very recent discovery that there are tens of millions of sisters and brothers in the Christian faith, over there in that "atheist" country that has been National Enemy Number One for over four decades, is a fact of enormous significance for U.S.-Soviet relations. The 1988 Millennium of the Russian Orthodox Church offered a unique opportunity throughout the American churches for the study of church life in the U.S.S.R., Orthodox theology and liturgy, Russian history, and the issues of war and peace between our two nations. Americans have been learning that there is no non-political way to understand the churches of the

U.S.S.R., nor is there any way to understand the Russian people without apprehending their Christian roots, nor is there any significant encounter with them that does not confront the unending burdens of war and persecution and the deep-souled passion for peace.

Two political leaders who might have been thought most unlikely to vivify this reality of brothers and sisters in the Christian faith did just that during the 1988 Millennium. On his first trip to Moscow, Ronald Reagan visited the Danilov Monastery, the new headquarters of the Russian Orthodox Church, met with both hierarchs and dissident priests, and hailed and encouraged ecumenical exchanges, which had previously been suspect to his administration and ideological allies. Mikhail Gorbachev, presumably the world's most powerful atheist, publicly boosted the Millennial celebrations, candidly acknowledged serious "mistakes" in past Soviet treatment of churches, directed the return and restoration of numerous closed churches and monasteries, announced that laws concerning religion would be rewritten and liberalized, met with the Patriarch and other church leaders to solicit their support for his moral reforms, and let it be known that his mother remains an Orthodox believer who faithfully attends liturgy back in the old home town of Privol'noye in the Stavropol region of Southern Russia. In a Paris news conference on July 5, 1989, he acknowledged: "I was baptized, I was christened. It was normal."

The Unending Perils

These hopeful developments in U.S.-U.S.S.R. relations, Soviet internal reforms, religious renewal, and ecumenical discovery gain their importance, of course, against the background of unending perils. The superpowers remain adversaries all around the globe. While Gorbachev's language of common humanity is largely purged of Marxist-Leninist pyrotechnics, the geopolitical rivalries of the superpowers continue to powerfully affect every continent and virtually every nation. The still-uncurbed arms race and numerous regional conflicts are prime obstacles to multinational cooperation on global problems of the economy, the environment, and finite resources. Above all, the apocalyptic power of these two mega-governments to destroy their own and all Earth's peoples may persist for many years.

If some diplomatic and ecumenical trends seem encouraging just now, they are still very vulnerable to political uncertainties in both countries. It is not at all clear that the Bush administration and a Democratic Congress will forge military and arms control policies that will assure a genuine détente, even if Soviet policy continues to be as forthcoming as it has been since 1986. Domestic politics within the U.S.S.R. is not only marked by efforts at reform; it is rife with powerful resistance to reform, ethnic unrest, widespread disgruntlement over a laggard consumer economy, and effusions of radical populism. The upsurge of pro-democracy movements, toppling communist regimes throughout Eastern Europe, presents an extremely difficult test of Gorbachev's leadership in both foreign policy and his party circles. Some American Sovietologists have conjectured that Gorbachev must achieve major economic and diplomatic successes very soon or seriously risk political demise. The downfall of Gorbachev might provoke a severe deterioration in U.S.-U.S.S.R. relations, especially if U.S. policy fails to grasp the opportunities offered by Gorbachev's unprecedented style of leadership. And a hardline turn in Soviet politics might burden religious life with renewed hardships.

So, hope remains balanced on the edge of precarious trends and unending troubles. The urgencies of superpower relationships remain. In many, many ways, the American public has been poorly equipped to cope with these relationships.

Enmity and Ignorance

Ignorance of another country's people, history, and institutions is typically a reflection of ethnocentric education, isolationist media, and downright indifference. Civil liberties in Uruguay, civil war in Sudan, poverty in

Indonesia, and politics in Portugal are not subjects that engage the passions of very many Americans.

Ignorance of the Soviet Union, however, is a very different matter. Most Americans have had a heavy emotional investment in their enmity with the Russians over the past four decades. Fear of "the Soviet threat" and antipathy to "godless communism" have constantly been invoked in American politics, religion, education, and even entertainment.

But fear and animosity do not necessarily motivate persons to seek a better understanding of those whom they fear and hate. For most of the Cold War years, most Americans have shared a profound ignorance of the Soviet Union and have mustered little resolve to inform and educate themselves more adequately.

The challenge of Sovietology is to overcome this widespread ignorance and the many other obstacles to mutual understanding between our two nations.

Soviet Obstacles

To be sure, there have been many obstacles on the Soviet side. The U.S.S.R. has been a largely closed society throughout both its pre- and post-revolutionary history. Not only in the Stalin years but on into the mid-1980s, Soviet media, education, arts, religion, and politics were subject to the harsh control of the state and the Communist Party. Soviet newspapers and textbooks have been loaded with crude, even absurd propaganda hostile to the United States. American news reporters on customary four-year stints in Moscow have usually been subjected to such heavy-handed treatment by Soviet authorities that their reports have understandably tended to be negative and cynical. American scholars seeking access to Soviet institutions have typically experienced severe frustrations—visa denials, closed libraries, bogus data, personal harassment. The repression and manipulation of religion have made credible study of Soviet churches particularly difficult; Western analyses of religion have therefore tended to be anecdotal and preoccupied with dissidents and martyrs.

Regime control in the U.S.S.R., however, has never been

19

complete. Soviet scholars and other elites have enjoyed access to Western scholarly and periodical works. Some scientists and church leaders have traveled widely and encountered Americans of many political persuasions. Millions of Soviet adults have been regular listeners to the BBC and the Voice of America.

The significance of *glasnost* ("openness" or "publicity") is precisely that the Soviet Union can no longer be accurately described as a closed society, even though it is far from becoming a liberal democracy. Soviet media, performing arts, and even official legislative bodies have become arenas for vigorous dissent. Official commissions are at work filling the "blank pages" of history. In 1988, student history exams had to be canceled because the textbooks needed to be rewritten. Stalin's prime purge victims like Nikolai Bukharin have been rehabilitated. American scholars and journalists now are burdened with a problem quite the opposite of their former predicament: an avalanche of data, sudden access to more events than they can attend, a multiplication of interview and exchange opportunities.

U.S. Education: Self-inflicted Ignorance

The obstacles to mutual understanding on the American side have been no less troublesome. Most of our public schools, colleges, and universities have been disinclined to accord high priorities to Soviet studies or Russian language. The now-familiar lament of those who care about foreign languages is that there are more teachers of English in the U.S.S.R. than there are students of Russian in the U.S. In an interview recently at Moscow's Institute for the Study of the U.S.A. and Canada, Director Georgi Arbatov said bluntly: "You Americans are lazy in foreign languages." Russians have to bear the heavier burdens of translation in most educational and ecumenical exchanges with Americans. From 1970 to 1985, a period during which there was a renewal of Cold War animosities in the U.S. (especially after 1976), there was actually a drastic decline in Russian studies in American universities. (There has been an upward trend since the mid-1980s.) In short, at the very time more knowledge and understanding were critically needed, including the schooling of more professionals in Soviet foreign policy, there was a diminishing supply. The ignorance of American education was thus self-inflicted.

A particularly dangerous aspect of this ignorance—and an aspect to which this volume devotes special attention—is the lack of awareness of significant chapters in the history of U.S.-Russian relations both before and after 1917. This sin of omission partakes of a more pervasive characteristic of American self-consciousness—a disinclination to take seriously the history of our own foreign relations. The result is that again and again we "innocent" Americans have found ourselves plunged into international crises with no notion that our country has had any part at all in the events provoking the crises—whether with Korea or Cambodia or Hungary or Lebanon or Iran or Angola or Cuba or Nicaragua. In such cases, ignorance is too often cloaked in self-righteousness and even in aggression and brutality.

The historical attention-span of Americans, especially with regard to other nations, is shorter than that of almost any other nation. This trait of our national character is especially exposed in our relations with the peoples of the Soviet Union. Each of the ethnic nations of the U.S.S.R. has a deeply rooted historical consciousness, a shared remembrance of glorious and bitter times, not only of living generations but also of ancient ones. So it is also with the Soviet peoples as a whole. They have a firm attachment to the icons, music, and palaces of the remote past, and they hold indelible memories of the Bolshevik Revolution; of the Civil War; of Stalin's forced industrialization and collectivization; of the purges, labor camps, and repression of religion; and of the Great Patriotic War. If much of Soviet history is overlaid with secrecy and political distortion, the profound sense of things past is not thereby displaced; it endures in the psychic depths of the people. It is also constantly on the agenda of the party, the priests, the artists, and the intellectuals. For many in the younger generation, however, the sense of history is clouded by

21

cynicism about the false chronicles of the communist years. Gorbachev's reforms are therefore accompanied by a determination to recover a morally credible sense of history.

Ignorance and Remembrance

All this is to say that historical seriousness is the first requisite for American understanding of the Soviet Union—not ideology, not economics, not penetration of the Politburo, not analysis of the military balance between the superpowers. When Americans meet Russians, Americans must be prepared for history lessons—or for historical polemics. Quite apart from understanding the treasures and burdens of Russian culture through the millennial centuries, Americans must come to know those flash-points in U.S.-Soviet relations from 1917 to date, moments of grievance and misjudgment on both sides, many of them "what-if" moments when our relations might have ameliorated instead of deteriorated. This is not to assert that there is a "moral equivalence" between the superpowers, in some arithmetical sense. Almost every effort in the 1980s by any American scholar, politician, or church body to acknowledge the possibility of some American fault at some point in the Cold War has been denounced by self-styled "neo-conservatives" as the sin of "moral equivalence." What is at stake in developing a historical seriousness about U.S.-Soviet relations is a precious sense of *moral ambiguities:* that, however they may be measured, the responsibilities for most international conflicts tend to be shared. The theological implications of that sensitivity will be sketched in our last chapter.

Most Americans do not remember, if they ever knew, that U.S. armed forces invaded Russia after the Bolshevik Revolution—but the Russians remember. Most Americans do not know that the Soviet Union, as a member of the League of Nations, was the most forceful advocate of collective resistance to Nazi aggression, but the U.S. never joined the League. Most Americans have never emotionally grasped the fact that the Soviet people bore the heaviest burdens and suffered the heaviest casualties of World War

II and that they were alone in fighting the main force of German armies in Europe for three years, but the Russians remember and still believe that the Western allies were indifferent to their fate. Most Americans have yet to learn that the Soviet government made all the major concessions in the SALT II negotiations throughout the 1970s (which is why the Joint Chiefs of Staff supported the treaty), but the prospects for treaty ratification were defeated by a lushly funded campaign of anti-Soviet untruths and distortions. When American church leaders trace their relationships with Russian churches to ecumenical exchanges in the 1950s, Russian church leaders remind them of the widespread Russian Orthodox churches in Alaska and California in the early nineteenth century and of the endurance of those churches to the present.

In all these matters, American forgetfulness (or ignorance) tends to confront Russian remembrance. The point is not to romanticize Russian virtues and to intensify American guilt: it is to plead for historical seriousness in understanding the other side of enmity.

Images and Asymmetries

Such understanding has been made even more difficult by the cultural manipulation of Russian images in American movies *(Rambo* and *Red Dawn,)* television (ABC's "Amerika" and commercials for Wendy's and Miller Lite), and innumerable spy novels (with titles like *The Red Fox, Red Omega,* and *Troika).* These stereotypical products are poor surrogates for what should be a much more plentiful American market for Soviet literature and other arts.

There is a severe asymmetry in cultural sharing. American literature is popular and plentiful in the U.S.S.R.—and not just Poe, Irving, Longfellow, Whitman, and Twain of the nineteenth century, but Ernest Hemingway, John Steinbeck, Kurt Vonnegut, James Baldwin, John Updike, Joyce Carol Oates, John Cheever, and Studs Terkel. Russian literature in U.S. educational institutions seldom gets beyond Dostoevsky and Tolstoy. The treasures of twentieth-century Russian literature, not only from the exiles but from those who have stayed and published in the U.S.S.R., often with extraordinary inspiration and courage, are just beginning to be discovered in a few American circles. A short list would surely include Mikhail Bulgakov, Yuri Trifonov, Chingiz Aitmatov, and Valentin Rasputin. The same asymmetry is to be found in films, although there is little occasion for American cultural pride in many of the popular, violent, and vulgar movie exports—not to mention TV series and rock videos. A research project undertaken by the U.S. government's International Communication Agency, based on interviews with Russian citizens, found that "Soviets have an insatiable interest in America and are disappointed because they perceive that Americans do not reciprocate."[4]

There have been serious media problems on the U.S. side: a lack of substantive Soviet expertise on the part of many reporters; preoccupation with personalities, dissidents, and anecdotes to the neglect of history, institutions, and social forces; columnists, like George Will, who sometimes seem to suppose that nothing important has really changed in the U.S.S.R. since Stalin; editorial policies of major metropolitan newspapers that seem to bend with the winds of domestic political change and to curry favor with policy elites.

In the past two decades, the decline of American self-confidence tended toward a resurgence of Cold War attitudes in the wake of military defeat in Indochina, energy and hostage crises, the collapse of the Nixon administration in the Watergate affair, congressional revelations of CIA and FBI abuses, and the fading of the American dream for millions of families whose real income declined as home ownership became more and more costly. To be sure, some aspects of Soviet behavior contributed to the deterioration of the détente of the early 1970s: the repression of dissidents, curbs on Jewish emigration, and the invasion of Afghanistan. It is very doubtful, however, that the national security of the United States was increasingly imperiled by these or other Soviet actions—yet the U.S.S.R. once again became the scapegoat for the frustrations of millions of Americans who became vulnerable to political demagoguery. George Kennan, former ambassador to Moscow and dean of Russian studies, put it this way:

> Observing, then, in the years of the late 1970s and early 1980s, the seeming inexorable advance of this hysteria of professed fear of and hostility to the Soviet Union, but finding so little objective reason for it, I could only suspect that its origins were primarily subjective; and this seemed to me to suggest something much more sinister than mere intellectual error: namely, a subconscious need on the part of a great many people for an external enemy—an enemy against whom frustrations could be vented, an enemy who could serve as a convenient target for the externalization of evil, an enemy in whose allegedly inhuman wickedness one could see the reflection of one's own exceptional virtue.[5]

Demagoguery and Diplomacy

This projection of extreme enmity—not without some basis in fact but subject to gross manipulation and fabrication—has provided an unending source of demagoguery in our domestic politics. Again and again, possible diplomatic openings in U.S.-Soviet relations have been slammed shut by storms of moral indignation in the general public, distortions of the historic record, skewed analysis of the military balance, and the most cynical interpretations of Soviet motives and intentions. The former U.S. ambassador to the Geneva-based Committee on Disarmament, James Leonard, has testified to his own frustrating experience of this perverse relationship between domestic politics and international diplomacy:

> The root of our problem in negotiating disarmament agreements is not the particular international framework or approach. . . . It's more fundamentally in our way of looking at our relations with the Soviet Union and with the world at large. It is, in particular, the extraordinary strength and resiliency of anti-Soviet sentiment in this country. . . . It has a particularly pernicious form, because it has

> become clearer and clearer to the leaders of the two
> parties . . . that the issue of our relations with the Soviet
> Union and the question of nuclear war . . . are extremely
> useful issues when it comes to running for president.[6]

Government officials themselves have frequently con-
founded public understanding and intensified anti-Soviet
animosities by falsifying history or by misrepresenting the
military balance. During the Reagan administration, National Security Council and Arms Control Agency staff
repeatedly flashed a chart on TV and in public briefings that
purported to show comparative trends in the arms race. By
focusing on the huge size and variety of Soviet land-based
missiles and highlighting the Soviet buildup of the 1970s,
while omitting the large overall U.S. lead in nuclear
weapons and the fact that the Soviet upcurve was largely a
matter of trying to catch up, the chart seemed clearly
designed to deceive the public and to justify further U.S.
escalation.

Styles of Sovietology

All these obstacles to understanding have been reinforced at the most sophisticated professional level by some
flawed styles of American scholarship in Soviet studies.
Teaching and research in Russian subjects were very
marginal priorities in higher education before World War II.
George Kennan was the very first foreign service officer to
receive special training in Russian studies—and for that he
was sent to the University of Berlin. The coming of the Cold
War roused Congress and academe to generous funding of
new programs, institutes, and research grants that would
enhance national security objectives. In the 1950s, Soviet
studies became a big business in partnership with the
foreign policy establishment. Academic integrity was
almost unavoidably compromised through that partnership. At least four widespread tendencies in Soviet studies
from that period on were quite problematical for both
education and foreign policy: (1) preoccupation with a
totalitarian model of analysis, which carried over from

studies of Nazi Germany and focused on elite personalities ("Kremlinology") while discounting institutional interests and factional politics; (2) a monolithic model of relationships among communist states (suggested by such labels as "Sino-Soviet bloc" and "Sino-Soviet studies"), which seriously underestimated the centrifugal force of nationalism and was slow to perceive the Sino-Soviet conflict and the historic antipathies between Vietnam and China; (3) a tendency toward gross exaggeration of the role of so-called "Marxist-Leninist ideology" on Soviet behavior, such as pretensions of world revolution and domination, at a time when ideological commitment and zeal were nearly exhausted; and (4) a disposition to disparage Soviet science and technology, presumed to be stultified by ideological constraints—until the shocking space orbit of *Sputnik* in 1957, after which skepticism suddenly yielded to alarmism and "agonizing reappraisals" of the Soviet threat.[7]

All these characteristics of Cold War Soviet studies— there were exceptions, of course—made for the relative neglect of history, nationalism, culture, and social analysis. In their hard abstractions, such studies tended to reinforce the dehumanization of the "enemy," which had generated such popular antipathies. Unlike many scholars in the field of Chinese studies (some from missionary families) who had lived much of their lives in China, who had acquired a deep appreciation of Chinese culture, and who had careers that would be ruined or constrained by McCarthyism, most of the new generation of Sovietologists had no first-hand experience of Russian culture and tended to discount if not despise it. This anti-Russian tendency was sharpened by the prominence of understandably embittered Eastern European emigres in Soviet studies: Poles, Czechs, and Hungarians whose homelands had come under the heavy hegemony of Stalinist Russia at the end of World War II—as well as Baltics and Ukrainians whose homelands were under Soviet sovereignty.

In short, several generations of students preparing for academic, intelligence, or foreign service careers were steeped in styles of Soviet studies that tended to warp their expertise, even while validating relentlessly belligerent attitudes toward the U.S.S.R.

Aggressive Think Tanks

As Soviet studies became less wedded to Cold War policies in the late 1960s and the 1970s, they experienced a decline in funding and enrollment. Just as serious, if not more so, was the onset of the Think Tank Revolution of the 1970s: the outflanking of university teaching and research by ideologically committed conservative institutes lavishly funded by corporations and right-wing foundations. Some of these institutes had nominal bases in universities—such as the Center for Strategic and International Studies at Georgetown University and the Hoover Institution at Stanford University—and operated on the fringes of faculty tolerance and academic integrity. However, it was the emergence of autonomous centers like the American Enterprise Institute, the Heritage Foundation, and the Committee on the Present Danger that brought to the political arena an intensely aggressive ideological style. Such institutes proved extraordinarily effective in seizing the initiative in both foreign and domestic policy. They became the vanguard of the zealous conservative revolt that captured the Republican Party, provided the Reagan administration with many of its top personnel and policy papers, repudiated détente, and revived the Cold War world view and rhetoric of the 1950s.

Of special import for the churches after the mid-1970s were several new conservative think tanks with an explicitly religious platform: the Ethics and Public Policy Center, the Institute on Religion and Democracy, the Center on Religion and Society, and the James Madison Foundation. These institutes shared the ideological orientation of the more secular ones mentioned above but have made a specialty of attacking, discrediting, and defunding the National Council of Churches (NCC), the World Council of Churches (WCC), denominational peacemaking programs, and the National Conference of Catholic Bishops. In particular, these institutes have portrayed ecumenical councils as too heavily influenced by liberation theology (which, in turn, is charged with being too heavily influenced by Marxism), too supportive of Third World revolutionary movements, too soft on Soviet communism, and too uncritical of Soviet policies on religion and human rights. Both Protestant and Catholic pronouncements are regularly charged with lacking both theological integrity and technical competence, and with making excessively specific policy prescriptions, most of which are said to be naive about Soviet or socialist evils and the realistic requirements of national security.

For the most part, these are very dubious allegations. They are especially vexing to church leaders because they are typically based on distortions and even blatant untruths. Hard-pressed denominational and ecumenical leaders tend to feel that they don't have the time and resources to cope with the endless barrage of assaults from the right wing. But such attacks seem increasingly to have come from within some denominations, as so-called lay committees and "evangelical" networks have targeted clerical and bureaucratic leadership. The Institute on Religion and Democracy has spawned front groups in several denominations (including the Presbyterian Church (U.S.A.), the United Methodist Church, and the Episcopal Church), which have intensified the hostility to progressive leadership on foreign policy issues, especially U.S.-U.S.S.R. relations, the arms race, and Central America.

The funding of these conservative para-religious think tanks has come primarily from non-church sources, especially major military contractors and conspicuously conservative foundations (such as Scaife, Smith-Richardson, John Olin, and Coors). No doubt these funders view their grantees as instruments of their corporate interests and ideologies, whatever may motivate the work of think tank staffs themselves.

The Varieties of Religious Enmity

There have long been more deeply-rooted religious antipathies toward the Soviet Union that have provided yet more obstacles to the nurturing of irenic understanding. For mainline Protestants, Wall Street lawyer John Foster Dulles—"Mr. Christian Layman," son of a Presbyterian preacher, influential in the Federal, National, and World councils of churches before becoming secretary of state in 1953—personified the ideological Cold War against "atheistic communism." The dominant political theologian of the 1940s and 1950s, Reinhold Niebuhr (once a pacifist and a socialist), was an influential advocate of nuclear deterrence and an anti-Soviet military buildup in the early years of the Cold War. Niebuhr's appeal was more to the "Christian realism" of balance of power politics than to the zealous ideological moralism represented by Secretary Dulles. Nevertheless, Niebuhr seriously exaggerated the Soviet threat, believing in "the missile gap" and in Soviet hegemony throughout much of the Third World. In the 1960s he did become an opponent of the Vietnam War. (Niebuhr's prestigious mantle was claimed by some neo-conservatives in the 1980s for a resurgent anti-Soviet crusade and a runaway arms race of which Niebuhr would hardly have approved.)

Protestant fundamentalists and other "evangelicals" have been inflamed since the 1940s by the Manichaean anti-communist preachings of Frederick C. Schwarz (founder of the Christian Anti-Communist Crusade), Billy James Hargis (the Christian Crusade), Billy Graham, Jerry Falwell, Pat Robertson, and Edmund Robb. In Graham's case, however, visits to the Soviet Union and other Eastern European countries in the past decade have greatly moderated his rhetoric. He has become a circuit-rider among Soviet Baptists, an advocate of nuclear arms reductions, and an honored guest at a Soviet-sponsored peace conference.

Edmund Robb, a leader of the "Good News" faction among conservative United Methodists and head of the Ed Robb Evangelistic Association, is also one of the founders and the board chairman of the Institute on Religion and Democracy. His 1986 book, *The Betrayal of the Church: Apostasy and Renewal in the Mainline Denominations* (coauthored with his daughter Julia Robb and published by Good News), is a direct attack upon those he calls "the Religious Left": denominational mission boards and peace-making programs, as well as Roman Catholic bureaucrats and the NCC and the WCC. "The Religious Left" is alleged to serve as "a public relations firm for the Soviet Union," thereby willing to "identify itself with totalitarians." Both Catholic and Methodist bishops are accused of selling out to "the Religious Left" in their pastoral letters on peace in which the bishops were "willing prisoners" of their staffs.[8]

For Roman Catholics, a decades-long uncompromising crusade against all forms of communism and socialism was given a firm platform by Pope Pius XI's 1937 encyclical, *Divini Redemptoris,* and was vigorously embodied in Cardinals Spellman of New York, Cody of Chicago, and McIntyre of Los Angeles. That crusade was bitterly sanctioned in the 1940s and 1950s in ethnic communities of Polish, Hungarian, and other Eastern European heritage. All these tended to make anti-Sovietism a sacred credo for Catholics. That is why Pope John XXIII's 1963 encyclical, *Pacem in Terris,* marked such a dramatic turnabout for many Catholics (including John F. Kennedy): the zealous crusade was terminated in favor of a more conciliatory approach that recognized significant changes in post-Stalinist Russia. Even so, the National Conference of Catholic Bishops as late as 1983 felt driven to toughen its pro-NATO, anti-soviet language in the final draft of its renowned pastoral letter, *The Challenge of Peace: God's Promise and Our Response,* in order to placate the more conservative bishops.

The Unification Church and allied enterprises associated with Sun Myung Moon (and heavily funded by South Korean sources) have developed multiple, increasingly sophisticated and covert strategies for infiltrating the theological, academic, publishing, and ethnic minority realms—therein to propagate severe anti-communist doc-trines.

Since the Six Day War in 1967, enmity between Israeli and Soviet governments, Soviet backing of Arab regimes, Soviet

31

curbs on Jewish institutions and emigration, and the not-yet-eradicated strains of anti-Semitism in the U.S.S.R. have been reflected in the emergence of a harsh neo-conservatism in the American Jewish community. One of the most potent sources of anti-Soviet sentiment has been *Commentary*, the journal of the American Jewish Committee edited by Norman Podhoretz who made the political transition from left to right in the 1970s. Podhoretz's journal and his omnipresence in other media have been devoted to zealous hyperboles of "the present danger" from the Soviet threat and opposition to disarmament.

The Influence of Pro-Sovietism

The main burden of this opening essay on Sovietology is to lift up the problems of understanding that stem from enmity and ignorance and that perpetuate excessive anti-Sovietism. In some earlier periods, it would have been appropriate to discuss more fully the problems created by excessive pro-Sovietism on the part of some groups. The Communist party in the U.S. has been an impotent organization since the 1940s. The romantic enthusiasm for Soviet social and economic planning that was shared by some American socialists and United Front groups in the 1930s turned to abject disillusionment after Stalin's purges and the Hitler-Stalin Pact of 1939. Some liberals who rejected the early Cold War policies of Harry Truman enlisted in the Henry Wallace Progressive campaign of 1948 and the Soviet-sponsored Stockholm Peace Appeal of 1950 and thereby became naively apologetic for Soviet policies, as did some revisionist historians in later years. In the moral and generational turmoil of the 1960s and the Vietnam war, some Americans became thoroughly alienated from their own nationhood and embraced the policies of Ho Chi Minh and/or Mao Zedong. And some earnest Christians have been rather uncritical participants in the Prague-based Christian Peace Conference that has been dominated by pro-Soviet pressures since 1968—although others have used their CPC participation for both ecumenical dialogue and candid political criticism.

None of these groups inclined toward pro-Sovietism has significantly influenced U.S. policy, public opinion, public education, or the mainline churches during the Cold War. They have all been on the outer fringes of American thought and action.

Enmity and Ambiguity

Altogether there has been a persisting pattern of mutual reinforcement among various sectors in almost all American institutions—media, entertainment, politics, academe, industry, religion—tending to perpetuate the language and the images of enmity.

It is nonetheless true that some journalists, TV and film producers, politicians, diplomats, scholars, industrialists, and religious leaders have labored long and hard to encourage a more moderate, more human, more clear-eyed view of the Soviet Union, Russian history and culture, and the shared history and interests of the superpowers. They have often done so in the face of great personal and institutional abuse. The most helpful among them have not ignored the tyranny and treachery of so much of the Russian past and even of the present. They have not thought it an easy matter to bridge the gulf between Russian and American experience. But they have helped greatly to strip away the stereotypes, to offer a balanced and properly ambiguous interpretation of the truth, to count the appalling costs of enmity, and to open up the most hopeful prospects for peacemaking. My roster of such persons will become evident in the chapters that follow.

CHAPTER 2

THE RUSSIAN STORY

The history of Russia is the story of a lonely nation. From the time of their conversion to Christianity in the tenth century until the present day, its people have lived in almost complete spiritual isolation.

—Nicolas Zernov[1]
The Russians and Their Church

It has been given to Russia to have observed with clarity, and with extraordinary sharpness and anguish to have lived through one of the most sudden turns of history, the turn which leads away from imperialism to the communist revolution. In a few days we utterly destroyed one of the most ancient, powerful, barbaric, and ferocious monarchies. . . . We have raised up the lowest strata of the toiling masses, who were oppressed by Tsarism and the bourgeoisie, to freedom and independence. We have inaugurated and strengthened the Soviet Republic, a new kind of state, immeasurably superior and more democratic than the best of the bourgeois parliamentary republics.

—V. I. Lenin[2]
"The Principal Task of Our Time"

Soviet novelist Yuri Trifonov, who died in 1981, once agreeably quoted William Faulkner in a Soviet literary journal. Faulkner, and then Trifonov, testified: "The past is never dead. It's not even past." Trifonov added: "History is not simply something that was. History is with us and in us."[3] The weight of that truth may indeed be similarly understood by American southerners (at least up to Faulkner's generation) and by Soviets of almost any nationality. Sensitive southerners have traditionally been deeply conscious of the moral and spiritual burdens of their own history.

Russians are a people whose past is never really past. The past weighs very heavily upon the present in the ineffable consciousness of belonging to Holy Mother Russia, the recollection of invasions from all directions, the enormity of remembered suffering and sacrifice, the rituals of remembrance at military monuments and cemeteries, the icons that celebrate the Communion of Saints, the firmness of an unchanging Orthodox liturgy, the intensity of cultural pride, the homage paid to poets and novelists, the continuity of rigorous traditions in the performing arts.

It is a major thesis of this book that history, especially pre-Revolutionary history, is more basic than Marxist or Leninist ideology in understanding the Soviet Union today. It is Russian-ness that counts most. Louis Halle's book, *The Cold War as History*, puts the matter sharply in accounting for the darker traits of Soviet conduct:

> The behaviour of Russia under the Communists has been Russian behaviour rather than Communist behaviour. Under the Communists Russia has continued to behave essentially as it behaved under the czars. There has been the same centralization and authoritarianism. There has been the same conspiratorial approach to international relations. There has been the same profound mistrust of the outside world. There has been the same obsession with secrecy and with espionage. There has been the same cautiousness, the same capacity for retreat. There has been the same effort to achieve security by expanding the Russian space, by constantly pushing back the menacing presence of foreigners across the Russian borders.[4]

Halle perhaps overstates the point—but the case for historical continuities is compelling.

Russian history is a vast, terribly difficult, and absolutely fascinating subject, which rightly engages legions of specialists on a huge variety of topics and periods. In the pages that follow, I can only offer some impressionistic narratives, a few diverse slices of history, and some reflections on the meaning of that heavy heritage.

A CURSORY CHRONICLE

For many centuries in the pre-Christian and the pre-Slavic years, nomads roamed the vast plains and boated the mighty rivers (the Dniester, the Dnieper, the Don, and the Volga) between the Carpathians and the Urals. Various tribes—Cimmerians, Scythians, Sarmatians, Goths, Huns—dominated those plains in successive waves of invasion and conquest. With the collapse of the brief but brutal Hun empire in the fifth century c.e. there was the great Migration of Peoples from the Balkan regions where the Huns had ruled. While new Slavic communities of Czechs, Slovaks, Poles, Serbs, Croats, Slovenes, and Bulgars were forming, other Slavs moved east and established trading towns on those great rivers in what is now the Ukraine and southern Russia. Those eastern Slavic settlements provided the precursors of Russian culture and nationhood in the heart of the Dark Ages from the sixth to the tenth centuries.

The Varangians

The political consolidation of this nascent Russia was more a Scandinavian than Slavic achievement. An invasion of Varangians (Vikings) in the ninth century, under Rurik, established a provisional capital at Novgorod (later known as "the Father of Russian Cities") and a ruling dynasty that lasted for seven hundred years. Culturally, however, these Scandinavian aliens became thoroughly assimilated and Slavicized.

Rurik's son Oleg moved the dynastic capital to Kiev in

882. Thus Kiev became the political seat of *Rus* (originally a tribal name), the seedbed of Russian identity. And Kiev became "the Mother of Russian Cities."

Excluding Novgorod, Russian history has often been abbreviated as a tale of three cities: Kiev, Moscow, and St. Petersburg-Leningrad. Kiev was the political and cultural center from the ninth to the thirteenth centuries. Moscow became the ascendant capital in the fifteenth century, to be displaced by Peter the Great's St. Petersburg in the early eighteenth century, then reclaimed as the seat of sovereignty following Lenin's revolution. After a brief name change to Petrograd (1914–1924) and Lenin's death in 1924, St. Petersburg became Leningrad.

Kievan Rus

In the tenth century, Kiev became much more than the political capital of Rus. It became the religious heart of Rus. In 988, *Prince Vladimir* adopted Eastern Christianity on the fervent counsel of his emissaries who were awed by the splendor and beauty of the Orthodox liturgy they experienced at the immense Saint Sophia Cathedral in Constantinople. It was the art and drama of the liturgy that gripped the aesthetic sensitivities of Rus and shaped the ecclesial style of Orthodox piety in Russia for a thousand years. Vladimir, who surely acted from a combination of political and marital motives, obliged his subjects to convert and be baptized in the River Dnieper—but he subsequently experienced a dramatic redemption of his own character and would become sainted. A towering figure of St. Vladimir bearing a large cross today dominates the Kievan heights above the Dnieper.

It was this baptism of Vladimir and Rus in 988 that was celebrated in 1988 as the Millennium of Russian Christianity. But it was more than an ecclesiastical anniversary for the Russian Orthodox Church. It was irresistibly the Millennium of Russian nationhood. The adoption of Christianity gave Rus a written language for its liturgy and literature, a language based on the Cyrillic alphabet developed by two Greek brothers who were missionaries to Slavic peoples in the previous (ninth) century, Saints Cyril and Methodius. This combination of unifying faith and language became the epochal political fact for the Russian people. It has been this decisive formation of Russian character and culture by deeply-rooted Christian identity and spirituality that, more than any other force, accounts for what it means to be Russian, to feel Russian, to think Russian—even in a country under atheist banners. So it was that Mikhail Gorbachev and other Soviet leaders felt compelled to hail and give practical support to the 1988 Millennium. From the very foundations of Russian nationhood, it has been impossible to separate religion from politics. Neither Orthodox theology nor political practice has warranted such a separation. In fact, Eastern Christianity proclaimed a doctrine of *symphonia* between church and state: harmony and collaboration reflecting the divine harmony of the whole Creation.

Within the present borders of the Soviet Union, however, there are much older nationalities and Christian churches than Russia and the Russian Orthodox Church. The origins and oldest surviving structures of Armenian and Georgian Christianity date back at least to the fourth and fifth centuries. (Armenian legend claims Christian roots in the first generation of the Apostles.)

Kiev became a splendid metropolis in the eleventh century—a walled city with dozens (perhaps hundreds) of beautiful churches, as well as the political, commercial, and agricultural center of Rus. Moreover, Kiev provided an early Russian window toward the West both through royal marriages with most of the ruling families of Europe and through international trade. This European consciousness of early Russia would be nearly wiped out by the ravages of Asian assault and oppression in the later Middle Ages. Vladimir's son, Yaroslav the Wise (1019–1054), whose energetic diplomacy secured those royal marriages and flourishing trade, proved to be not so wise after all, for he decreed a pattern of inheritance in which the realm was rotated and eventually divided among his sons. With the passing generations, the glories of Kiev were dissipated in family feuds among the nobility. The realm of Rus was dismembered, making it increasingly vulnerable to banditry and invasions.

Mongol Hordes and Monastic Saints

It was this shattered and weakened Rus that fell victim to Mongol (Tartar) conquest in the thirteenth century, beginning with a 300,000-man invasion in 1236 and the sack of Kiev in 1240. The onslaught was led by Batu, son of Genghis Khan, and was brutally reinforced by Tamerlane in the fourteenth century. There followed a pattern of alien, absolutist rule that lasted until 1480. These were centuries of devastation, much killing and suffering, and forced tribute to the Mongol Khans.

There were also assaults from the north and the west, some of which provided later generations with the romance of remembered glories. While Kiev was suffering its Tartar destruction in 1240, the legendary *Prince Alexander Nevsky* of Novgorod defeated Swedish invaders on the banks of the Neva River (from which he took his name). Two years later, Alexander's forces routed the Teutonic Knights on the frozen surface of Lake Peipus ("The Battle on the Ice"), thereby hurling back an imperial Germanic and Roman Catholic crusade.

These were also the centuries of Renaissance in the West, from which Russian clerics, scholars, and artists were almost totally isolated. Isolated from both the West and Mongol hegemony were the great forests of the Russian north, where a renascent church inspired the renewal of nationhood. It was a kind of liberation from exile. There in ascetic intimacy with the cold and dark of raw nature, a monastic and mystical revival slowly generated the power of a new messianism during the "silent centuries of Russian history."[5] The incarnation of this revival was the most spiritual of all Russian saints, *St. Sergius of Radonezh* (1314–1392), who in 1337 founded the Holy Trinity Monastery at Zagorsk (which in recent decades provided the seat of the patriarchate as well as the Moscow Theological Academy). By the end of the fifteenth century, 150 new monasteries had been established, most of them starting as spiritual retreats in the forests. It was Sergius who inspired the Golden Age of Iconography from the fourteenth to the sixteenth centuries, the most celebrated exemplar of which was Andrei Rublev (1370?–1430?). Sergius was both a spiritual and political mentor, remembered especially for his blessing and material aid to Prince Dmitri of Moscow who defeated the Tartars in the epic battle of Kulikovo in 1380. The first Russian victory over Mongol forces, Kulikovo did not end Mongol domination, however. It took exactly another century of gradually dissipating Mongol power before Moscow was strong enough to throw off the yoke of the East.

Russian sainthood has typically combined spiritual, political, and military virtues. Thus Sergius is venerated not only for monastic retreats but for being an inspirer of culture, a booster of Moscow's development, and even as "the Builder of Russia."

Moscow as The Third Rome

As Kievan Rus was largely undone and as Mongol control gradually faltered, Muscovy emerged to claim the seat of Russian power in the fifteenth century. While only a modest village, Moscow had built its first kremlin (fortress) as far back as the twelfth century. In the early fourteenth century, the Metropolitan See of the Russian Orthodox Church moved from Kiev to Moscow. New churches were built within the Kremlin.

It was *Ivan III (the Great),* the first duke of Moscow to call himself "tsar," who most decisively overcame the Mongols and centralized the Russian state. His reign (1462–1505) followed just after the fall of Constantinople to the Turks in 1453, which meant the effective separation of the Russian Church from Greek authority. Now Moscow began to conceive itself as "The Third Rome," the final and only true guardian of the Christian faith. Ivan claimed divine right for his own authority and added yet more cathedrals, as well as palaces and towers, to the Kremlin.

Ivan IV (the Terrible), grandson of the Great, is justly remembered as terrible for his massive terror, slaughter of innocents, and institution of serfdom during his half-century reign (1533–1584). He murdered both Metropolitan Philip and his own son and namesake; the horror of the latter murder was given a grisly and famous portrayal in Ilya Repin's bloody 1885 painting. But he was a pious murderer. The Terrible commissioned the building of Russia's most conspicuous national symbol (at least for TV newscasters), St. Basil's Cathedral in Red Square. And he began the conquest of Siberia that would be completed by his successors in the next century.

The trouble with hereditary monarchies is heredity itself; it often gives birth to poor leadership. Rurik's seven-hundred-year-long dynasty came to an inglorious end when the Terrible's last son, Feodor, proved weak and incompetent and Boris Godunov became regent. Feodor died in 1598. There followed fifteen years of peasant revolts, rival pretenders to the throne, hostilities among the nobility, and invasions by Polish and Swedish armies. Altogether a chaotic interval deservedly known ever since as the Time of Troubles.

The Romanovs

Monarchy was restored with the election of Tsar Michael in 1613, the first of the Romanov dynasty that would rule for three centuries, finally to be liquidated by the Bolsheviks in 1917. Now to a very selective history of the Romanovs and their most notable doings.

Peter the Great (1682–1725), brilliant and brutal, forced Russia to overcome its centuries of political and cultural isolation by importing Western science, engineering, and culture; by building a very Western new capital more or less named for himself, St. Petersburg, "a window on Europe"; by developing extensive world trade and a strong army and navy; by promoting industry and mining; by rationalizing the bureaucracies of government; by establishing the Academy of Sciences and many educational institutions. In 1721, Peter abolished the Patriarchate of the Russian Orthodox Church, which the Metropolitan of Moscow had claimed since 1589. Thus the Church came under the tsar's personal authority, exercised through a chief procurator. The Patriarchate would not be restored until the collapse of the monarchy in 1917.

Catherine the Great (1762–1796), a German princess who

married and then may have contrived the murder of Russia's Peter III, established French as the language of high society and built the Hermitage Palace and the Smolny Institute in St. Petersburg. Her armies seized Poland, the Ukraine, and Crimea. She gave moral support to the American Revolution—and shared her bed with dozens of lovers.

Alexander I (1801–1825) suffered Napoleon's invasion and the burning of Moscow but survived to help conceive the Holy Alliance and the century of semi-peace that lasted from the Congress of Vienna (1815) until World War I. Alexander also fought victorious trans-Caucasian wars against Persia and Turkey, in consequence of which Russian rule was extended over Georgia, Armenia, and Azerbaijan. A war against Sweden resulted in the acquisition of Finland. Somewhat more liberal in his early years than his predecessors, he promoted education, abolished the secret police, and authorized some releases from serfdom. In his later years, however, Alexander regressed toward a tighter autocracy and religious fundamentalism. That regression provoked a progressive group of aristocratic army officers to become advocates of a more democratic constitutional monarchy. Upon Alexander's sudden death in December 1825, these officers attempted a coup in St. Petersburg but were speedily put down. The leaders of that military revolt, the "Decembrists," were tried and executed by the authorities of the new tsar, Nicholas I.

Nicholas I (1825–1855) offered three decades of repressive and merciless despotism. He resurrected the secret police. He was also an aggressive interventionist against revolutions in Poland, Hungary, and Romania. That aggressiveness was disastrously pressed to vindicate claims to intervene as protector of Orthodox peoples in the Ottoman Empire, resulting in the Crimean War (1853–1856) against Turkey, Britain, and France. Nicholas died before that war ended in defeat and the forced withdrawal of Russian forces from the Black Sea area.

Notwithstanding the tyrannies and aggressions of Nicholas, the decades of his reign would be remembered as the Golden Age of Russian culture. The intelligentsia became a self-conscious class of dissidents—a galaxy of literary and philosophical stars with names like Pushkin, Lermontov, Turgenev, Dostoevsky, Gogol, and Herzen.

Alexander II (1855–1881) was clearly the most progressive of all the Romanovs. He decreed the emancipation of twenty-three million serfs in 1861, reduced censorship, reformed the courts, expanded education, and built railroads and industry. Had his successors followed his trends, the modern history of Russia might have been much less cataclysmic. But his legacy is ambiguous. His very reforms roused insatiable demands for more sweeping changes. Alexander II also completed the conquest of Islamic Central Asia. His assassination in 1881 led to new intensifications of official terror under *Alexander III* (1881–1894) and *Nicholas II* (1894–1917).

Comes the Revolution

In those last regressive years of tsarist rule, rapid industrialization was the catalyst to a rising class consciousness and political mobilization among urban workers. Neither terror nor token reforms could withstand the onrush of revolution. There was a spate of modest labor legislation in the 1880s and again in 1900 and 1903. Following a series of strikes and the "Bloody Sunday" massacre of peaceful demonstrators in St. Petersburg in 1905, Nicholas II decreed the establishment of an elective assembly, or *Duma,* which proved essentially powerless. A civil rights manifesto proved virtually meaningless. The unpopular and disastrous Russo-Japanese War of 1904–1905, the continuing strikes, the harsh suppression of new workers' councils *(Soviets),* radical terrorism that led to some assassinations, and public outrage at the bizarre influence on the royal family of a licentious mystic named Rasputin all contributed to the momentum of systemic change. But it was finally the monarchy's woeful mismanagement and millions of Russian casualties in the war of 1914–1918 that set the stage for cataclysmic revolution.

Among the conspirators in a botched assassination attempt on Tsar Alexander III in 1887 had been a young St.

Petersburg student named Alexander Ulyanov who, facing a sure sentence of execution at his trial, made this portentous statement:

> Only the terrorist is in a position to defend the right to think freely and the right to participate intellectually in the life of society. Terror . . . is the sole defensive weapon which a minority can resort to in order to demonstrate . . . the consciousness that it is fighting for justice. . . . Among the Russian people, you will always find ten men so devoted to their ideals and with such a burning sympathy for the sufferings of their country that they will not consider it a sacrifice to lay down their lives for the cause.[6]

Alexander Ulyanov was the idolized older brother of Vladimir Ilyich Ulyanov, whom the world would come to know as V. I. Lenin, leader of the October Revolution of 1917 and first ruler of the modern Soviet state. The hanging of brother Alexander, following shortly after the death of his very devout Orthodox father, perhaps helps to explain a remark Lenin made twenty years later: "I was sixteen when I gave up religion."

Lenin: The Idol of Leadership

From the age of twenty-three, Vladimir Ulyanov was a professional revolutionary. A lowly law clerk in St. Petersburg by day, he frequented Marxist study groups by night. Assuming the name Nikolai Petrovich (the first of many aliases), he conducted statistical studies of working conditions, wrote pamphlets on the role of the Russian proletariat in world revolution, and traveled all over Europe meeting other radicals and revolutionaries. His plans to establish a workers' newspaper called *Rabocheye Dyelo* (The Workers' Cause) were discovered by police; he was imprisoned for a year, then exiled to the Siberian village of Shushenskoye, north of Mongolia, for three years. It was there that he assumed the name Lenin, after the great Siberian river Lena.

In 1900 at the age of thirty, Lenin began publishing a

newspaper called *Iskra* (The Spark) as a vehicle for building up a strongly organized radical socialist party. To keep publishing *Iskra* and to evade the police, Lenin moved to Leipzig, Munich, London, and Geneva. In 1902, he published his most important revolutionary tract, *What Is to Be Done?* That work invoked Karl Marx's ideas of economic determinism and class struggle—but its *political* philosophy of elitist, conspiratorial revolution owed more to the writings of a fanatical young revolutionary of the 1870s, Sergei Nechayev, whose main legacy was a document titled *The Revolutionary Cathechism.* This divergence of the ruthless, conspiratorial Lenin from Marxist thought is much elaborated in Michael Harrington's modern classic, *Socialism*, in which the case is made for understanding the mature Marx as a person essentially committed to evolutionary, democratic social change.[7] For Lenin, Marx's early rhetoric about the "dictatorship of the proletariat" was transmuted into the dictatorship of the party over the proletariat and, ultimately, the dictatorship of a small, tight intellectual elite over the party and the proletariat. Moreover, there was nothing in the works of Marx to suggest that world revolution could successfully begin in Russia. He believed that advanced capitalist industrial development in a country like Germany would be the catalyst to socialist triumph.

The magnitude of this divergence of Lenin from Marx is the measure of how misleading it can be for Americans to accept the Soviets' own invocations of "Marxist-Leninist ideology" as if there really were such a unified, integrated body of political and economic thought. There has been an unwitting partnership between Soviet leaders who have ritually recited the canons of that purportedly coherent "Marxist-Leninist" dogma and those whose hostility to the Soviet Union is primarily based on the mistaken presumption that such an ideology is the prime determinant of Russian behavior. Here, as in so many relations among nations, animosity is peculiarly vulnerable to illusion, even to the unconscious aid of hated adversaries. As we shall note further on, there is a similar problem of ill-informed interpretation of Marx's views on religion and of Lenin's divergence from them.

In 1903, Lenin's Social-Democratic Party, meeting in Brussels and London, split into its Bolshevik (majority) and Menshevik (minority) factions as Lenin tightened his personal grip on the machinery and money of the party. During the next fourteen years, his operations moved to Paris, Cracow, Berne, and Zürich.

During all those years of exile, Lenin had no direct part in the dying days of tsarist rule. Yet he had somehow maintained and consolidated his authority among the Bolsheviks and masses of workers back in Russia. He was in Zürich in March 1917 when a Polish friend rushed into his apartment and shouted: "Haven't you heard the news? There's a revolution in Russia!" A month later, he was welcomed at the Finland Station in Petrograd by thousands of workers, soldiers, and sailors and forthwith assumed direction of the Bolshevik strategy to undermine the Provisional Government of Alexander Kerensky that had replaced the monarchy. Kerensky's relentless but disastrous prosecution of the war against Germany helped Lenin's cause. By November (October by the old Julian calendar) the Bolsheviks succeeded and Kerensky had fled.

Lenin headed the new Soviet government as Chairman of the Council of People's Commissars. On the very first day of the October Revolution, a Degree on Peace was issued, which unavailingly urged the Allies to join in negotiations to end the war. The Bolsheviks announced a policy of War Communism, which attempted central control of all production, distribution, and finance. They then sued for peace with Germany, which was secured with the Treaty of Brest-Litovsk on March 3, 1918—a treaty which cost Russia control over Poland, Lithuania, Latvia, Estonia, and Finland. But there would be no internal peace for three years. Civil war commenced in the summer of 1918. The Bolsheviks' new Red Army, organized by Leon Trotsky, was embattled by diehard monarchists, Cossacks, church leaders, ethnic minorities, Polish forces, and World War I Allies—those Allies ambiguously intervening to keep military supplies out of German hands and, perhaps, to undo the new Bolshevik regime. Early in that civil war in July 1918, the deposed Nicholas II, his wife, and four children were executed in the Asian town of Ekaterinburg (now Sverdlovsk) as pro-monarchist forces drew near. By early 1921, the Red Army had defeated its chaotic array of opponents.

In the spring of 1921, Lenin acknowledged such "poverty, ruin, and exhaustion" of the Russian economy that an expedient retreat from communist centralization was necessary—a measure of free enterprise in farming, small factories, retail trade, and foreign investment. This New Economic Policy (NEP) did much to restore the productivity and stability of the country. The Bolsheviks, having reconstituted themselves as the Communist Party in 1918, and having launched fervent propaganda for world revolution, also retreated from that expectation and agitation, thereby gaining diplomatic recognition from most European powers by 1924.

Lenin was only fifty-two when he suffered a stroke in 1922, but he managed to retain his preeminent leadership through long months of deteriorating health until his death on January 21, 1924.

While the name and person of Lenin have been idolized in the decades since his death—conspicuously in the daily throngs visiting Lenin's mausoleum in Red Square and in his omnipresent icons in buildings, parks, and other public places—it is clear that he was greatly and genuinely esteemed by his Bolshevik colleagues. He was a zealously dedicated leader who was profoundly outraged by the sufferings of workers and peasants in tsarist times. His was a charismatic personality and an eloquent voice. He was both a brilliant theorist and a practical genius in organization and administration. He maintained a modest life style and, while intellectually arrogant, showed little if any interest in self-glorification or personal rewards. Lenin had an undoubted capacity for ruthless discipline, bitter invective, and brutal expediency, but these qualities were almost always enlisted for the ends of the revolution as he saw them.

Every Soviet leader since Lenin has sought to wrap himself in the aura and rhetoric of Lenin. For many Soviet citizens in recent years (especially with the resumption of the de-Stalinization process), all Lenin's successors from Stalin to Chernenko have seemed to be unworthy of succession—thus lifting Lenin to a still higher place in national remembrance. Mikhail Gorbachev's political audacity, reformist zeal, multiple talents, and engaging personality still confront stubborn resistance, ethnic dissensus, and popular discontent, but it is possible to imagine that he may yet achieve the public distinction of being Lenin's worthiest successor. That is, if the new wave of de-Stalinization and de-Brezhnevization doesn't sweep on to become de-Gorbachevization or even de-Leninization. In 1989, some citizens of Leningrad made the sacrilegious suggestion that the name of their city should revert to Petrograd. That would surely leave the Russian Revolution without its own icons.

THANATOPSIS AND RESURRECTION

The sweeping narrative just concluded barely hints at a crimson story that courses throughout the thousand years of Russian history: the grisly procession of numberless unnatural deaths.

A ceaseless meditation on the meaning of death—a *thanatopsis*—is peculiarly and politically imperative in Sovietology. It is also one of the surest clues as to what is central in the theology and liturgy of the Russian Orthodox Church, as well as in the beliefs and prayers of Russian Protestants.

One of the core functions of any theology is to cope with the reality and meaning of death, and death's implications for life and for faith. For American Protestants preoccupied with a piety of personal guilt and salvation, there is a stunning contrast in Russian Orthodoxy's stark concentration on themes of life, death and resurrection.

For some Americans, however, death and dying have almost become faddish topics in recent years—in college courses, parish study groups, and pastors' institutes. Usually the focus is on the individual and family experience of dying and death. But a few theologians have focused on cultural, ethnic, national, and potentially global experiences of death. The Jewish Holocaust and the specter of nuclear holocaust have transformed the issues of death into the meaning, if not the meaninglessness, of human history itself.

Any encounter with Russians over issues of war and peace is bound to call forth the bitter memory of twenty million Russian deaths in World War II. That has become such a ritual act that it sometimes desensitizes those who hear it for the fifth or the tenth time. Much less familiar, however, is the enormity of unnatural death throughout the whole of Russian history. That history is cruelly loaded with invasions, civil wars, peasant rebellions, famines, assassinations, purges, and scorched earth policies.

The Mongol conquests of the thirteenth to fifteenth centuries, whatever their immediate ravages of human life, bequeathed a pattern of autocracy that made political death a commonplace in later centuries. Curiously, the Mongols were religiously tolerant: Orthodoxy became more and more the faith of the masses in those generations of political subjugation.

Ivan the Terrible, suspecting the people of Novgorod of Polish sympathies in 1570, assaulted that "Father of Russian Cities" and slaughtered sixty thousand inhabitants. The very next year, a Tartar assault on Moscow drove Ivan out, burned the city, incinerated or otherwise massacred many thousands of inhabitants, and carried off many other thousands of survivors as slaves. Eventually, Ivan returned to Moscow's Kremlin where, before he died in 1584, he boasted of deflowering a thousand virgins and murdering thousands of his own begotten children.

Within the next three years, regent Boris Godunov,

governing in place of Ivan's mentally and physically unfit son Feodor, tortured, executed, or exiled rival boyar (noble) families and publicly beheaded some of Moscow's leading merchants.

Famines early in the seventeenth century decimated millions and reduced some of the survivors to cannibalism. And that was during the utterly chaotic "Time of Troubles" when peasant wars, Polish and Swedish invasions, and the armies of rival pretenders produced uncountable carnage, and rival tsars were assassinated.

In the mid-seventeenth century, the tyrannical Patriarch Nikon imposed such trivial ritual reforms as crossing oneself with three fingers instead of two—enforced by executing or exiling dissenting clerics. Archpriest Avvakum, who led the opposition to Nikon's reforms, was burned at the stake. Thus came the *Raskol*, the rupture or schism within Orthodoxy that has persisted to this day in the unyielding fundamentalism of the Old Believers.

Peter the Great in 1698–1699 put down rebellions by roasting many rebels over slow fires and by personally involving his mighty seven-foot frame in the axing of twelve hundred others.

There were hundreds of peasant revolts against the tsars of the seventeenth to nineteenth centuries, with incalculable death tolls. The bloodiest of these was the 1773–1775 uprising against Catherine the Great led by a Don Cossack named Emelian Pugachev, who pretended to be Tsar Peter III, the murdered husband of Catherine. Pugachev promised to liberate serfs and forced laborers, and rallied over twenty thousand men for a guerrilla war that seized the cities of Saratov and Kazan, plundered landed estates, and hanged landowners. Eventually, the uprising was mercilessly crushed by Catherine's armies. The captured Pugachev was carried in a cage to Moscow where Catherine had his body dismembered. She thus may have won the double-distinction of having dispatched both her real and pretended husbands.

Three of Catherine's six successors were assassinated.

Nineteenth-century Russia has long been characterized as "autocracy tempered by assassination."

Leo Tolstoy's novel, *War and Peace*, is not all fiction. Its sanguinary portraits of the Franco-Russian War of 1812 vivify the sheer quantity of dying and death as had no previous work of history or literature. Of the Battle of Borodino, Tolstoy wrote:

> Some tens of thousands of men lay sacrificed in various postures and uniforms on the fields and meadows . . . where for hundreds of years the peasants of Boro-dino . . . had harvested their crops and grazed their cattle. . . . The grass and earth were soaked with blood. . . . Storm clouds had gathered, and a drizzling rain began to fall on the dead, on the wounded, on the panic-stricken, and exhausted, and hesitating soldiers. It seemed to say: 'Enough, enough; cease. . . . Consider. What are you doing?'
>
> To the men on both sides, alike exhausted from want of food and rest, the doubt began to come whether they should still persist in slaughtering one another . . . but . . . some unfathomable, mysterious force still led them on . . . and the cannon balls flew as swiftly and cruelly from each side and crushed human flesh, and kept up the fearful work.[8]

Tsarist pogroms of the 1880s led to the planned killing of one-third of the Jewish populations in cities like Kiev and Kirovo. Again in 1903 pogroms were promoted by Nicholas II's minister of interior, Plehve, with the announced purpose of "drowning the revolution in Jewish blood."

On Bloody Sunday, January 22, 1905, in St. Petersburg, 150,000 workers bearing icons and portraits of the tsar marched peacefully for an end to war with Japan, civil liberties, amnesty, and an eight-hour day. When the tsar's police stopped firing on the unarmed marchers, more than a thousand lay dead in the streets and thousands more were wounded. That was the spark that lit the flame of the Russian Revolution.

Not many Americans have a clear picture of the relationship of that revolution to the First World War and its aftermath. The scale of death was unprecedented in the history of warfare. At the very beginning of World War I in August 1914, the Russians suffered 170,000 casualties and surrendered nearly 100,000 soldiers in the disastrous Battle of Tannenberg. Only ten months into the war, casualties mounted to more than three million. On and up went the toll, even after the February Revolution of 1917 when the hapless Provisional Government under Kerensky launched its futile offensives that were so suicidal that the prospect of a truly democratic regime died with them.

> There is something unassimilable about the spectacle of the Russian army at war. . . . The numbers involved are too vast; a flat anonymity descends upon those endless bodies of men, and where one can comprehend the suffering of a thousand, a million is too much. They vanish like ghosts into the awful icy wastes of Poland. . . . A second million men follows the first and is swallowed up, and so the process goes mercilessly on until, in the end, one is left with . . . an enormous abstract. Too much is crowded onto this canvas, every face is lost in the mass; it is, quite simply, too inhuman and too big.[9]

That Great War was not only an international conflict for the Russian people. It also collapsed into revolution and then into savage civil war. Bruce Lincoln continues the story of blood and vengeance in *Passage Through Armageddon:*

> All across the Russian land killing raged, as brothers fought brothers, and sons fought fathers, leaving regions twice and thrice devastated. Never had the Great War seen such raw cruelty, as Reds and Whites tortured and killed each other with unmatched callousness.[10]

The Reds' new secret police, the Chehka, unleased a campaign of terror that killed fifty thousand or more civilians—while the White Terror was even less restrained, leading on one occasion to the slaughter of fifty-two railroad carloads of prisoners. Admiral Kolchak's retreat from the Red Army across Siberia with his White troops and masses of civilians in the bitter winter of 1919 led to the deaths of a million or more men, women, and children—more from starvation, disease, and cold than from military action.[11]

Civil war was immediately followed by a drought in the lower Volga area, which alone took more than five million starved lives in 1920–1921. Nikita Khrushchev's first wife died in that famine.

Altogether, in seven years of war, revolution, civil war and famine—1914–1921—perhaps more than twenty million Russians perished—maybe even more than in World War II.

Nor was there any respite in the interwar years. Stalin's forced collectivization of agriculture and liquidation of independent farmers, the kulaks, in 1929–1933 cost ten to fourteen million more lives through executions, forced migration, and starvation. That was the "Forgotten Holocaust," which was remembered fifty years later in 1984 by ten thousand Ukrainian-Americans in Washington who marched from the Washington Monument to within a block of the Soviet Embassy to commemorate the genocide of perhaps seven million or more of their people at Stalin's hands—brutalities accompanied by a fresh wave of religious persecution and executions.

When that awful work was done, Stalin launched the immeasurable purges of 1934–1938. Lenin had spent his whole revolutionary life developing and building up a political party; Stalin destroyed that party for the sake of his despotic and paranoid personal power. The purges not only annihilated most revolutionary colleagues in political and military posts but indulged in massive murders of hundreds of thousands, probably millions, who were killed on the very eve of another war that would cost twenty million more lives, and that would force Stalin to enlist the churches in the defense of Holy Mother Russia and to restore the consolations of the churches for such vast suffering. But not before a third wave of religious persecution that had closed thousands of churches and taken the lives of many more bishops and priests.

Even the twenty million deaths in the Great Patriotic War of 1941–1945 don't tell the full story of the loss of life. A heavy legacy of the war and its privations was an increase in civilian mortality and a massive net loss in potential births.

If the Battle of Stalingrad marked the military turning point of World War II and was horrendous in its casualties and physical devastation, it was perhaps the Nazi siege of Leningrad that most vividly exemplified Russian suffering and death during the war. Harrison Salisbury's account of that siege, *The 900 Days*—magnificent in its portraits of both horror and heroism—contains a chapter grimly titled "Death, Death, Death." Salisbury estimated total deaths in the city at between 1,300,000 and 1,500,000 persons. The vast majority were civilians who died from starvation, scurvy, freezing, and German bombardment. "More people had died in the Leningrad blockade than had ever died in a modern city—anywhere, anytime; more than ten times the number who died in Hiroshima."[12]

It was the first winter of the siege in 1941–1942 that witnessed the worst of the death. Salisbury gives dead flesh and bones to the statistics:

> Death stalked Leningrad at winter's end. The city was filled with corpses. They lay by the thousands on the streets, in the ice, in the snowdrifts, in the courtyards and cellars of the great apartment houses. . . . There were corpses in the gardens of the Anichkov Palace, . . . on the Fontanka and in the vaults of the Alexandrinsky Theater. There were twenty-four bodies in the Nikolsky Cathedral, awaiting delivery to a cemetery—one in a coffin, twenty-three wrapped in sheets and rags. Bodies had piled up in the hospitals. . . . In March the Leningrad Funeral Trust buried 89,968 persons. In April the total rose to 102,497. . . . No exact accounting of bodies was possible in Leningrad during the winter months, when thousands of corpses lay in the streets and were picked up like cordwood, transported to Piskarevsky, Volkov, Tatar, Bolshaya Ohta, Serafimov, and Bogolovsky cemeteries and to the large squares at Vesely Poselok (Jolly Village) and the Glinozemsky Zavod for burial in mass graves, dynamited in the frozen earth by military miners.[13]

In a thoroughly depressing epilogue, Salisbury tells the postwar story of Stalin's personal hatred of Leningrad and his paranoia toward Leningrad's political, military, and cultural leaders who had managed to survive the siege. Stalin not only caused the epic itself to be largely suppressed: he engineered another of his awful purges, which led to the extermination of perhaps two thousand or more survivors of the nine-hundred day ordeal.[14]

In sum: during the lifetime of the Soviet Union's oldest senior citizens today, perhaps sixty to seventy million of their compatriots have suffered unnatural deaths. One must keep saying "perhaps" because nobody knows the precise numbers.

I do not know what all this death means to the psyches and spirits of those we have called "enemies" for so many years. I only suspect we must take it very, very seriously and that we must deeply ponder the possibility that there is a uniquely Russian sense of the preciousness of human life on the part of many persons in that officially atheist state. Surely we have here a clue as to why, in the faith of Russian Christians, the power of the Resurrection of Jesus Christ is such a central theme. Nicolas Zernov tells the Russian story in this light:

> Every spring a Russian witnesses the resurrection of Nature. After six months of immobility and death, life comes back to the Russian land. With noise and triumph, the rivers and lakes burst the ice which has kept them imprisoned for half a year. Grass and flowers appear over-night in the fields, which for many months have been covered with a thick white mantle; the birds begin to sing; the air becomes scented; men and animals feel exhilarated and reborn. Life proves once more to be stronger than death. This yearly experience of the resurrection of Nature has a striking parallel in the history of the Russian people, for, as a nation, they, too, were weighed down, deprived of freedom, overwhelmed for two centuries by the Mongol invader. Then a spring day came; the nation burst its heavy chains and returned to life and light. And this resurrection was achieved by the spiritual force of Christian faith which was mightier than the military skill and numerical strength of the Tartars.
>
> This power of resurrection in Nature and history assumed for the Russians its full meaning in the light of Christ's victory over sin and death, and therefore Easter is celebrated

by them with a joy and splendour unequalled in any other Church. In Russia, not a few devout people only, but the nation as a body has for centuries praised and thanked God for Christ's Rising from the tomb. The service on Easter night is an experience which has no parallel in the worship of other nations. Only those who have been present at this service can realise all that the Resurrection means to the Russian people.[15]

OF RUSSIAN GRACE AND BEAUTY

A recounting of the horrors of Russian history, so crucial to humane understanding, nevertheless risks the overcoming of empathy with yet more antipathy. That is why a very positive appreciation of Russian culture is absolutely imperative to round out the human story.

Suzanne Massie's enchanting volume, *Land of the Firebird: The Beauty of Old Russia*, seriously underestimates the endurance of beauty and creativity in post-1917 Russia, notwithstanding all the harshness of Stalin and the cultural commissars and the stifling orthodoxies of "socialist-realism." The music of Prokoviev and Shostakovich; the virtuosity of Sviatislav Richter, David Oistrakh, and Mstislav Rostropovich; the persisting glories of Russian ballet; the literary treasures of Boris Pasternak, Alexander Solzhenitsyn, Andrei Voznesensky and Yevgeny Yevtushkenko (and others mentioned in the last chapter) attest to the fact that the flow of genius has hardly been shut off. The cultural thaw under *glasnost* has permitted the celebration of Marc Chagall, the resurrection of avant-garde abstractionism, the publication of Pasternak and Nabokov, the rehabilitation of artists-in-exile, the release of anti-Stalinist films like *Repentance*—and has already contributed enormously to the healing of cultural wounds.

But Massie's paean to pre-Soviet culture is too true and too powerful to pass by:

Nations, like individuals, have the right to be judged not only on their faults and failings, but also on their

57

achievements and glories. There was injustice in old Russia, as there was and is in every nation. But it was a many-textured society, characterized also by a full measure of grace and beauty. . . .

Russian culture has much to offer us. The Russians know the darker side of humanity, but they also understand the extraordinary capacity of the human soul for sacrifice and love, and they have the ability to accept both sides of man with greater equanimity than we in the West. They know how to take a long view, something we have all but forgotten in our anxious desire for immediate gratification. . . . They have approached God in a spirit of meekness; they have loved nature. They have revered poets and poetry with a passion equaled by few other peoples, and have produced a poetic literature of extraordinary richness and variety. Their knowledge of suffering and their understanding of human weakness have made their 19th-century novels probably the greatest in world literature. They . . . turned ballet into an uplifting and popular art, one that is particularly modern. Their music has stirred hearts all over the world. These manifestations of beauty which old Russia produced so brilliantly, permeated by the spiritual qualities of the Russian people, are perhaps what we most need to rediscover now, to offset the coldness and impersonality of an increasingly heartless, technological and materialistic modern world.[16]

The second half of this book is largely devoted to "the spiritual qualities of the Russian people" as they are expressed in religious life and thought. One of the most fascinating features of contemporary Soviet life, however, is the blurring of the lines between religious and non-religious persons in that supposedly atheist state. An aspect of this blurring is the profound absorption of a new generation of Soviet writers in problems of spirituality, tradition, alienation, and moral values.

Perhaps the most popular of these writers is a professed atheist, Chingiz Aitmatov from Kirghizia in Soviet Central Asia, a member not only of the Writers' Union but also of the Communist Party and the parliament (the Supreme Soviet). Aitmatov's novels are marked by the quest for a new religious faith that is sensitive to the pilgrimages of earlier generations but more truly liberating than traditional dogmas, a faith that might fill the spiritual void created by the barren materialism of a decaying Marxist-Leninist ideology. His 1986 novel, *Plakha* (The Executioner's Block), offers the story of Avdii (Obadiah) Kallistratov, an Orthodox seminary student in search of God but also of "emancipation from dogmatism." After expulsion from both church and seminary, Avdii continues his search as a religious humanist and newspaper reporter who crusades against drug addiction and alcoholism, only to be crucified by a drunken criminal gang whose leader is the image of a brutal Stalinist thug. Aitmatov's message seems to be that neither the church nor the party meets the moral and spiritual needs of the younger generation.

A modern parable for Soviet-American relations is contained in Aitmatov's earlier novel, *The Day Lasts More Than a Hundred Years*, first published in Moscow in 1980 and now available in English. There is a kind of double-story in the novel. Traditional religious and communal values collide with modern technology, but it is a science fiction sub-plot that speaks to the enmity of our two peoples. A Soviet cosmonaut and an American astronaut are sent on a joint space mission to a remote planet. They are amazed by the nobility of the people they discover there. Together they transmit from that extra-terrestrial, highly sophisticated society up there (perhaps a metaphor for God) an invitation to a peaceful intergalactic exchange. Alas, the joint Soviet-U.S. mission command rejects the offer and hermetically seals off the Earth from outside contacts. But the first report of these two space travelers, radioed back to Earth, excitedly depicts the extraordinary people they have discovered:

> Listen, listen! We are sending a trans-galaxy transmission back to Earth! . . . The people of Lesnaya Grud', we consider, are a unique race of rational beings. . . . the remarkable thing is that they do not know of states as such; they know nothing of weapons; they do not even know what war is. We do not know; perhaps in the distant past they had wars and separate states and money and all the

social factors of a similar character; but at the present time they have no conception of such institutions of force as the state and such forms of struggle as war. If we have to explain the fact of our continuous wars on Earth, will it not seem inconceivable to them? . . . They have achieved a level of collective planetary consciousness that categorically excludes war as a means of struggle. . . . It is possible that they have achieved a level of scientific development which will one day allow the humanization of time and space to become the main purpose of rational human beings, and so allow the world to evolve to a new, higher, eternal phase.[17]

CHAPTER 3

BETWEEN THE REVOLUTIONS

A more virtuous man, I believe, does not exist, . . . nor one who is more enthusiastically devoted to better the condition of mankind. . . . I am confident that Russia (while her present monarch lives) is the most cordially friendly to us of any power on earth, will go furthest to serve us, and is most worthy of conciliation.

—Thomas Jefferson[1]
Referring to Tsar Alexander I in 1807 letter to William Duane

The inconsistency and complexity of the Russian soul may be due to the fact that in Russia two streams of world history—East and West—jostle and influence one another. The Russian people is not purely European and it is not purely Asiatic. Russia is a complete section of the world—a colossal East-West.

—Nicholas Berdyaev[2]
The Russian Idea

Once upon a time there was a great invasion of North America from Siberia. There were no Americans there to shout, "The Russians are coming! The Russians are coming!" For those who invaded became in fact the first Native Americans. To be sure, they weren't called "Native Americans" or "Indians," nor had they ever been called

"Russians" either. That's because they came about thirty thousand years ago.

In seeking the sources of superpower conflict in the twentieth century, it becomes evident that neither rivalry nor harmony well describes U.S.-Russian relations in past centuries. The connections were mostly episodic, even anecdotal, during the eighteenth and nineteenth centuries. There were a few moments of diplomatic tension, and there were moments of political convergence. There were more comedies than tragedies. Occasionally, there were outpourings of sentimental rhetoric and even poetry that purported to celebrate a friendship that never really had deep roots. Russia was, above all, preoccupied with its ancient enemies and allies in Europe and Asia and viewed the United States as a possible adjunct to such preoccupations. The United States was preoccupied with its internal development in extraordinary isolation from most Old World conflicts—although there were moments of intense engagement with Britain, France, and Spain. There was little reason in either Russia or America to anticipate a global rivalry in which the fate of the whole Earth would be at stake.

Yet there remains a rather fascinating, if hardly fateful, record of U.S.-Russian relations before 1917 that sheds some light on more recent events—not least because Russians typically are more likely to recall that history than are Americans. What is especially striking is the discovery that in almost every major U.S. foreign policy dating from the American Revolution of 1776 to the Russian Revolution of 1917, there is at least a peripheral element of Russian-American engagement—the American Revolution itself, the War of 1812, the Monroe Doctrine, the American Civil War, the acquisition of Alaska, the Spanish-American War, the Open Door policy in China, the settlement of the Russo-Japanese War, the Great War of 1914–1918. All these chapters in American history included some Russian-American connection, however trivial or inconsequential.

The Russians Came

There was a second invasion of North America from Siberia in the 1700s, this one indeed by Russians. The domain of the tsars having extended to easternmost Siberia in the seventeenth century, there was a Russian migration across the Bering Strait to Alaska in the eighteenth century. The Russians came—explorers, traders, trappers, settlers, Orthodox missionaries. There were marriages with native American descendants of those earlier migrants from thirty thousand years before. Russified villages spread across the Alaskan landscape. A Russian-American company was formed and established a trading monopoly of Alaskan products. The Russian drive continued down the Pacific coast to regions later known as the states of Washington, Oregon, and California as new settlements and trading posts penetrated an area already in dispute between Britain and the United States. The southernmost Russian establishment was Fort Ross, on Bodega Bay just north of San Francisco.

The Monroe Doctrine of 1823 was not only concerned with the removal of Spanish and Portuguese imperialism from Latin America and with British, French, and Dutch intervention in the hemisphere: it was also partly aimed at Russian intrusion. In fact, it was in the context of discussing American relations with Russia that President Monroe set forth the cardinal principle of his doctrine: "the American continents, by the free and independent condition which they have assumed and maintain, are henceforth not to be considered as subject for future colonization by any European power." When the Russian minister in Washington proposed to Tsar Alexander I that the Russian government protest the Monroe Doctrine, the tsar declined—with lofty disdain:

> The document in question enunciates views and pretensions so exaggerated, it establishes principles so contrary to the rights of the European powers, that it merits only the most profound contempt. His Majesty therefore invites you

to preserve the passive attitude which you have deemed proper to adopt, and to continue the silence which you have imposed upon yourself.[3]

What might have been a serious conflict was quickly forestalled by a treaty in 1824 under which the Russian government agreed to withdraw its posts and settlements northwestward to Alaska. Before long the Russians even began to contemplate their withdrawal from Alaska.

Apocalyptic Visions

Throughout the nineteenth century there were few if any signs that either the Russian or United States government felt seriously threatened by the other. But a wise and famous French observer, Alexis de Tocqueville, ended the first volume of his 1832 classic, *Democracy in America*, with these astonishingly prophetic words:

> There are at the present time two great nations in the world, which started from different points, but seem to tend towards the same end: . . . the Russians and the Americans. Both of them have grown up unnoticed; and while the attention of mankind was directed elsewhere, they have suddenly placed themselves in the front rank among the nations, and the world learned their existence and their greatness at almost the same time. . . . Their starting-point is different and their courses are not the same; yet each of them seems marked out by the will of Heaven to sway the destinies of half the globe.[4]

A more fearful, even sinister forecast came a few years later from a fervent Maryland abolitionist (later a member of Congress), Henry Winter Davis. His 1837 book, *The War of Ormuzd and Ahriman in the Nineteenth Century*, prophesied a coming great conflict that threatened the survival of America, thereby anticipating the apocalyptic anti-Sovietism of the early Cold War more than a century later. Davis wrote of Russia: "Her interest, her ambition, her hate, the principles of her Czar, the proud hope of taming Europe to the yoke of absolute power, all combine to impel her into active hostility against this republic. . . . She only waits the auspicious solution of the European problem to seize the first invitation of internal discord or foreign embarrassment, to begin the plot that is to end with our ruin."[5]   Now for a word about the title of that book. In ancient Zoroastrian theology (as all readers of this book will surely know), *Ormuzd* represents the good spirits and *Ahriman* the evil spirits, with both engaged in cosmic struggle. For Henry Winter Davis in 1837, Russia was the incarnation of *Ahriman* and therefore an evil empire.

Diplomatic Beginnings

These dark forebodings of the 1830s would seem to have found little diplomatic or military evidence to warrant them. Soviet publicists in the 1980s, determined to soften the hardline "evil empire" attitudes of some influential Americans, recalled with considerable hyperbole that Tsarina Catherine the Great had given moral support to the U.S. Revolutionary War.[6] Indeed there was a Russo-American affinity of sorts—but certainly not based upon a common enthusiasm for revolution or democratic constitutions. Rather, its essentially negative basis was mutual hostility to the British Empire. For Catherine and her predecessors and successors, British sea power imposed the most serious barriers to Russian imperialism. Perhaps an independent American empire could develop a navy powerful enough to divert the British and help promote Russian ambitions. As it happened, early American empire-building was much more continental than maritime.

A cordial correspondence between President Thomas Jefferson and Tsar Alexander I followed the tsar's 1804 intercession through Turkey to seek release of the crew of the American ship *Philadelphia*, imprisoned in Tripoli after the ship had run aground. Jefferson's letter of appreciation to Alexander began, "Great and good friend." It continued, "What has not your country to hope from a career which has begun from such auspicious developments!"[7] This and subsequent letters apparently prepared the way for official

Russian recognition of the U.S. in 1809, whereupon John Quincy Adams was dispatched to St. Petersburg as the first U.S. ambassador. While Adams gained the esteem of Russian authorities and the diplomatic corps, and was conspicuously sympathetic to the Russian cause in the face of Napoleon's onslaught in 1812, his later and higher responsibilities would place him in a somewhat more adversarial role.

The War of 1812–1814, a folly for both American and British interests, proved to be inimical to Russian interests. Both Moscow and Washington were torched during that war. With Napoleon and his huge multinational army having just captured Moscow, Tsar Alexander I in September 1812 sought to enlist more British assistance against France. To that end, he offered to mediate the conflict between the U.S. and Britain. That overture was warmly welcomed by President James Madison who was commanding a very unpopular war. Britain, however, declined to permit Russia to interfere in its "internal" affairs in America. Nevertheless, in order to placate the tsar and to keep New World conflicts out of Old World politics, the British Foreign Office proposed direct peace negotiations with the U.S. It was not until August 1814 that peace talks actually got under way in Ghent, Belgium (the very month the British invaded Washington and burned the Capitol and the White House), with John Quincy Adams in charge of the U.S. delegation. A peace treaty was signed on Christmas Eve. The tsar's initiative perhaps merits some credit for helping to end the war.

As Secretary of State under President Monroe in 1819, Adams was approached by the Russian minister in Washington with the startling proposal that the U.S. join the Holy Alliance of European powers that Tsar Alexander had piously formed in 1815: a covenant in which European sovereigns pledged to be guided in all their policies by "the duties which the Divine Saviour has taught to mankind." Many years later in his memoirs, Adams published the text of his dispatch to the U.S. minister in St. Petersburg indicating the reasons for refusing to join Europe:

For the repose of Europe as well as of America, the European and American political systems should be kept as separate and distinct from each other as possible. If the United States as members of the Holy Alliance could acquire the right to ask the influence of its most powerful members in their controversies with other states (as suggested by Alexander), the other members must be entitled in return to ask the influence of the United States for themselves or against their opponents. In the deliberations of the League they . . . must occasionally appeal to principles which might not harmonize with those of any European member of the bond. This consideration alone would be decisive for declining a participation in that league, . . . although [President Monroe] trusts that no occasion will present itself rendering it necessary to make that determination known by an explicit refusal.[8]

So the United States gently but firmly declined the invitation to join Europe and become Russia's ally. Both the invitation and the declination provide special ironies in view of Soviet efforts in recent years to keep the U.S. out of Europe and U.S. resolve to stay in.

It was also Secretary of State John Quincy Adams who was responsible for that portion of the Monroe Doctrine that aimed to remove Russian influence from North America. After Tsar Alexander issued an imperial edict in 1821 forbidding non-Russian vessels to approach within 100 miles of the coast of Russian America (Alaska), Secretary Adams delivered a sharp warning to the Russian minister in Washington: "I told him specially that we should contest the right of Russia to *any* territorial establishment on this continent, and that we should assume distinctly the principle that the American continents are no longer subjects for *any* new European colonial establishments."[9] That language reappeared, virtually verbatim, in President Monroe's Doctrine just four months later.

Global Domination?

Whatever the credibility of forecasts by Tocqueville and Henry Winter Davis in the 1830s, the expansionist policies of the United States in the 1840s and 1850s under cover of the Monroe Doctrine provoked bitter comparisons with tsarist imperialism from some Latin Americans. A Chilean writer named Bilbao in the late 1850s declared:

> Look at the empires which pretend to resuscitate the old idea of the domination of the globe, Russia and the United States. The first is very far away; the second is very near; Russia is limiting her warlike operations [after defeat in the Crimean War]; the United States are extending theirs every day. . . . We have already seen fragments of America fall into the clutches of the Anglo-Saxon boa constrictor, and involved in its coils; yesterday Texas, after that northern Mexico and the Pacific salute a new lover; today the advance guard of guerrillas scour the isthmus, and we see Panama, that future Constantinople of America, hang in suspense, view its destiny in the abyss, and ask 'Will there be a south, will there be a north?'[10]

That Latin protest was a painful anticipation not only of contemporary U.S. troubles in Central America but of much Third World sentiment, which today pronounces a "plague on both your houses" judgment on Soviet and American militarism and interventionism.

The Crimean War

Russia was marginally implicated in U.S. anti-British sentiment and policies in the 1850s and 1860s, specifically with regard to the Crimean War and the U.S. Civil War. The British declaration of war on Russia in 1854 received very little sympathy from Americans, especially not from burgeoning Irish communities in eastern cities that had become bulwarks of the Democratic Party, then led by President Franklin Pierce. Three hundred Kentucky riflemen sent word to the Russian minister in Washington that they were prepared to go to Crimea and fight against England. When the British tried to recruit American volunteers to compensate for their own troop shortages, there arose the strange specter of Americans fighting Americans on Russian territory—but that didn't happen.

When the British Foreign Office proved unresponsive to U.S. protests against this recruitment activity, President Pierce in 1856 dismissed John Crampton, the British minister in Washington, along with three consuls. Britain's wrath was constrained by the dependence of its textile industry on imports of Southern cotton. The controversy faded as the Crimean War ended.[11]

"God Bless the Russians!"

It was the vital economic connection between Britain and the American South that may help explain one of the most extraordinary episodes in the whole history of U.S.-Russian relations. The boundary between fact and fancy in that episode was problematical at the time, and it remains so. In 1863, as the Civil War ground on cruelly and indecisively, Russian fleets were welcomed to the harbors of New York and San Francisco. War also seemed imminent between Russia and Britain (perhaps allied with France). Because of England's supposed sympathy for (and implicit threat to intervene for) the Confederacy, the Russian fleets were enthusiastically greeted as evidence of Russian support for the Union and as a deterrent to British and French intervention. Secretary of the Navy Gideon Welles bespoke popular Union sentiment in crying "God bless the Russians!" Perhaps the Russians had mixed motives, but there was certainly a Russian interest in keeping Tsar Alexander II's ships from being bottled up in the Baltic Sea by the British navy. Helping the Union cause may not have been the primary motive after all. At any rate, Russian sailors were feted at dinners and parties and were transported on special trains to Boston, Philadelphia, and Baltimore. Ippolit Tchaikovsky, naval officer and brother of composer Peter, recalled: "Every Yankee thought it his duty to stop us in the street, raising his right hand and calling it Russia, then his left, calling it America, then noisily clapping both hands above his head and shaking them to illustrate the strength of our union."[12]

A recent issue of *Soviet Life* offers an entirely benign interpretation of the whole affair. Recalling that President

Lincoln had addressed an appeal for aid to the Russian Chancellor, Prince Alexander Gorchakov, the Soviet magazine reports this reply from Gorchakov to Lincoln:

> When your country was just born, Russians stood at her cradle like guardian angels at the time of George Washington, your first President. We do not want America divided into a Union and a Confederacy: Only the United States of America will satisfy us.

The report acknowledges that Russian ships did not actually engage British or French fleets in battle. In truth, the threat of intervention was past and the tsar's navy was old and obsolete. There was, however, a happy sequel. At the end of the Civil War in the summer of 1865, several U.S. ships sailed through the Baltic Sea to St. Petersburg, purportedly to express gratitude for Russian aid. Their crews were royally received by brass bands and banquets and taken on tours of several Russian cities. They were invited to the residence of Moscow's Governor-General where (according to this colorful account) "they were met by imposing gentlemen in red coats and powdered wigs. The Americans bowed again and again, not realizing that the gentlemen were actually the doormen." *Soviet Life*'s concluding generalization is to claim proudly that "Russia came to America's aid in the critical moments of the latter's history."[13]

Whatever the unembellished truth in that Civil War episode, the current interest of Soviet propagandists in praising tsarist diplomacy toward the United States as proof of long-lasting friendship seems evidence of Soviet seriousness about renewing détente. It certainly reflects the relaxation of ideology in foreign policy. (True, the Soviet writers obviously couldn't resist a bit of comical condescension in their account.)

In the immediate post-Civil War years, there were repeated expressions of amicability on both sides. In 1866 poet Oliver Wendell Holmes penned this verse in his "America to Russia":

> Though watery deserts hold apart
> The worlds of East and West,
> Still beats the selfsame human heart
> In each proud Nation's breast.[14]

Also in 1866 Tsar Alexander II cheerfully declared that the Russian and American peoples "have no injuries to remember." When Grand Duke Alexis visited the U.S. in 1871, poet Holmes was at it again with lyrics for the nation's public schoolchildren to sing—"Welcome to the Grand Duke Alexis!" sung to the familiar tune of the Russian national hymn:

> Bleak are our shores with the blasts of December,
> Fettered and chill is the rivulet's flow;
> Throbbing and warm are the hearts that remember
> Who was our friend when the world was our foe.[15]

The Grand Duke was indeed warmly greeted by large crowds. But the highlight of his trip may have been a buffalo shoot in Nebraska.

The Selling of Russian America

For a brief time in the last third of the nineteenth century, Russian-American friendship enjoyed considerable popular enthusiasm in the U.S. It was a relationship that seemed to have fresh moral sanctions on both sides, for Alexander II had emancipated the serfs in 1861 and Lincoln the slaves in 1863. Russian monarchy seemed increasingly enlightened and progressive.

This aura of friendship, the persistence of mutual antipathy to Britain, the imperialist drive of Manifest Destiny, and the imminent bankruptcy of the Russian American Company all contributed to the U.S. acquisition of Alaska in 1867. But there were also fervent anti-expansionist sentiments and congressional resistance to be overcome. Russia was clearly anxious to sell. The tsar's ministers wished to shorten the lines of their military commitments: Sitka was 10,000 miles from St. Petersburg. Alaska was just not proving profitable—the fur supply seemed exhausted, and the mineral resources had yet to be exploited. Subsidizing the Russian American Company in an indefensible arctic wasteland seemed increasingly like a very bad idea. The challenge was to keep Alaska out of British hands and persuade the United States to buy it.

Baron Edouard de Stoeckl, Russian minister in Washington, had no difficulty persuading Secretary of State William Seward, a fervent expansionist, that Alaska should be bought for $7.2 million. Having obtained Tsar Alexander's consent for the sale, Stoeckl stopped by Seward's house on a March evening and proposed that the treaty be drafted at the State Department on the morrow. Seward couldn't wait: "Why wait until tomorrow, Mr. Stoeckl? Let us make the treaty tonight!"

"But your department is closed. You have no clerks, and my secretaries are scattered about the town."

"Never mind that," urged Seward. "If you can muster your legation together, before midnight you will find me awaiting you at the Department, which will be open and ready for business."

Having gathered their aroused staffs, the American secretary of state and the Russian minister toiled through the night and, at four o'clock on the morning of March 30, 1867, they concluded their draft treaty and signed it.[16] Not all Russo-American agreements would be so happily or speedily concluded in later generations.

Seward's enthusiasm and impatience were not fully shared by Congress and the press. The treaty was called "Seward's Folly." Alaska was disparaged as "Polario," "Frigidia," and "Walrussia." It took a nationwide "educational" campaign by Seward, along with Russian bribes of some well-selected Congressmen (reported by Stoeckl to St. Petersburg as "secret expenses"), to secure Senate consent to the treaty and House appropriations to buy Russian America.[17] Not many years would pass before Alaskan gold, fish, and furs would make "Seward's Folly" a very profitable investment. Neither Russian diplomats nor

American politicians in 1867 viewed the sale in geopolitical terms—but its consequences for superpower relations in the next century would seem very large indeed.

An ethnic and ecumenical legacy of Russian America today is the endurance of seventy widely scattered Russian churches in Alaska, now belonging to the Orthodox Church in America and served by a bishop in Sitka, along with a seminary in Kodiak. The breakdown of traditional culture in those parishes is a source of much pastoral sensitivity and public concern.

In that special heritage of Russian America, it is particularly notable, and ecumenically symbolic, that Patriarch Tikhon, in whom the Russian Orthodox Patriarchate was restored in 1917 after two centuries of its abolition by Peter the Great in 1721, had previously served in 1898–1907 as bishop of North America and the Aleutian Islands. Orthodox congregations in the United States sometimes sing the hymn to Saint Herman, of Russian origin, whose missionary labors helped establish the Orthodox Church in North America:

> O Blessed Father Herman of Alaska,
> North Star of Christ's Holy Church,
> You planted the cross firmly in America.
> The light of your holy life and great deeds
> Guides those who follow the Orthodox way.[18]

Imperial Rivalry

The purchase of Alaska and the Aleutians presaged the ascendancy of the United States as an imperial power in the Pacific and East Asia in the last decade of the nineteenth century. U.S. conquest of the Philippines in the Spanish-American War and a more assertive diplomacy vis-a-vis both China and Japan naturally enough occasioned responses from Russia, then as now an ambitious Asian and Pacific power. Russia indicated it was "friendly" toward U.S. acquisition of the Philippines as more desirable than their seizure by any European power, which might have provoked a more militant response. President William McKinley held parallel views (in addition to his purported enthusiasm for Protestant evangelistic opportunities). He apparently feared that U.S. withdrawal from the Philippines could cause such a scramble among the imperialistic Europeans that a world war might result.[19] (Decades later, the Philippines and U.S. forces there would become involved in a world war in 1941–1945. In yet two more decades the Philippines would become a major base for U.S. intervention in Vietnam, confronting the Soviet Union in a bitter, protracted proxy war, a war which not only resulted in U.S. defeat but left the U.S.S.R. in possession of new military bases in Southeast Asia. In 1989, Mikhail Gorbachev offered to withdraw from the U.S.-constructed naval base at Cam Ranh Bay in Vietnam if the U.S. withdrew from its naval base at Subic Bay in the Philippines.)

It was a collision between the U.S. "Open Door" policy and Russian expansionism in China in the late 1890s that provoked the most serious diplomatic conflict between the two growing world powers prior to 1917. Zealously promoted by Secretary of State John Hay in 1899–1900, the two basic "Open Door" principles were: (1) respect for Chinese integrity and independence against imperial "spheres of influence" and dismemberment; and (2) equal commercial opportunity in a Chinese free market. This was a particularly vivid example of the moral dualism that has so often characterized American diplomacy: moralistic exhortation to other nations mixed with material self-interest. In this case, the mingled enthusiasms of missionaries and businessmen urged the government to take firm action against Russian, German, and French pressures, which threatened the partition of a politically weakened China and thereby also threatened American and British opportunities in China.

The Open Door policy proved ineffective, not only because it lacked any means of enforcement, but also because Secretary Hay made fatuous claims about its approval by the various imperial powers. Russia was particularly evasive and, in fact, continued to oppose the policy.

As the imperialists' exploitation continued unchecked, violent antiforeign passions mounted among the Chinese. In June 1900, an uprising fomented by a secret society known to Westerners as "Boxers" launched a campaign to expel the "foreign devils." More than 200 Christian missionaries and their family members were killed, many by swords and spears. Foreign legations in Peking were besieged under a reign of terror. An international rescue expedition of 20,000 troops (including 2,500 Americans), commanded by a German general, lifted the siege after nine weeks—and also plundered the city. Theodore Roosevelt justified U.S. intervention as necessary "to secure for our merchants, farmers, and wage-workers the benefits of the open market."[20]

The Russian government was not entirely displeased by this turn of events, citing the Chinese uprising as a warrant for further intervention. When Russians were attacked by Boxers in Manchuria, the Russian minister of war exulted: "This will give us an excuse for seizing Manchuria."[21] Within three months, Russian forces had gained control over the whole of Manchurian territory. That development caused Secretary Hay to press Russia to pledge that American business would not be discriminated against in Manchuria.

Peacemaking, Face-saving, and Face-losing

It was this Russian domination of Manchuria, as well as its perceived threat to Korea, that led Japan to seek negotiations with Russia to sort out their spheres of influence in Northeast Asia. When the negotiations broke down, Japan attacked the Russian fleet in the southern Manchurian harbor of Port Arthur (now Lushun) and the Russo-Japanese War was on. Largely because of Russia's blatant disregard of the Open Door policy, Americans tended to support the Japanese. They seemed to back the winner as Japan inflicted a series of humiliating defeats on Tsar Nicholas II's forces. But the war virtually bankrupted both belligerents. Japan finally requested President Theodore Roosevelt to take the initiative in seeking the tsar's consent to negotiations. Nicholas, burdened not only with financial woes but also with the political upheavals of the 1905 revolution, readily agreed to negotiate. Roosevelt thereupon met with Russian and Japanese diplomats at Portsmouth, New Hampshire, and secured a treaty under which Russia withdrew from Korea and Southern Manchuria and surrendered half of Sakhalin Island to Japan. Japan, however, had initially demanded the whole of Sakhalin and a large monetary indemnity, rousing the Japanese public to expect these prizes as the rewards of military victory. Roosevelt persuaded the Japanese representatives to compromise by dropping these demands.

The acceptance of Roosevelt's terms for the Treaty of Portsmouth won the president the gratitude of Russia for the face-saving settlement, and a Nobel Prize in 1906. For many Japanese, however, the settlement seemed a humiliating loss of face. There were anti-American riots in Japan, which were answered by an upsurge of anti-Japanese sentiment in the United States. A reciprocal animosity thus arose that continued through World War II.

So, both the Open Door policy and the Russo-Japanese War, which marked America's debut in the high imperial politics of Europeans-in-Asia, and which greatly intensified U.S.-Russian diplomacy, proved to be something less than totally auspicious for American interests.

The Tsar and the Hague

Nicholas II had accompanied his militaristic adventurism at the end of the nineteenth century with a fervent, apocalyptic advocacy of disarmament, a feat of moral dualism not too difficult for many political leaders to have managed in subsequent generations. His purported passion for disarmament was apparently roused by his familiarity with (if not his reading of) a seven-volume analysis of modern warfare (in 1897) by one of his own subjects, Ivan S. Bloch, a Polish banker and a Jew: *The Future of War, in Its Technical, Political and Economic Relations*. Bloch wrote, "The very development that has taken place in the mechanism of war has rendered war an impracticable operation." He was concerned with much more than physical destruction. He believed that the technology of modern warfare (already a century ago) would produce political, economic, and social destruction beyond recovery. He accurately foretold the futile character of the First World War:

> At first there will be increased slaughter—increased slaughter on so terrible a scale that it will be impossible to get troops to push the battle to a decisive issue. . . . Certainly, everybody will be entrenched in the next war. . . . The first thing every man will have to do will be to dig a hole in the ground. Battles will last for days, and at the end it is very doubtful whether any decisive victory can be gained.

Bloch concluded: "War, therefore, has become impossible except at the price of suicide."[22]

Tsar Nicholas was reportedly so moved by Bloch's gloomy analysis that he issued an imperial rescript on August 24, 1898, summoning the whole world to its first general disarmament conference. His rescript emphasized the self-defeating nature of military technology and urged "an end to these incessant armaments," which "though today regarded as the last word of science, are destined tomorrow to lose all value in consequence of some fresh discovery." Nicholas also lamented the economic costs of "this massing of war material": already a "crushing burden, which the peoples have more and more difficulty in bearing."[23] (Ninety years later, in his book *Perestroika: New Thinking for Our Country and the World*, Mikhail Gorbachev pointedly asked whether the West wants "to overstrain the Soviet Union economically by accelerating the arms race," while noting that U.S. arms spending is the prime cause of the federal debt that "will have to be repaid by many generations of Americans." He added: "We are saying openly for all to hear: we need lasting peace in order to concentrate on the development of our society and to cope with the tasks of improving the life of the Soviet people.")[24]

The World Disarmament Conference did meet in the Hague May through July of 1899. At first, the McKinley administration indicated a reluctance to participate. However, a growing peace movement—anti-imperialistic, pro-disarmament, fervent for arbitration—succeeded in persuading the government to send a delegation. The official U.S. posture at the Hague was that disarmament was basically a European matter. Nevertheless, U.S. and Russian officials sat down together for the first time to discuss the issues of disarmament, an exercise that has sporadically engaged them for nearly a century.

No significant measures of disarmament resulted from either the 1899 conference or its sequel in 1907, also called by Tsar Nicholas II. There were resolutions and declarations designed to "humanize" the conduct of warfare, which moved Mr. Dooley (the fictional creation of Chicago editor Finley Peter Dunne) to remark that the 1907 conferees discussed "th' larger question iv how future wars shud be conducted in th' best inthrests iv peace."[25] A positive result of the first Hague Conference was the establishment of a Permanent Court of Arbitration in the Hague, for which Andrew Carnegie built the Peace Palace that now houses the World Court. An American capitalist thus produced the most visible and enduring memento of the world's first disarmament conference, a conference summoned by a Russian emperor.

The Great Migration

Perhaps more than any foreign policy issue, it was the domestic policies of the last two tsars that most influenced U.S.-Russian relations in the years from 1881 to 1917. Those policies resulted in a veritable mass invasion of the United States by more than three million Russian subjects in that period. (Unlike the invasion of thirty thousand years ago, or the settlement of Russian America in the eighteenth century, both of which involved crossings of the Bering Sea to Alaska, this invasion was mostly by trans-Atlantic steamship.) Political repression and anti-Jewish pogroms within the Russian Empire (which then included Poland,

Finland, and Lithuania), especially after the accession of Alexander III in 1881, spurred the Great Migration, which peaked just before the outbreak of World War I. In 1913 alone, nearly 300,000 emigrants from the realm of Nicholas II came to America. Polish and Lithuanian Catholics, Finnish Lutherans, and Jews from Poland, Lithuania, Byelorussia, and the Ukraine constituted most of these refugees. It was not until the Bolshevik Revolution of 1917, with its atheism and religious persecution, that large numbers of Russian Orthodox emigrants fled their homeland.[26]

The Great Migration unquestionably had significant impact on public attitudes, political movements, and government leaders in the U.S. There was increasing outrage against tsarist repression, thereby predisposing many Americans toward a positive view of a possible Russian revolution. There was also an infusion of radicalism into the body politic from dissenting exiles (including some hardened revolutionaries) and thousands of emigre socialists, especially Jews who settled in Eastern cities, organized trade unions that became adjuncts to both Democratic and Socialist parties, founded journals of social philosophy, and taught in the burgeoning social science departments of urban universities. Some had been, or became, communists. Some communist celebrities like Leon Trotsky and Nikolai Bukharin had settled in New York, only to return to Russia after the outbreak of revolution.[27] Like Lenin from Zürich, they were to join in making the October Revolution a return of exiles.

Response to Revolution

When the February Revolution of 1917 deposed the last of the tsars, few Americans retained any sentiments of friendship for the Romanov dynasty. Those bonds had never really been strong and steady for most Americans anyway. Most of the time between the revolutions of 1776 and 1917, Russia had been a power on the remote periphery of the nation's consciousness. It was largely the decadence and brutality of the last years of tsarist rule that made many

Americans sympathetic to the first stages of the Russian Revolution. President Woodrow Wilson voiced such sympathy in his very first public comment on the Revolution. It came in a passage in his April 2, 1917 address to Congress asking for a declaration of war against Germany. It was Woodrow Wilson in all of his most romantic idealism:

> Does not every American feel that assurance has been added to our hope for the future peace of the world by the wonderful and heartening things that have been happening within the last few weeks in Russia? Russia was known by those who knew it best to have been always in fact democratic at heart, in all the vital habits of her thought, in all the intimate relationships of her people that spoke her natural instinct, their habitual attitude towards life. The autocracy that crowned the summit of her political structure, long as it had stood and terrible as was the reality of its power, was not in fact Russian in origin, character, or purpose; and now it has been shaken off and the great, generous Russian people have been added in all their naive majesty and might to the forces that are fighting for freedom in the world, for justice, and for peace. Here is a fit partner for a league of honour.[28]

Remember that Wilson was referring to the February (actually the March) Revolution and the forced abdication of Nicholas II.

On the very first day of Lenin's October Revolution seven months later, the all-Russian Congress of Soviets in its very first official act issued its Decree on Peace. That decree called for an immediate armistice and for the Allies to renounce any territorial gains and to free all their imperial colonies (which they were hardly eager to do). George Kennan, commenting on these developments in his magisterial book *Russia and the West Under Lenin and Stalin*, wrote, "I hold the first World War to have been *the* great catastrophe of Western civilization in the present century. I think it an endless pity that it did not cease in November 1917, when the Bolsheviki called for its termination." While the ideological cast of the Decree on Peace was clearly unacceptable to the Western Allies, their leadership failed "to see the strategy and futility of the war itself and to bring the struggle to an end . . . on a basis of compromise."[29]

There is no way of knowing how subsequent history might have unfolded if such a compromise peace had been sought in 1917. The belligerents had stumbled without purpose or direction into that war in 1914. They kept on stumbling pointlessly throughout 1917 and 1918. The last year of that horrible war of attrition, that suicidal and "impracticable operation" foreseen by Ivan Bloch, then the ill-advised and incoherent Allied military intervention in Russia, the growing estrangement between Soviet leaders and the Western democracies, and the unjust follies of the Treaty of Versailles thus became prime causes of the emergence of totalitarian regimes and of another and even more devastating world war within a very short generation. And prime causes, too, of a subsequent Cold War that would last for a very long generation.

The beginning of moral wisdom in world politics is to learn how to assess the burdens of history. That is an exercise for which too many Americans have a trained incapacity. In the primordial resources of Jewish-Christian faith, however, there are lessons and powers and graces for that task.

CHAPTER 4

BETWEEN THE WARS

Let us not repeat the mistake of believing that either good or evil is total. Let us beware, in future, of wholly condemning an entire people and wholly exculpating others. Let us remember that the great moral issues, on which civilization is going to stand or fall, cut across all military and ideological borders, across peoples, classes, and regimes—across, in fact, the make-up of the individual himself. No other people, as a whole, is entirely our enemy. No people at all—not even ourselves—is entirely our friend.

—George Kennan[1]
Russia and the West Under Lenin and Stalin

The complete victory of the socialist system in all spheres of the national economy is now a fact. This means that exploitation of man by man is abolished—liquidated—while the socialist ownership of the implements and means of production is established as the unshakable basis of our Soviet society. . . . The Constitution of the U.S.S.R. is the only thoroughly democratic constitution in the world.

—Joseph V. Stalin[2]
Speech on the 1936 Constitution to the
Extraordinary Eighth Congress of Soviets, November 24, 1936

It may surely be doubted whether any epochal event anytime, anywhere has ever been engulfed in more complex and confusing events than the Bolshevik Revolution during its very first years. The Bolshevik leadership itself was fragmented on many issues, even while facing bitter opposition from various factions not only of the old monarchist regime but also of the moderate, displaced Provisional Government of Alexander Kerensky. Having come to power in the midst of the Great War that still raged mercilessly, the new Soviet government conducted on-and-off negotiations with both Germany and the Western Allies seeking at least temporary advantages from both, but eventually leading to the Treaty of Brest-Litovsk. That treaty was soon followed by the eruption of the Russian Civil War and by invasions of Russian territory by British, French, American, and Japanese forces, some of which remained embattled with the new Red Army many months beyond the Armistice of November 11, 1918. While the Paris Peace Conference in the winter and spring of 1919 was fractured by disputes among the Allies, the Russian Civil War continued and a new socialist government was formed in Germany—only to be immediately threatened by a pro-communist uprising by the Spartacus League whose leaders Karl Liebknecht and Rosa Luxemburg were murdered by reactionary vigilantes. A short-lived Bavarian Soviet Republic was engineered then put down, and a Hungarian communist coup was crushed by Romanian forces. In the very same season, the Bolsheviks created the Communist International (Comintern) to promote world revolution by propaganda and subversion, and a great Red Scare swept through England, France, and the United States, making diplomacy even more difficult and severely curbing civil liberties in the democracies. In 1920, the Soviets were at war with Poland. In 1921, the terrible drought-induced famine claimed millions of lives.

Whether the genius of Lenin and Trotsky, or the disarray of their many antagonists, better accounts for Bolshevik survival into the 1920s is a question this modest volume cannot answer.

Civil War and U.S. Intervention

The Russian Civil War of 1918–1921 saw many-sided domestic confusion compounded by stunning international events. Political scientist Frederick L. Schuman said of it: "No magic of political or social science can reveal with any precision what factors played what roles in determining the outcome of any such disorderly combat as raged over Russia between 1918 and 1921."[3]

The first serious strain in U.S.-Soviet relations after the Bolshevik Revolution, particularly as Russians remember it, was occasioned by American military action within Russia in 1918–1919 during the Civil War. United States forces intervened in two regions: northern European Russia and eastern Siberia.

Both the motives for, and circumstances of, intervention remain disputable among historians and between Soviet and U.S. accounts. The Soviets have repeatedly portrayed the U.S. role as part of a multinational imperialist conspiracy to destroy their government in its infancy. A typical Soviet account, published in *Pravda* at a time of sharp Cold War antipathies in 1957, offered this bitter, ideologically loaded description of the intervention:

> [The imperialists] saw in the victory of the Socialist Revolution a threat to their own parasitical existence, to their profits and their capital, to all their privileges. In the effort to throttle the young republic of the Soviets, the imperialists, led by the leading circles of England, the U.S.A., and France, organized military campaigns against our country. From all sides—from north and south, east and west—the attacking hordes of interventionists and White Guards poured onto our territory. . . . For over three years the Soviet Republic was obliged to fight off the mad armed attack of the combined forces of the imperialist beasts of prey and the internal revolution.[4]

That version remains a grievance that some Russians continue to repeat in conversations with Americans, though not always with the purple prose of that account.

There were various purposes at work in the intervention

by Allied forces. As Russia sued for peace with Germany, Britain and France were particularly determined to sustain Russian military resistance on the Eastern front so that the full weight of German forces would not shift to the Western front. There was Allied suspicion that the Bolsheviks were really tools of the Kaiser, especially after Lenin was permitted to travel through Germany on a sealed train en route from Zürich to St. Petersburg in the spring of 1917. The Allies had also dispatched massive military supplies to the Provisional Government in the summer and fall of 1917 and were understandably anxious that those supplies not fall into German hands, or be seized by Soviet forces and thereby lost to the Allied war effort. Before the Revolution, a British naval force had been based in the far Russian north at Murmansk to help protect supply lines in view of the German navy's blockade of both the Baltic Sea and the Dardanelles. After the Treaty of Brest-Litovsk, Britain sent six hundred soldiers and two hundred marines to bolster its presence in the north.

Beyond these shared Allied concerns, French Premier Georges Clemenceau and British War Minister Winston Churchill (joined by some British officers and doubtless many others in the West) harbored hopes that intervention, in combination with the White Army under Admiral Kolchak, might indeed lead to the collapse of the Bolsheviks. Moreover, British and French funds were given to a variety of anti-Soviet groups in Russia after the Civil War broke out in May 1918.

The initial British request to President Woodrow Wilson was to send American troops solely for the purpose of protecting Allied war materiel. Wilson arranged to reinforce the British garrison at Murmansk with 150 U.S. marines in June 1918, joined by a French battalion in July. Also in July, however, the Allied War Council upped its appeals to Wilson as German forces drove toward Paris. An additional consideration for Wilson was the apparent opportunity offered by two crack divisions of the Czech Legion that had defected from the Austrian army, been captured by the

Provisional Government, released, and were now prepared to fight for the Allies if they could get safe conduct across Siberia to Vladivostok, then sail around to the Western front. There was also a vast store of 600,000 tons of military supplies in Vladivostok.

Wilson replied that he rejected intervention as a matter of principle and was opposed to fighting the Bolsheviks, not wanting to "add to the present sad confusion in Russia." But he nevertheless judged that the limited purposes of safeguarding munitions and helping the Czech Legion would somehow not constitute intervention, so he announced: "The Government of the United States is glad to contribute the small force at its disposal for that purpose."[5] In August, seventy-five hundred Americans landed at Vladivostok. In September, three U.S. battalions arrived in the port of Archangel. And so it was that American forces became implicated in the Allied intervention, somehow without "intervening." Wilsonian idealism got coopted by other governments to help legitimize their more opportunistic aims.

In the meantime, however, the Czech Legion had actually begun fighting against the Red Army instead of against the Germans and had joined the White Army in a drive on Moscow. The Japanese had landed a major force of seventy-two thousand troops in Vladivostok. Japan had extra motives: revenge for the Portsmouth terms of 1905, economic domination of Eastern Siberia, and displacement of Russian influence in Manchuria. It wasn't until 1922 that the Japanese reluctantly withdrew the last of Allied troops from the Soviet Union.

The Armistice November 11, 1918 terminated the wartime pretexts, if not anti-Soviet designs, for intervention. But Allied forces (including those of the U.S.) remained for many months without clear directives, pending postwar settlements in Paris. Early in 1919, Britain even sent additional munitions and advisers to the White Army—and the U.S. extended to Admiral Kolchak the war loans previously granted to Kerensky and also sent more arms to the White Army in Siberia.

As the dubious legitimacy of intervention became more and more intolerable to Soviet authorities, direct military conflict for U.S. forces became more and more probable. American troops in the Archangel region were at last attacked by the Red Army at Shenkursk on January 25, 1919, when the temperature was 30 degrees below zero. In that battle, the following precipitous retreat, and other actions in the area, U.S. forces suffered 244 dead and 305 wounded. There had also been a mutiny in the 339th U.S. Infantry, "since nobody knew what he was fighting for in the frigid wastes of North Russia."[6] Wilson finally withdrew American troops from North Russia in July, 1919, eight months after the Armistice. When the White Army collapsed that fall, the British also withdrew.

Not until April 1, 1920 did the last American troops leave Vladivostok. General William Graves wrote in his memoirs: "I was in command of the United States troops sent to Siberia and, I must admit, I do not know what the United States was trying to accomplish by military intervention."[7]

Allied intervention in the Russian Civil War achieved none of its various and conflicting purposes. Lenin succeeded in taking Russia out of the Great War and its alliance with the West. The new Soviet government was not defeated or overthrown. The ill-coordinated White Army units collapsed one after another. In time, the majority of the Russian people, less for reasons of proletarian ideology than for war weariness, acquiesced in their new leadership. If it is true that the United States was the least belligerent of the major Allies—and that Woodrow Wilson was earnestly committed to the principle of nonintervention—the legacy of the *fact* of intervention is that Soviet resentment was intense and long-lasting. And so was Soviet contempt for the disarray and ineptitude of the intervention. George Kennan, who has refused to grant Soviet claims that all the Allied governments conspired from the start to overthrow the Bolsheviks, nevertheless renders a hard judgment on the whole affair:

Never, surely, have countries contrived to show themselves so much at their worst as did the Allies in Russia from 1917 to

1920. Among other things, their efforts served everywhere to compromise the enemies of the Bolsheviki and to strengthen the Communists themselves. So important was this factor that I think it may well be questioned whether Bolshevism would ever have prevailed throughout Russia had the Western governments not aided its progress to power by this ill-conceived interference.[8]

Paris and Moscow 1919

It was still a chaotic, warring, fearful world when the Paris Peace Conference got under way in January 1919. Not only did civil war rage in Russia, but there were also other attempted revolutions in Europe and Red scares everywhere in the West. These external events combined with the Allies' vindictiveness, greed, and lack of common purpose to intensify antagonisms with the Soviets, sow the seeds of Nazism, and compound the troubles that would lead to a Second World War in just twenty years.

Both parties to the Treaty of Brest-Litovsk, Germany and Russia, were vengefully excluded from the Paris Conference—most pointedly because of the stubborn vetoes of French Premier Clemenceau. The predictable consequence was that neither Germany nor Russia was given any positive stake in helping to construct a stable peace. In the German case, even though the kaiser had abdicated two days before the Armistice and a new republic under democratic socialist leadership had been established, exclusion was followed by such major punishments as loss of homeland territory and all overseas colonies, forced demilitarization, and the cruel folly of a food blockade for a year. Two years later, Britain and France sought to impose on Germany the further burden of exorbitant reparations, 132 billion gold marks, which Germany had no conceivable prospect of paying.

So, instead of fostering conditions for building a stable and peaceful democratic Germany, the Allies excluded, humiliated, and crippled their former and future enemy. Before long, the festering grievances of the German people would be demagogically exploited by a deranged Austrian veteran who had fought in the German army as a corporal. In time, his power and his policies would cause both Allied and Russian peoples, the Jews of his own country and in all of Europe, and many other peoples to share in the most ghastly slaughter in history.

The vacant Russian chair in Paris was haunted by the inevitable specter of Russian assertiveness in virtually all the diplomatic issues of the post-Armistice world. Lenin was physically absent but a constant political presence. One of the earliest acts of the Russian Revolution had been to open the tsar's archives and shock the world with exposure of imperialistic treaties with the Allies, casting a cynical shadow on their righteous wartime rhetoric about democratic principles. President Wilson's Fourteen Points before Congress on January 8, 1918, were prompted by those revelations and were, at least in part, a propagandistic effort to recapture the high moral ground of the Allied war effort.[9] The sixth of Wilson's Points was conspicuously solicitous for the new Soviet government, asking the nations of the world to obtain for Russia

> an unhampered and unembarrassed opportunity for the independent determination of her own political development and national policy and assure her of a sincere welcome into the society of free nations under institutions of her own choosing; and, more than a welcome, assistance also of every kind that she may need and may herself desire. The treatment accorded Russia by her sister nations in the months to come will be the acid test of their good will, of their comprehension of her needs as distinguished from their own interests, and of their intelligent and unselfish sympathy.[10]

A year later in Paris, Wilson and British Prime Minister David Lloyd George both pressed for Russian representation, believing it to be essential to any viable political settlement in Europe. But (just to put the conference in its proper zoological perspective) "Tiger" Clemenceau absolutely refused to have any dealings with what "British

Lion" Winston Churchill called "the foul baboonery of Bolshevism."[11] Clemenceau did yield, however, to a British proposal (relayed by Wilson) for an Allied meeting with representatives of both Red and White factions in the Russian conflict, not in Paris but on the island of Prinkipo in the Sea of Marmara. The Prinkipo suggestion was preconditioned on acceptance by both Reds and Whites of a ceasefire in Russia. The Whites refused, the Soviets equivocated, and the proposal died.

At the suggestion of journalist Lincoln Steffens (and without informing Clemenceau), Wilson then decided to send a low-level representative to Moscow for informal, exploratory talks with Soviet leaders. The president dispatched a twenty-eight-year-old attaché, William C. Bullitt (accompanied by Steffens), just after U.S. troops had suffered defeat and most of their casualties from the Red Army in North Russia. Wilson clearly wanted to terminate both Allied intervention and the Civil War itself. So it was that in March 1919 Bullitt met with Lenin and other Bolsheviks. After a rather surprising and rapid meeting of minds, Lenin produced a document that might well have stabilized, if not reconciled, U.S.-Soviet relations. The draft's terms were clearly advantageous to both sides: an end to both civil war and intervention, amnesty for Russians who had aided the Allies, procedures for diplomatic communication if not recognition. An inspired Bullitt returned to Paris—only to find that Wilson declined even to see him, pleading a headache after a recent nervous collapse. Bullitt's earnest representations to junior officials met with skepticism and downright opposition. The French, having belatedly learned of the Bullitt mission, accused the British of complicity in underhanded diplomacy. Lloyd George, who may have privately welcomed the proposed terms, publicly disowned the mission in the face of a Conservative anti-communist firestorm in Parliament.[12]

The first serious American attempt at peacemaking with the Soviet Union ended in the bitter politics of Paris and London. Bullitt's own bitterness led him to resign in protest against Wilson's lack of support and the president's compromises with France and Britain on other issues. Fifteen years later, Bullitt returned to Moscow as Franklin Roosevelt's first U.S. ambassador.

While Bullitt was off in Moscow in March 1919, another U.S. initiative toward the Russians began to germinate in Paris. Herbert Hoover, director of postwar food relief in Belgium and other countries, had warned, "The wolf is at the door of the world." He proposed the creation of a relief commission for the Russian people, among whom starvation was widespread. But, whether or not Hoover thought of food as a political weapon (as it sporadically has been by U.S. policymakers for decades), he suggested hard preconditions of such a program: the Bolsheviks must stop fighting anti-communist groups at home and must also cease communist propaganda abroad. Wilson and all of the Big Four accepted the idea but attached even more political strings: the plan would not confer official recognition on Soviet authorities, yet Allied forces must be in direct control of transportation and distribution within Russia, in addition to which there must be local autonomy in consulting on food distribution without interference from Moscow.

Even Clemenceau could endorse such an anti-Bolshevik program so tied up with political strings. The proposal was drafted and intended for dispatch to Lenin. But French radio operators balked and refused to send it. By circuitous means, the proposal arrived days later in Moscow and was promptly and vehemently rejected on the understandable grounds that it constituted intolerable political interference in Russian internal affairs and offered no assurance that Allied troops would withdraw from Russian territory.[13]

Herbert Hoover's food relief plan of 1919 was the first, but would hardly be the last, U.S. diplomatic gambit toward the Soviet Union that was set forth with benevolent purposes but with nonnegotiable terms. Soviet leaders, of course, have played that same game very often and very skillfully.

If the Paris Peace Conference ended without genuinely peaceable arrangements for Germany and Russia, it did produce a covenant of collective security through a new League of Nations. That happened only because Woodrow Wilson absolutely, eloquently, relentlessly, and uncompromisingly insisted upon it—only to have his own compatriots repudiate membership. But Germany was not only excluded from the Paris Conference: it was denied membership in the League until 1926. The Soviet Union, also excluded from Paris and initially from the League, was finally admitted to the League in 1934, only to be the one nation expelled, in 1939. Among major powers, only Britain and France maintained continuous membership throughout the League's two troubled decades.

In the League itself, as at the Paris Conference, the biggest problem was the empty chairs that needed delegates from great nations. Had there been continuous membership by both the United States and the Soviet Union, each with an active stake in collective security against aggression, a half century of world history might have been spared a fair measure of its misery.

Relief, (Non-) Recovery, and (Non-) Recognition

Notwithstanding Herbert Hoover's fervent anti-communism, he found himself in Russia in 1921-22, after all, as director of a massive, strictly non-political American Relief Administration operation. This was a food program in response to the famine that struck the Ukraine and Southern Russia in the spring of 1921. If millions perished, millions of others were surely saved by American aid. All this happened while the United States government was in the early months of a fifteen-year refusal to recognize the Soviet government—a refusal that was constantly expressed in shrill tones of moral principle and indignation. The uncomplicated humanitarian spirit of that famine relief program offered an opportunity to reckon on some degree of Russian appreciation to diminish Bolshevik cynicism and to contemplate diplomatic recognition. But that opportunity was not about to be grasped by a Harding administration that wallowed in the "normalcy" of righteous isolationism and unbridled materialism. It was another of those historic "what-ifs" in which domestic preoccupations precluded wise diplomacy.

Famine was only one part of the desperate economic crisis Lenin faced in 1921 when he launched the New Economic Policy that made major concessions to private enterprise. That policy was accompanied by a round of requests to Western countries for economic and political measures that would enhance Russian recovery: more trade, financial credits, diplomatic recognition. On trade, Britain was first to respond, agreeing to a landmark Anglo-Soviet Trade Agreement in March 1921. Most other European governments followed suit by the end of the year. But the United States declined to go along. Herbert Hoover, serving not only as relief administrator in Russia but also as Harding's Secretary of Commerce, asserted that normal trade was impossible unless the Soviets were prepared to "abandon their present economic system."[14] In fact, however, Lenin permitted American business ventures to open and substantial U.S. trade to develop throughout the 1920s, beginning with mining concessions to a very young entrepreneur named Armand Hammer in 1921. (In the 1980s, octogenarian Hammer was still doing business with the Russians.) Ford, General Electric, and Westinghouse corporations each invested millions of dollars in various Soviet projects.

Moscow was much less successful in securing financial credit and diplomatic recognition. These benefits were being withheld because the Bolsheviks had disowned the foreign debts they inherited from the tsar and the Provisional Government—and also had nationalized foreign properties whose erstwhile owners pressed claims against the Soviet government. This highly charged issue of debts and claims was repeatedly invoked by the U.S. throughout the Harding, Coolidge, and Hoover administrations as a matter of honor and morality and therefore a prime reason for nonrecognition. The European Allies were no less adamant than the U.S. in withholding capital until getting satisfaction on debts and claims. After a season of Western pressure, the Soviets responded by submitting to

Allied governments an enormous bill of charges for damages allegedly caused by their military intervention.[15]

These unresolved conflicts, along with all the other burdens of reconstruction from the Great War, led to the Genoa Conference on Economic Recovery in April 1922. This time, both Russia and Germany were invited, offering some promise of their reintegration into the European community. The Genoa agenda of aid and trade, debts and claims, relief and reparations provided the opportunity to create a big, bold European recovery program on the order of the Marshall Plan a generation later. But the Harding administration boycotted the conference altogether, assuring the general failure of the unhappy deliberations in Genoa. France and Britain maintained a vengeful disposition toward the hard-pressed young German government.

There was, however, an extraordinary sideshow. Russian and German delegates, losers in the economic stakes, slipped away sometime after midnight on Easter morning for their famous "pajama party" at the coastal resort of Rapallo. There they drafted and signed a treaty of diplomatic recognition, reciprocal trade, and cancellation of claims. In effect the treaty also legitimized a secret process of military cooperation already under way for some months. For the next decade, Germany's military elite provided the Red Army with technological expertise and staff training. In return, the Germans were furnished Russian training sites for tank crews and airplane pilots, thereby implicating both governments in violations of the Treaty of Versailles from which their participation had been excluded.

These two recent enemies, mutual diplomatic outcasts after the Great War, both governed by radically changed postwar regimes, were thus drawn together, not really in a military alliance but in a non-ideological pact of convenience. When word of the Rapallo Treaty reached British and French delegates back in Genoa, moral indignation was added to the dismaying impasse on economic issues. The conference broke up in total frustration. Clearly, the Soviets had succeeded in dividing the powers of Western Europe.

Germany was once again regarded as the incarnation of treachery. Governments, press, and public in both London and Paris were outraged at this "unholy alliance." The Rapallo partners were outcasts again. And the war-weary and impoverished peoples of Europe, both West and East, were denied the fruits of a generous and constructive recovery program.

The Rapallo Treaty did not stabilize Russian-German relations for long. They teeter-tottered throughout the 1920s, then were undermined by Stalin's subversions and Hitler's ascendancy, only to be cynically and superficially patched up in the bizarre Hitler-Stalin Pact of 1939 on the eve of their mutual conflagration.

The Long Road to Recognition

German recognition of the Soviet Union in 1922 did not prove to be a deterrent to other European governments doing so. Ramsay MacDonald, Britain's first Labour Prime Minister, extended recognition in January 1924, just several days after the death of Lenin. Italy immediately did the same. By the end of 1924, France, Norway, Sweden, Denmark, Austria, Hungary, and Greece had joined the parade of recognition. The United States delayed doing so for another decade.

It would be untrue to claim that the American policy of nonrecognition, originally a very moralistic one, began with the Harding administration. Whatever Woodrow Wilson's personal views after his breakdown while campaigning for the League in September 1919 and his extraordinary isolation thereafter, his administration was represented as opposed to recognition de jure. In August 1920, his new secretary of state, Bainbridge Colby, replied to an Italian inquiry into American policy that "the existing regime in Russia is based upon the negation of every principle of honor and good faith, and every usage and custom, underlying the whole structure of international law."[16] In later years under Republican administrations, the issue of unpaid war debts and claims would be more frequently raised to sustain the shunning of the U.S.S.R. But morality and money, that enduring dualism of American policy, continued to rationalize the non-recognition policy.

Material interests began to play a different role in the late 1920s. U.S. trade with the Soviet Union increased steadily so that by 1930 it amounted to the largest share of Soviet imports, about 25 percent.[17] American engineers, labor leaders, industrialists, and machines became important factors in the Soviets' new five-year plans. Some Americans became enthusiasts for the enormous process of social and economic transformation under way in Russia—a process that unquestionably claimed vast resources of idealism and sacrifice from many Russians, even while brutalizing millions.

The election of Franklin Delano Roosevelt to the presidency in 1932 opened a new chapter in American diplomacy. Both more pragmatic and more internationalist than Herbert Hoover, he was responsive to trade issues and liberal opinion. He was also confronted with the surging militarism of Japan (aggressively shown in the conquest of Manchuria in 1831) and the advent of Adolf Hitler in Germany. Recognition of the Soviet Union was seen as a timely counter to these developments. The U.S.S.R. publicly acknowledged that its concern about Japanese expansionism on the Siberian periphery motivated its desire for recognition.[18]

Roosevelt's reception of Soviet Foreign Minister Maxim Litvinov on November 15, 1933, secured assurances on two points: no Soviet subversion or propaganda in the United States and no restrictions on freedom of worship for Americans in the U.S.S.R. The issue of debts and claims was postponed—and never really resolved.

FDR's pursuit of the issue of religious freedom with Litvinov, who came from a Jewish background, provided one of the more memorable and amusing dialogues in the annals of U.S. diplomacy:

> Now you know, Max, your good old father and mother, pious Jewish people, always said their prayers. I know they must have taught you to say prayers. You must know all the good old Jewish psalms and prayers.

Litvinov was conspicuously nonplussed and embarrassed by this little homily. Roosevelt continued:

> Now you may think you're an atheist. You may think you don't have any religion, but I tell you, Max, when you come to die do you know what you're going to think of? You're going to be thinking about what your father and mother taught you. That's what you'll think of when you're dying.

Litvinov reportedly blustered and laughed nervously, and may have worried that he was committing a crime against official Marxist-Leninist doctrine by continuing to listen to Roosevelt's preaching. But FDR went on:

> In America nobody can understand this idea that people shouldn't have access to religion—any kind they want. That's all I ask, Max—to have Russia recognize freedom of religion.[19]

Two days later on November 17, 1933, Roosevelt personally announced the establishment of diplomatic relations with the Soviet Union. He appointed William C. Bullitt as his ambassador—the same Bullitt whom Woodrow Wilson had sent to Moscow fifteen years before and then refused to see upon his return to Paris. (Bullitt's enthusiasm about his return to Moscow later turned to a consuming antipathy to Stalinism.)

Whatever FDR's hopes for terminating the mutual isolation of the two governments, the times just ahead would see a resurgence of Soviet propaganda in the U.S., as well as a new round of religious persecution and Stalin's most ghastly purges in Russia. The continued divergence of foreign policies, especially concerning Germany and Japan, would contribute incalculably to the most awful convulsions of human history within a dozen years.

Weimar

There is a particularly grim chapter in the unending centrality of Germany in U.S.-Soviet relations in those interwar years: the tragedy of the Weimar Republic,

Germany's brief experience of democratic, libertarian government, 1918–1932. It was an exhilarating time of cultural ferment and social transformation. But post-monarchical politics was very fragile and vulnerable to economic distress and ideological exploitation.

In an immediate sense, the Weimar Republic was destroyed by Hitler, an event that led to World War II. In a larger sense, capitalist America and communist Russia, in something like equal measure—not because they had a common policy, for these were years in which they had no diplomatic ties—must bear much of the responsibility for destroying the Weimar Republic. One of them, America, not by any willful intention but by its undisciplined economy and rambunctious materialism during the 1920s when its official foreign policy was isolationist but its commercial institutions decisively affected every other nation. The other, Soviet Russia, by the very willful intention to smash a genuinely social-democratic system and replace it by a communist regime it could control. It was, after all, the collapse of the U.S. economy and the North American Depression, which was inevitably exported to Europe, that left a majority of German workers unemployed, and that wiped out the lower middle class economically, thus providing Nazism with its greatest political base. And it was Stalin's nihilist strategy after 1928 to wreck democratic socialism politically, by obstructionist parliamentary tactics in the Reichstag, vicious propaganda, and violence in the streets. The aim was to usher Hitler into a very temporary period of power, which, after the destruction of all civil institutions, might clear the way for a Soviet Republic of Germany. So the German Communists fought against the Social Democrats instead of fighting against the Nazis, right up to Hitler's accession to the chancellorship in January 1933.[20] In a way, it was an attempted replay of Lenin's sabotage of the Provisional Government in Petrograd in 1917. It was perhaps Stalin's worst blunder, for which his people would pay a terrible price.

George Kennan, who served in Germany during the late stages of the Weimar Republic, recalls:

> Here was a brave experiment in democratic and republican government in a country which had never known anything of this sort before. All the odds were against it. The Weimar Republic had to combat the effects of the bitterness of defeat, the wartime losses, the biological disbalance, the economic disruption, the inflation, the social upheaval, the great spiritual bewilderment; as well as the vindictiveness and indifference of the Western Allies, the anti-republican prejudice of the army officers' corps, the general lack of any real democratic tradition. . . . [and a] Communist party . . . violently oriented against the whole success of the experiment and utterly unscrupulous in its determination to wreck it at any cost.[21]

Such was the tragedy of Weimar.

Stalin, Hitler, the Pope, and Collective Security

Stalin's inability to manipulate Hitler and control events in Germany after 1932 led to major changes in Soviet foreign policy: diplomatic relations with the United States (1933), membership in the League of Nations (1934), pacts with France and Czechoslovakia for mutual defense against Germany (1935), and Comintern formation of a United Front with Western socialists and liberals to oppose Nazism and Fascism (1935). In March 1936, citing the Franco-Soviet Treaty of 1935 as a provocation, Hitler marched his troops into the Rhineland in violation of the Treaty of Versailles. France was disposed to resist militarily but couldn't get British or League support and declined to act alone.

Soviet efforts to build an anti-Nazi coalition with the West were severely tested in the Spanish Civil War, which broke out in July 1936 when the Fascist movement of Francisco Franco staged a coup against the Republican government. Stalin was initially reluctant to intervene; but when Franco's forces received increasing military support from Mussolini's Italy and Hitler's Germany, thousands of Soviet military and civilian personnel, along with tanks and guns, were joined to the Republican cause. Once again, France and Britain declined to become involved. The United States, seeking to remain detached, imposed an embargo on arms to Spain. But thousands of French, British, and American volunteers joined an international brigade and fought side by side with Spanish Loyalists and Russian communists. Their idealism was fired by the belief that this was the last chance to stop international Fascism. It turned out to be the dress rehearsal for the worst of world wars.

By 1939, the Loyalists had lost to the Fascists, the Soviets had withdrawn, and the non-communist liberals had been tainted by association with the communists. If that taint later proved to be a bitter legacy for American liberals besieged in the Cold War and battered by the cruelties of McCarthyism, its reverse twist was immediately and literally deadly for many Russians who had fought in Spain and had survived. Precisely their association with Western liberals and socialists gave them new hope for the liberalization of Bolshevism back home, only to lead to their becoming special victims of Stalin's purges and exterminations.[22]

This ironic and double tragedy of the anti-Fascist forces who had enlisted in the cause of Republican Spain was also steeped in religious hostilities. The Vatican and the Spanish bishops gave their blessings to Franco's Falange because the new Republican constitution had disestablished the Catholic Church and created a social democratic state. The American hierarchy strongly supported the congressional embargo on arms to Spain—arms that might have enabled the Republican government to survive. In both Spain and America, official Catholic support for Franco was marked by the harshest of anti-Soviet, anti-communist, and anti-socialist anathemas. Many individual Catholic liberals in both countries supported the Republicans and deplored the behavior of their bishops.

On March 28, 1939, the day Generalissimo Franco's army marched into Madrid and claimed its victory, Pope Pius XII sent this message of gratitude:

101

> Raising our hearts to God, we thank Him and your
> excellency for the desired victory of Catholic Spain and pray
> that this beloved country, having found peace, may renew
> with vigor her ancient Christian traditions which made her
> so great. With these sentiments we send your excellency and
> the whole Spanish people our Apostolic blessing.[23]

Franco's victory merged with all the other events that were reinforcing Nazi and Fascist aggression and weakening the powers of resistance to it. Not only had Stalin's intervention in Spain failed to enlist the West: it had actually increased the gulf between the U.S.S.R. and the democracies. Forty years would pass before Spain itself recovered genuinely democratic institutions.

In the Munich crisis over Czechoslovakia in 1938, after Chamberlain's accommodation to Hitler, the League again could not muster concerted resistance to Hitler. The 1935 Soviet treaty with Czechoslovakia required common action against Germany by both France and the U.S.S.R.—but France again refused to act.

In these fateful opportunities for collective security to prove itself against Nazi aggression—when almost any resistance might have halted the aggression, weakened Hitler within Germany, and prevented World War II—the person who pleaded again and again for united action at Geneva's Palais des Nations was the eloquent Foreign Minister of the Soviet Union, Maxim Litvinov. Whatever Stalin's motives, Litvinov's earnest anti-Nazi convictions could not be doubted. There were still empty chairs where American delegates might have been seated.

These failures of the League of Nations (more precisely failures of both its members and non-members, not of its Covenant) portended even more than the devastation of Europe and the Holocaust. They led to Nazi occupation of all the European neighbors of the Soviet Union, which in turn led to the massive Soviet reaction that remained the heavy reality of Eastern Europe from 1945 to 1989: nine nations in the grip of Soviet power.

Yes, Stalin seized Eastern Europe in the 1940s. But Hitler prepared the way. And the moral responsibility for what

Hitler did is widely shared among the nations and churches of the West as well as by Joseph Stalin.

Stalin's dismay over the failure of Allied action against Nazism was in the immediate background of one of his most cynical moves—but a move which revealed that cynicism may sometimes be a synonym for illusions: the Nonaggression Pact with Hitler signed August 24, 1939. Just one more week, and German troops, tanks, and planes attacked Poland, and Europe was at war again.

A further word about the Hitler-Stalin Pact is in order. By the spring of 1939, as German forces were preparing to move into Bohemia and Moravia, Stalin had lost all confidence in alliances with France and Britain, as well as in the League of Nations and its schemes of collective security. He could have had no doubt that Hitler's appetite had been whetted for more ambitious conquests; he surely wanted to reinforce any of Hitler's inclinations to strike westward rather than eastward. It then must have seemed fitting to remove his rather idealistic, passionate Jewish foreign minister, Maxim Litvinov, in order to come to some accommodation with Hitler. The new man was the old Bolshevik robot, V. M. Molotov, who worked out the astounding deal with Joachim von Ribbentrop, Hitler's foreign minister, who came to the Kremlin. The deal was humiliating for Communists and Socialists of the United Front in the West who had presented themselves as the strongest champions of resistance to Hitler. The United Front itself was shattered. One sometime Socialist who had enlisted in various United Front groups was Reinhold Niebuhr of New York's Union Theological Seminary. For Niebuhr, the Hitler-Stalin Pact was "a bitter blow" that had "stunned everyone." While his balance-of-power approach to world politics granted that Stalin's move was "understandable enough," Niebuhr judged it to reveal the ultimate "degradation of communism." What the Soviet Union had done, "as the fatherland of socialism, to which millions of United Fronters in every nation have given their devotion, is despicable."[24]

Conflicts and Consequences

Striking a fair moral balance between the Soviet Union and the Western Allies in their relative responsibilities for Hitler and all the inhumanities of World War II is thus no easy matter. If the Russians could fairly charge the West with a failure of nerve in the mid-1930s, several years later the defeated French, the valiant British, and those Americans who really cared about all this at the time could fairly be dismayed that Stalin turned Hitler loose for such horrors in the West. But after June 22, 1941, when Hitler's merciless "Operation Barbarossa" was inflicted on the Russians, and it would be three whole years before the invasion of Normandy during which time the Russians bore the most brutal burdens of the war, the scales of justice tilted once again.

Looking back over those brief years of one short generation between two world wars—assessing the political consequences and moral burdens of the Russian Civil War and Allied intervention, of the simultaneous disarray of the Paris Peace Conference, of the dismal controversies over post-war relief and recovery and recognition, of the annihilation of Weimar social democracy by Nazism, and of the inability of the West and the Soviets to concert their response to aggression—it is not too difficult to identify sources of U.S.-Soviet conflict. For unlike the years before 1917 during which Russian-American relations were mostly marginal on both sides and peripheral to the major struggles of world politics, the inter-war years were full of crucial turning-points, of "what-if" moments, which now still make you weep because you know that the fates of many nations and millions of people might have been pointed in much happier directions, depending on what the United States or the Soviet Union decided, or what these two nations might have done together. But the persistence of an immature and irresponsible isolationism on one side, and a ruthless and cynical despotism on the other side, hardly made an amiable alliance possible.

These two superpowers-in-process-of-becoming were finally drawn together, belatedly, not by ideology or by trade or by religion, but by the man whom the modern world loved to hate more than any other, Adolf Hitler.

CHAPTER **5**

THE PERPETUAL POST-WAR NON-PEACE

The greatest menace to our civilization today is the conflict between giant organized systems of self-righteousness—each system only too delighted to find that the other is wicked—each only too glad that the sins give it the pretext for still deeper hatred and animosity. The effect of the whole situation is barbarizing, since both sides take the wickedness of the other as the pretext for insults, atrocities, and loathing; and each side feels that its own severities are not vicious at all, but simply punitive acts and laudable matters of judgment.
—Herbert Butterfield[1]
Christianity, Diplomacy, and War

I have seen the Russians close up. Their hopes and desires are for peace—and an apartment.
—Adlai E. Stevenson[2]
Friends and Enemies

The twentieth century has been relentlessly hailed as the century of the most radical changes in the whole course of human experience—political, economic, social, cultural, and especially technological changes, which have driven all the others. But that truism doesn't capture a contradictory fact. For nearly half of this century there has been a remarkably constant political fix in which two great powers have engaged each other across the whole spectrum of rivalry and conflict except that of total war. While it has not been a wholly static condition, the elements of constancy in policy and strategy on both sides are almost startling in the long view of modern history.

From the 1940s to 1990, the United States and the Soviet Union have sustained a global controversy that has not only drastically restructured their domestic institutions and priorities but has decisively affected the welfare and security of every other nation. It is a controversy presaged by the devastation of World War II, which not only crushed the might of Germany and Japan but crippled the imperial powers of Britain and France. The world arena then staged a stark bipolarity. The United States, having been spared the direct ravages of war in its homeland, had mobilized its industrial resources for extraordinary feats of military production but would soon generate unparalleled prosperity and a dominant role in the world economy. The imperious power of the United States was magnified by its atomic weapons. While the Soviet Union had suffered the heaviest casualties of the war and its western portions had been wasted by both obliteration battles and scorched earth policies, the residual strength of Soviet industry beyond the Ural Mountains and the Red Army's occupation of Eastern Europe had left Russia the preeminent power on the Eurasian mainland. Moreover, it soon became apparent that the United States would lose its nuclear monopoly.

So it was that this unending post-war period became a forever-threatening, potential *pre-war* era of debilitating rivalry that was neither war nor peace, which Walter Lippmann called the "Cold War" and John Kennedy called a "long twilight struggle." The struggle more and more became a forever escalating arms race, which strategists of nuclear deterrence claimed was peacemaking by "mutual terror" or even "mutual assured destruction." It was this capacity for total annihilation, not only of each other but of the whole human family, that obtained for the U.S. and the U.S.S.R. the pretentious appellation "superpowers."

The specter of nuclear annihilation did not, however,

prevent the superpowers from engaging in numerous proxy wars, nor lesser powers, various tribes, and militant movements from waging dozens of sub-nuclear wars, nor most of the nations from getting caught up in the swirling currents of militarization, conventional arms races, and the arms trade. Some of the lesser powers—nobody could be sure how many—also acquired nuclear weapons or the potential to produce them. Some developed chemical weapons and even waged chemical warfare. Ballistic missile technology spread to more and more countries. And tens of millions of persons were casualties of the wars in this post-war non-peace era—not counting tens of millions of other casualties from the poverty, hunger, disease, and racism that were compounded by the gross militarization of this seemingly permanent and woefully misnamed "post-war period."

The Will of Heaven?

Was the Cold War inevitable? Was it indeed "the will of Heaven," as Tocqueville foretold it in the 1830s, that Russia and America would sway the destiny of the whole earth between them? Louis J. Halle, who served on the Policy Planning Staff of the State Department in the Truman years, came close to such a fatalistic perspective in *The Cold War as History*, his illuminating 1967 study. Halle viewed the Cold War as a tragic predicament of terrible dilemmas that demanded sympathy for both sides—a predicament in which World War II and its aftermath

> put Russia in the role of challenger—superficially, at least, in the role of aggressor. But the historical circumstances, themselves, had an ineluctable quality that left the Russians little choice but to move as they did. Moving as they did, they compelled the United States and its allies to move in response. And so the Cold War was joined.[3]

Halle's tragic view of things is appealing in its humane sensitivities and tempered judgments. It comes close, however, to a historical determinism that diminishes both freedom and responsibility in the political arena. A tragic historical consciousness need not assume that aggression or war is inevitable, or that a demonic view of enemies is excusable. Neither Soviet nor American conduct since 1945 should be so readily exempted from moral assessment.

An open view of history, which takes both freedom and responsibility with radical seriousness, while knowing that choices are almost always limited and that consequences are seldom fully imaginable, must ask: When did the Cold War begin, and why? What were the moments of real choice, the "what-if" moments, when other and better decisions were possible? Is the world doomed to permanent hostility between the superpowers, if not a doomsday holocaust?

The case for accepting the "perpetual post-war non-peace" as really permanent, or at least relentless beyond any reckoning, rests on such assumptions as the following: (1) There is an irreconcilable conflict of fundamental values between democratic America and totalitarian Russia. (2) The Soviet system is fundamentally static and incapable of genuine transformation. (3) The technology of nuclear weaponry is here to stay forever; it cannot now be uninvented. Therefore, nuclear deterrence is the fixed foundation of national security.

Those assumptions add up to the strange metaphysical notion that history, at least world political history, has virtually stopped—that neither political imagination, nor social change, nor technological progress can significantly alter superpower relationships.

No Single Sarajevo

Perspectives on the future of Russian-American relations are shaped by the dimensions of inquiry into the past. If the beginning of the Cold War is traced only to Soviet occupation of all "the ancient states of Central and Eastern Europe," as dramatized in Winston Churchill's "Iron Curtain" speech in Fulton, Missouri, March 5, 1946—or conversely traced to the March 12, 1947 pronouncement of the militant Truman Doctrine supporting "free peoples who are resisting attempted subjugation" by communist forces—many antecedent decisions and events that pointed toward such a conflict may be unwisely ignored or forgotten. For the Cold War had no single Sarajevo or Pearl Harbor. Its origins were diffuse and cumulative from 1918 on.

Nevertheless, by 1945 there had been some accommodations that might have been better cultivated to preclude a hardening hostility between the two nations. Diplomatic relations had been established. The U.S. and U.S.S.R. became wartime allies in 1941. Both peoples were propagandized into friendship and solidarity, not all of which was fatuous. There had been strategic summits for Roosevelt, Churchill, and Stalin in Teheran (November 1943) and Yalta (February 1945), and for Truman, Churchill, Attlee, and Stalin in Potsdam (July 1945). The U.S. and U.S.S.R. collaborated in designing the structures of the United Nations, both sides accepting compromises in the process.

Lend-Lease Aid

From 1942 to 1945, the U.S. sent eleven billion dollars in Lend-Lease aid to the Russians, an amount that covered 427,000 trucks, 13,000 combat vehicles, 35,000 motorcycles, jeeps, tanks, planes, nearly 2,000 locomotives and 11,000 rail cars, four million pairs of army boots, nearly three million tons of petroleum products, almost five million tons of food, and a billion dollars worth of machinery. While the decisive military turning-point came at Stalingrad before American aid had arrived in significant volume, the Russians' final defeat of German armies on the Eastern front was greatly speeded by U.S. aid, especially transport equipment.[4]

From the beginning, wartime aid to the Russians was a matter of fierce political and religious controversy. There was particularly strong Roman Catholic opposition. Roosevelt sought to soften Catholic resistance by sending Myron C. Taylor on a special mission to Pope Pius XII in November 1941 to solicit the Church's understanding of what was at stake in Lend-Lease. Taylor, former board chairman of the

U.S. Steel Corporation and a leading Protestant layman, had been appointed FDR's "special representative" to the Vatican in 1939, an appointment greeted by much Protestant criticism. The 1941 mission, intended to allay Catholic antagonism, revived criticism from Protestant clergy and politicians. In a notably cynical but silly moment, Republican Congressman Hamilton Fish of New York proposed that Roosevelt invite Stalin to Washington and have him baptized in the White House pool—apparently oblivious to or forgetful of the fact that Stalin had been baptized and once was a seminary student.[5] The pope, having been advised that Roosevelt was an apologist for communism, was not as responsive to Taylor's visit as FDR had hoped. The Vatican did manage to suggest to Catholics that there might be a distinction between aiding Russians and aiding communism.[6]

There can be no doubt of the importance Roosevelt and his military chiefs attached to alliance with Russia. In March 1942, when FDR was informed that Lend-Lease shipments to the U.S.S.R. had fallen far short of scheduled goals, he declared:

> I would go out and take the stuff off the shelf of the stores, and pay them any price necessary, and put it in a truck and rush it to the boat. . . . Nothing would be worse than to have the Russians collapse. . . . I would rather lose New Zealand, Australia or anything else than to have the Russians collapse.[7]

Admiral Ernest J. King, U.S. Fleet Commander in Chief, strongly supported the aid program, saying in November 1942: "In the last analysis, Russia will do nine-tenths of the job of defeating Germany."[8]

Such comments match the Russians' claim, ever since 1945, that they played the major role in winning the war against Hitler. But such comments also reveal that, contrary to some Russian complaints, U.S. officials assigned a very high priority to the alliance and to Lend-Lease. By another accounting, a total of 2,660 shiploads of Lend-Lease supplies was sent, with seventy-seven ships sunk, mostly by German submarines and aircraft on the dangerous route around the north capes of Norway.[9]

No Clash of Interests?

On November 14, 1945—three months after Japan's surrender ended the war—Dean Acheson, then Under Secretary of State, addressed the National Council of American-Soviet Friendship in New York and offered a very positive assessment of prospects for a continuing alliance. "For nearly a century and a half we have gotten along well—remarkably well, when you consider that our forms of government, our economic systems, and our social habits have never been similar." Acheson cited "immutable facts of history and geography" to demonstrate why there had never been a war between Russia and America, nor any clash of vital interests in any place—"and there is no objective reason to suppose that there should, now or in the future, ever be such a place."[10] Whatever the accuracy of that assessment in late 1945, it would be overtaken by the rush of Cold War hostility in 1946 and 1947. Just two years after Acheson's optimistic speech to the National Council of American-Soviet Friendship, that organization was listed as subversive by the Attorney General of the United States.

It would be a serious short-circuit of historical accounts to suggest, however, that the Cold War began de novo in 1946 and 1947. In addition to the accumulation of mutual grievances in the years 1917–41, a series of decisions and events during the course of the Second World War produced considerable dissonance between the U.S. and the U.S.S.R.

Unconditional Surrender and the Cold War

A fundamental U.S.-British decision on the very aims of the war itself, a decision ironically prompted by concern to placate the Russians, helped shape the geopolitical context of the post-war Cold War. At Casablanca in January 1943, Roosevelt and Churchill announced the policy of prosecuting the war until the "unconditional surrender" of both

111

Germany and Japan. At the time, Soviet armies were embattled at Stalingrad, Stalin was pressing hard for an Anglo-American second front in western Europe, and assurances seemed imperative that the war against Hitler would be waged to total victory and would not end in an appeasing compromise. The unconditional surrender policy was thus intended as an affirmation of wartime solidarity with the Russians. Its post-surrender implications were not seriously considered.

In the judgment of Louis Halle, it was just this policy of unconditional surrender, requiring the elimination of German power from central Europe, that "laid the foundations of the Cold War."[11] The policy was indeed pursued to total victory so that by May 1945 German military and industrial power had been destroyed and the very structure of German government had totally collapsed. A power vacuum was left in central Europe that was only temporarily filled on one side by General Eisenhower's American, British, and French armies. While the U.S. rapidly demobilized under public and congressional pressure, the U.S.S.R. maintained a sizable military presence in all of the countries occupied by the Red Army late in the war. Faulty American intelligence, however, greatly exaggerated the size of these residual Soviet forces (anticipating the mythical claims of a "bomber gap" and then a "missile gap" and yet again a "window of vulnerability" in the years to come). Stalin, too, undertook substantial demobilization, but it would have been unrealistic to expect Stalin to withdraw all his forces, deployed as they were across the whole of eastern Europe and so soon after recapturing their own devastated territory. It proved to be shortsighted in the extreme to suppose that western Europe could reconstruct its own security without reference to a reconstructed Germany.

Both a prime cause and the most serious consequence of the dogma of unconditional surrender was the compulsion to demonize the enemies. That meant the righteous incapacity to recognize that there were either "good Germans" or early prospects for an armistice with Japan that would preclude the use of A-bombs.

Here, then, was one of the most terrible ironies of the twentieth century. A supremely tough, militant, no-compromise, fight-to-the-finish wartime policy, that of demanding unconditional surrender for the sake (it was said) of an enduring peace, set the stage for both the Cold War in Europe and the nuclear arms race.

Bell and Bonhoeffer

The possibility of negotiating peace with Germany short of unconditional surrender was understandably unthinkable as long as Hitler remained in power, for it was clear that his maniacal mind was absolutely bent on either the conquest of all Europe or Germany's own *Götterdämmerung*, a twilight of the gods. But, as the world would learn only slowly after the war, there was an impressive corps of anti-Hitler resistance leaders who sought contacts with the Allies in hopes of an early peace, given a successful overthrow of Hitler. It was in that honorable German effort that two church leaders, Dietrich Bonhoeffer in Germany and George Bell, Anglican Bishop of Chichester, played such potentially crucial roles. In clandestine visits to Willem Visser't Hooft in Geneva (Visser't Hooft was General Secretary of the provisional World Council of Churches) and to Bishop Bell in Stockholm, Bonhoeffer outlined the hopes of the resistance and sought support from Britain and the United States. Bishop Bell tried to persuade British Foreign Secretary Anthony Eden of the viability of the resistance, while publicly appealing for the formulation of peace aims that envisioned a European future with a positive role for post-Nazi Germany, unlike the vengeful Treaty of Versailles.[12] But such was the commitment to unconditional surrender, along with the identification of the whole German nation with Hitler, that these messages went unheeded at the upper levels of Allied government. When the July 20, 1944 plot against Hitler failed, the unconditional surrender policy no longer faced a serious challenge. Bonhoeffer was hanged for his role in the resistance. We are left with another haunting "what if": wondering what the shape of Europe, and the shape of

U.S.-U.S.S.R. relations, might have been after 1945 if Bonhoeffer and Bell had been taken more seriously.

At war's end, the vacuum in central Europe might still have been offset by the construction of a reunified and demilitarized Germany. But that would have taken political imagination and planning that, in the understandable but excessive militarization of wartime decision-making in both Britain and America, was almost impossible to come by. Typical and especially portentous was the purely military judgment, shared by Eisenhower, that the devastated city of Berlin was strategically unimportant—with no anticipation that Berlin's political and symbolic importance would make it a persistent focus of perilous conflict in the years ahead.

Germany was indeed demilitarized—but divided, not unified. The U.S., too, demilitarized. All too soon, the felt security needs of western Europe would lead to the return of large American forces to Germany, and then to the remilitarization of Germany itself. And Germany, instead of helping to balance and heal the powers of Europe, became instead the agonizingly fractured center of Cold War confrontations.

Second Front Delayed

The announcement of the unconditional surrender policy in January 1943 did not wholly succeed in diverting Soviet demands for a second front in western Europe. For a year and a half, the Russians had suffered the brunt of German assault by two hundred divisions of the Wehrmacht. Another year and a half would pass before D-day and the Normandy invasion. For three years, then, from June 1941 until June 1944, Hitler was able to concentrate his forces on the Eastern front. The Allied campaigns in North Africa and Italy engaged only one-tenth the forces Germany had committed to the Russian front. Stalin repeatedly and bitterly pleaded for action in the west to relieve pressure in the east.

That three-year-wait, the costliest period of the war in

Russian lives and livelihood, remains a deep grievance against Britain and America nearly a half century later. While the Red Army decimated German divisions in the battles of Kursk, Orel, and Kharkov in the summer of 1943 and began to recover large regions of lost territory, Russian casualties continued to total hundreds of thousands every month. Soviet leaders suspected that the Western Allies deliberately wanted Russian power so weakened that it would not command respect in the post-war years. That mistrust and bitterness underlay the early tensions of the Cold War.

Meanwhile, the U.S. government as early as 1944 had become preoccupied with "the Soviet threat." Louis Halle, then an official in the Department of State, later testified that "there was no time when the danger from the Soviet Union was not a topic of anxious conversation among officers of the State Department; and by the winter of 1944–1945, as the day of victory approached, it became the predominant theme in Washington."[13] That statement stands as a clear refutation of later demagogic charges by Senator Joseph McCarthy, Richard Nixon, and others that the State Department was either naive or riddled with communists.

FDR's Last Months

The Big Three rallied for an impressive show of Allied unity at the Yalta (Crimea) Conference in February 1945, primarily a military summit to coordinate final strategies for defeating Germany and Japan, but with post-war politics and territorial settlements also on the agenda. In the late 1940s and after, some zealous anti-communist crusaders would make Yalta an acrimonious symbol of the Cold War and of alleged U.S. appeasement. Some Roman Catholic clerics and politicians, especially those of eastern European heritage, were particularly harsh, as were some Protestants with missionary backgrounds in China and Korea. Such vociferous critics seriously misrepresented the historical context and conclusions of FDR's last summit.

Especially controversial in later years was the political

status of eastern European countries liberated from German occupation by the Red Army. Winston Churchill had gone to Moscow in October 1944 and obtained Stalin's approval of a cold arithmetical formula for dividing spheres of influence in the region: Russia 90 percent "predominance" in Romania, 75 percent in Bulgaria, Britain 90 percent in Greece, 50 percent each in Yugoslavia and Hungary.[14] That Churchill, who was prepared to make such expedient concessions to Stalin months before Yalta, should later come to be regarded as the personification of anti-Stalinist resolve is a bit of a twist of imagery. At Yalta, however, Roosevelt secured agreement on the principles of free elections in Poland and "democratic institutions of their own choice" for other countries in the region. It was clearly beyond the power of the United States to thwart the U.S.S.R.'s violations of those principles, as Stalin's political manipulations, backed by the Red Army, secured control of Poland, Romania, Bulgaria, and Hungary. The latter three had no heritage of democratic government and had joined Hitler as Axis satellites. The Russians obviously were determined to gain buffer states against any possible repetition of their incomparable wartime suffering.

For months before Yalta, there had been much domestic clamor in the U.S. for the administration to secure Soviet entry into the war against Japan—the American parallel to the earlier Soviet demand for a second front. At Yalta, Stalin promised such entry within three months of the defeat of Germany (a promise kept). He was assured that two island territories lost to Japan in earlier conflicts, the Kurile Islands and the southern half of Sakhalin, would be returned to Russia, along with certain port and rail concessions in Manchuria. That assurance would later be branded a "sellout" and a "betrayal of China" that a weak and dying Roosevelt couldn't resist—and the brand would come precisely from those who had most vociferously demanded that Roosevelt act to get the Russians to join the fight against Japan.

FDR was undoubtedly optimistic about his own powers to hold the wartime alliance together in the works of peace. But his life ran out only six weeks after returning to the

States from Yalta. Two questions loomed very large after his death on April 12, 1945: Was Roosevelt naive in his optimism about post-war U.S.-Soviet relations? If Roosevelt had lived out his fourth term, could he have prevented the Cold War from developing?

There is no way of knowing a certain answer to such questions. There was a rash of antagonistic messages between Roosevelt and Stalin in those last weeks, messages that indicate both the President's awareness of serious conflicts and his determination to overcome them. The conflicts concerned Soviet actions in Poland and Romania, American prisoners of war in areas liberated by the Red Army, the circumstances of German surrender on the Western front, and plans for the founding conference of the United Nations in San Francisco. For some reason, Stalin delayed American access to U.S. POWs undergoing physical distress, prompting this cable from Roosevelt:

> Frankly I cannot understand your reluctance to permit American officers and men to assist their own people in this matter. This Government has done everything to meet each of your requests. I now request you to meet mine in this particular matter.[15]

On March 29 FDR cabled Stalin that continued Soviet imposition of its pro-communist regime in Warsaw was "unacceptable" and might crush the hopes raised by the Yalta Conference. When Stalin complained that separate surrenders of German forces to the Anglo-Americans would allow transfer of German armies to the Russian front, Roosevelt replied April 4 in astonishment and indignation: "Frankly, I cannot avoid a feeling of bitter resentment toward your informers, whoever they are, for such vile misrepresentations of my actions or those of my trusted subordinates."[16] That last message to Stalin barely a week before FDR's death suggests that he was hardly oblivious to the possible breakdown of alliance trust and cooperation.

The death of Franklin Roosevelt shocked Stalin into extraordinary efforts to reaffirm the alliance and the organization of the peace. Public and very personal mourning seemed universal among the Russian people and was unprecedented for any foreigner. The Supreme Soviet rose in silent tribute after hearing a declaration that concluded, "let us insure that in future the friendship between our peoples will stand as a memorial."[17]

The Loan and the Bomb

The Soviets received early signals of Harry Truman's long-time antipathy to the U.S.S.R. Just ten days after Roosevelt's death, Truman berated Foreign Minister Molotov over Russian pressure on Poland in such strong language that Molotov complained: "I have never been talked to like that in my life." That brought an angry cable to Truman from Stalin, who referred to "the blood that the Soviet people freely shed on the fields of Poland for the liberation of that country. . . . To put it plainly, you want me to renounce the interests of the security of the Soviet Union."[18]

Two other holdover issues Truman inherited from Roosevelt intensified the growing mistrust. One was economic and humanitarian. The other was military and apocalyptic.

In January 1945, the U.S.S.R. requested a six billion dollar U.S. loan to aid in the post-war reconstruction of its devastated regions and the resettlement of twenty-five million homeless people. A U.S. response was delayed for some months while Ambassador W. Averell Harriman and the State Department argued that economic aid should be used as a diplomatic weapon to compel Soviet political concessions (a reminder of the political strings Herbert Hoover sought to attach to post–World War I relief). The loan issue was made captive to the escalation of mistrust in the spring of 1945.[19] Truman declined to act on the request. Moreover, he abruptly terminated Lend-Lease aid on May 8—a decision he later rescinded after Russian protests, and after he confessed he hadn't read the termination order before signing it.[20]

Whether generous American participation in the costs of Russian reconstruction in 1945 and after would have improved political relationships and prevented the Cold War is another one of those poignant "what-ifs." The Cold War itself was to become so much more costly than any conceivable aid program that, with benefit of hindsight, the Soviet loan request seems still to have been a badly missed opportunity. The Russian response to its rejection was not limited to resentment. Rejection was claimed as a license to plunder eastern Europe, especially East Germany, of vast amounts of industrial and railroad equipment. In a few years, West Germany would benefit from substantial Marshall Plan aid while East Germany struggled to recover from Soviet "reparations." The long-lasting economic imbalance between the two Germanys thus was not simply a matter of capitalist success and socialist failure: It had much to do with their opposite predicaments of reconstruction. The Berlin Wall needs to be viewed, at least in part, as a consequence of this lack of economic parity. From the political division of Germany in 1949 until the Wall was built in 1961, more than 2,600,000 persons had left East Germany for the increasingly prosperous West Germany, with severe economic consequences for the East. Labor shortages impaired both industry and agriculture; the flight of professionals depleted education, health care, and social services.[21] (As Communist authority in East Germany abruptly disintegrated in late 1989, another such exodus prompted the regime to open the Wall in a desperate move to win public support and entice exiles to return. The reunification of Germany, an untouchable topic for forty years, suddenly became a vexing issue for U.S.-U.S.S.R. relations, NATO, and the Warsaw Pact.)

Much more important in President Truman's mind than aid to the Russians were the post-war implications of the atom bomb. A momentous question is whether the final decision to drop the bomb on Japan was invested with high expectations concerning its political impact on the Russians. The development of atomic weapons had been a secret shared only by the U.S. and Britain—or so they thought. When Truman sought to impress Stalin at Potsdam on July 24 with "casual mention" of a new weapon

119

of "unusual destructive force," he could not have known that Stalin knew all about the bomb. Klaus Fuchs, a brilliant German refugee physicist, had been a Los Alamos insider and simultaneously a very successful Soviet spy. U.S. attempts to conceal the bomb from the Russians had actually increased Stalin's suspicions and his desperation to develop the Soviets' own atomic weapons.

Whether the bombing of Hiroshima was also, or even primarily, viewed as the political bombing of Moscow remains an unsettled controversy. Revisionist historians Gar Alperovitz, Martin Sherwin, and Peter Wyden all have pressed the thesis that Russia was a psychological target of the bomb and that, militarily, the bombing of Hiroshima was unnecessary to end the war with Japan in the summer of 1945. McGeorge Bundy's recent review of atomic decision-making is remarkably indignant in seeking to discredit that thesis.[22]

Truman's conduct at Potsdam was plainly influenced by Secretary James F. Byrnes who believed that "rattling the bomb might make Russia more manageable."[23] Secretary Byrnes went off to the London Council of Foreign Ministers' meeting in September 1945 emboldened by "the bomb in his pocket" to make no concessions to the Russians and to force concessions from them, especially in Eastern Europe. He didn't succeed. It was a rancorous meeting, so much so that John Foster Dulles, who attended as an adviser, regarded that as the beginning of the Cold War.[24]

The Soviets surely knew that the Baruch Plan of 1946 for the international control of atomic energy, presented to the United Nations, was not a totally serious offer in the minds of some top U.S. policy-makers, who correctly predicted that the Soviets would reject it anyway. The plan would have allowed the U.S. to maintain a monopoly of atomic weapons technology indefinitely while denying the U.S.S.R. the opportunity to develop such weapons and threatening intrusive inspection and punishment (perhaps by U.S. atomic weapons). Andrei Gromyko responded with a counter-proposal: an immediate outlawing and destruction of all atomic bombs, under a system of inspection and control that included a veto power. No doubt the Russians knew the Americans would reject that plan—which, of course, is what happened.

Cold War Policy and Machinery

In February 1946, the U.S. deputy chief of mission in Moscow, George Kennan, dispatched a sixteen-page document (later known as the "Long Telegram") to Washington that offered a balanced and coherent picture of U.S.-Soviet relations. That document provided an intellectual foundation for the policy of *containment*—although the term "containment" was not then mentioned. The "Long Telegram" underscored the national and historical roots of Soviet power, rather than ideological ones: Marxism was described as merely "the fig leaf of . . . moral and political respectability" for Stalinist policies that were brutal and unscrupulous. Stalin's paranoia and fear of "capitalist encirclement" were emphasized, along with the hope of Stalin's demise as an opportunity for significant change. Kennan appealed for efforts to promote public understanding and a positive vision of the American future and warned against a mindless anti-communism:

> I am convinced that there would be far less hysterical anti-Sovietism in our country today if the realities . . . were better understood by our people. . . . The greatest danger that can befall us in coping with the problem of Soviet Communism is that we shall allow ourselves to become like those with whom we are coping.[25]

Nearly a year and a half later, Kennan published substantially the same analysis in *Foreign Affairs* (July 1947) under the title "The Sources of Soviet Conduct" and the mysterious pseudonym, "Mr. X." By then he had become the first director of the State Department's Policy Planning Staff under Secretary George Marshall. It was the "Mr. X" article that introduced the word "containment": "the main element of any United States policy toward the Soviet

121

Union must be that of a long-term, patient but firm and vigilant containment of Russian expansive tendencies."[26]

These passages hardly warranted the ideological zealotry with which John Foster Dulles and others prosecuted U.S. policy in the 1950s, nor did they prescribe a primarily militaristic response to Soviet power, nor could they ever excuse the assaults on civil liberties by the government and in the universities, the media, and the churches, all in the name of anti-communism, which blotted those same years.

Elaborate new U.S. policy machinery for the Cold War was established by the National Security Acts of 1947 and 1949: a National Security Council based in the White House, a Department of Defense to coordinate the armed services, a Central Intelligence Agency with both analytical and operational functions. Military and paramilitary priorities increasingly dominated diplomacy. And nuclear priorities increasingly dominated both military and diplomatic policies.

The Marshall Plan

The Cold War was also waged with economic weapons. In the spring of 1947, Kennan's Policy Planning Staff formulated proposals for the European Recovery Program that would come to be known as the Marshall Plan. Originally that program may have had the potential for helping to reconcile the divisions between Western and Eastern Europe. The Soviet Union and all Eastern European nations were invited to participate. Politically, however, the plan was double-edged. Its peacemaking possibilities were offset by its anti-communist promotion. The plan appealed to Western countries like France and Italy where communist parties were exploiting economic weakness and aggravating political chaos. Congress and the American public were sold on the plan by the dualistic appeal of humanitarian aid and anti-communist self-interest.

Stalin's paranoia, of course, was aroused by these political as well as economic stakes in the European Recovery Program. He rejected participation not only for the U.S.S.R. but for all countries under his sway. One ironic and deeply tragic consequence of this conjunction of European recovery and the Cold War concerned Czechoslovakia. A decade after Hitler had seized that beleaguered democratic nation, Stalin repeated the offense. The Soviet-imposed coup in Prague in February 1948 followed the unanimous decision of the Czech cabinet to accept the invitation to participate in the Marshall Plan. Instead of being drawn into cooperative relationships with Western Europe, this fragile democracy was undone and enclosed behind the Iron Curtain. The Czech coup dismayed and disillusioned Western liberals who had labored to curb Cold War hysteria.

The Berlin Blockade and NATO

After the breakdown of four-power negotiations over the future of Germany in December 1947, followed by Russian withdrawal from the Allied Control Council in Berlin in March 1948, the Western powers proceeded to plan for the separate rehabilitation of West Germany. The first step was a currency reform initiated in June without Soviet consultation. The Russians responded by stopping all road and rail traffic between the West and Berlin, whereupon the Western powers stopped all rail freight between West and East. The Berlin Blockade lasted nearly a year, until May 1949. It was the first direct military confrontation of the Cold War and threatened to become the first battle of World War III. The U.S. Air Force transferred sixty long-range bombers to Britain. West Berliners were sustained by the prodigious airlift of food, coal, and other supplies.

Before the blockade ended, the Western Allies had signed the North Atlantic Treaty in Washington April 4, 1949. The Soviets had not only been defeated in the effort to force the Western powers out of Berlin: they had provoked the creation of a new military alliance against them. The admission of West Germany to NATO in October 1954 and its subsequent remilitarization put off indefinitely any serious thought of German reunification. In 1955, the U.S.S.R. and its satellites constituted a counter-NATO alliance, the Warsaw Treaty Organization. Rival military blocs increasingly defined the essence of the Cold War.

Cold War and Hot Wars in Asia

Paralleling the European conflicts were those of East Asia. Following the communist triumph in China in November 1949, some politicians and church folk became vengeful vigilantes in seeking to expose those Americans responsible for the "loss" of China. There was fervent opposition to diplomatic recognition and UN membership for Mao Zedong's China for three decades.

The outbreak of the Korean War in June 1950 may well have been a surprise to Mao Zedong—but its escalation provoked massive Chinese intervention. As General Douglas MacArthur's forces, lacking clear policy direction from Washington, threatened to extend the war into Manchuria, China sent 180,000 troops across the Yalu River and sent American and South Korean troops reeling in retreat. While the war ended in stalemate, the hostility toward Mao's China, the simultaneous guarantee of Chiang Kai-shek's security on Taiwan, and the deployment of the U.S. Seventh Fleet off the China coast became long-term features of the Cold War.

In the background of the Korean War and the bitterness of relations between Washington and Peking was U.S. post-war policy concerning Japan. George Kennan's memoirs suggest that the unilateral U.S. occupation of Japan, the exclusion of the U.S.S.R. from the Japan peace treaty, and the establishment in Japan of the major U.S. military base in Northeast Asia were serious policy blunders that probably led to Stalin's decision to sanction and support the North Korean invasion of the South. Stalin had good reason to believe the U.S. would not respond militarily because Korea had been declared beyond "the defense perimeter" by Secretary of State Dean Acheson in January 1950. Kennan believed in 1948 that the neutralization and demilitarization of Japan, through U.S.-U.S.S.R. negotiations, would have been a more prudent security policy in the region. However, he did support limited U.S. military action once the invasion had taken place.[27]

Harry Truman's memoirs tend to confirm Kennan's thesis that Japan policy was conceived in anti-Soviet terms. Speaking of the last weeks of World War II, Truman reflected:

> Anxious as we were to have Russia in the war against Japan, the experience at Potsdam now made me determined that I would not allow the Russians any part in the control of Japan. . . . I made up my mind that General MacArthur would be given complete command and control after victory in Japan. We were not going to be disturbed by Russian tactics in the Pacific. Force is the only thing the Russians understand.[28]

Stalin was surely made aware of Truman's hard line on Japan.

Once again we are invited to contemplate a very heavy "what-if." If Kennan's surmise is correct, and had his own policy views prevailed, the Korean War might never have occurred, U.S. relations with China might have normalized much sooner, and—dare one imagine it?—the Vietnam War might have been precluded, or at least mitigated. Fundamental to the U.S. rationale for the Vietnam War was the containment of "Asian communism," presumably controlled by China. Louis Halle's review of the disasters of U.S. east Asian policy up to 1950 offers this lament:

> Misunderstanding, misconception, mistake—these are inevitable in all international controversy. In the history of the Cold War as it developed in the Far East, however, they are consistently predominant. Americans, Russians, and Chinese, time and again, completely mistook the situation with which they had to deal. Time and again they acted on false premises, often with catastrophic consequences from which they could not afterwards extricate themselves. Bloody conflicts took place that neither side had intended, that neither side wanted, and that neither side could end. The Korean War was the greatest of these.[29]

Had Halle written his book a bit later, he might have said that the Vietnam War was the greatest of these.

Cold War Blueprint

It was in April 1950 that the National Security Council drafted a secret document (only declassified a quarter century later) that would be the U.S. blueprint for waging the Cold War until the détente of the 1970s. Known as NSC-68, the document was highly ideological and militaristic. It was opposed by Kennan as too rigid, bellicose, and simplistic, but he was overruled by Secretary of State Dean Acheson who wanted to seize the initiative in the Cold War and also to "shut up critics at home." The premises of NSC-68 were "the polarization of power which inescapably confronts the slave society with the free" and an alleged Soviet design for world conquest. The blueprint advocated development of hydrogen bombs, a rapid buildup of conventional forces, strong military alliances, a vague strategy to undermine the "Soviet totalitariat" from within, and a policy of non-negotiation until the Kremlin was prepared to "change its policies drastically."[30] Principal author of the crusading rhetoric of NSC-68 was Paul Nitze, who nearly three decades later would spearhead the fight against the SALT II Treaty by the Committee on the Present Danger and still later serve as arms control adviser in the Reagan administration.

Détente, Now and Then

Our discussion of this "long twilight struggle" has focused on the origins and defining events of the Cold War. It is beyond the scope of this volume to add narrative details for the years 1950–1970, although those years were also loaded with "what-if" moments. The U-2 incident, which shattered the promise of the Paris summit in May 1960—an occasion when Dwight Eisenhower and Nikita Khrushchev might have reached breakthroughs on Germany and disarmament issues—was one such moment. The Cuban Missile Crisis of October 1962 staged the Cold War's most anxious hours when some policy-makers on both sides believed a nuclear war was imminent—but mercifully found a formula for extrication. While that crisis is remembered as a triumph of American diplomacy, its costs proved to be long-lasting: Castro gained a guarantee of security and the Soviets were spurred to escalate their strategic missile buildup, which would achieve nuclear parity with the United States by 1970.

In each of a number of intermittent periods of apparent détente, some hopeful persons have declared the end of the Cold War.

There was Eisenhower's "Spirit of Camp David" when Khrushchev came calling in 1959—the spirit that was undone by U-2.

There was John Kennedy's "Strategy for Peace" address at American University in June 1963, pleading for a positive change of attitude toward the Soviet Union and its legitimate security interests, followed in a few weeks by the Partial Test Ban Treaty prohibiting atmospheric nuclear tests.

There was Lyndon Johnson's "Spirit of Glassboro" in June 1967 when Alexei Kosygin and LBJ reached virtual agreement on the draft of a nuclear Non-Proliferation Treaty, followed up a year later by a joint announcement to start Strategic Arms Limitation (SALT) Talks, which, alas, were put off after the Warsaw Pact invasion of Czechoslovakia August 21, 1968.

Then Richard Nixon offered his "generation of peace." While prolonging the Vietnam War four years, he went to China and also managed a season of détente that produced the first SALT accords with the Soviet Union. The political climate in Europe had been transformed by the *ostpolitik* of West German Chancellor Willy Brandt, which secured treaties with the U.S.S.R. and Poland and facilitated a four-power agreement normalizing the status of West Berlin.

The achievements and non-achievements of SALT I in 1972 produced starkly ambiguous results that got projected all the way to the 1990s and perhaps beyond. The most vital achievement of SALT I was the ABM (Anti-Ballistic Missile) Treaty, for two reasons: (1) The ABM Treaty recognized the defenselessness of the so-called "superpowers" in the

Nuclear Age—a recognition that would later be repudiated by Ronald Reagan's drive for space-based defenses. (2) The ABM Treaty established some very useful grievance machinery in Geneva, the Standing Consultative Commission. After years of mutually satisfactory service to both the U.S. and U.S.S.R. during the Nixon, Ford, and Carter administrations, that commission was virtually disabled by the shrill propaganda and specious charges of the Reagan administration. SALT I also produced a five-year interim freeze on offensive missiles, intended to set the stage for a SALT II treaty curbing such missiles.

However, the great failure of SALT I was that the Nixon administration (more especially Henry Kissinger) failed to face up to the consequences of deploying MIRVs that the U.S. began in 1970. The "multiple independently-targetable re-entry vehicles" mounted on both land-based and sub-based missiles were central to the general failure to accept and stabilize nuclear parity with the U.S.S.R. and thereby contributed to the demise of the détente of the 1970s. It was another one of those "what-if" moments. While the U.S. presented various proposals to limit MIRVs, they were always loaded with "provisions that ensured their unacceptability" to the U.S.S.R. "as Kissinger well understood and intended."[31] Kissinger allied himself with the Pentagon's technological fix on MIRVs instead of with the strong opposition to MIRVs in Congress and the Arms Control and Disarmament Agency.

Kissinger's failure has proved absolutely critical for all subsequent efforts at arms control. It meant that, far from weakening the U.S. nuclear arsenal in the 1970s (as some prevaricators still like to claim), 5,000 more nuclear weapons were added. And it meant that the U.S.S.R. would be challenged to follow suit, as it did after about five years. And it is the specter of those MIRVed Soviet missiles that was repeatedly invoked to oppose SALT II and to promote still another generation of U.S. missiles.

The Nixon administration's preoccupation with the Watergate scandals in 1973 and 1974 dimmed prospects for sustaining détente. A special irony in that period was the

The Saviour (Spasskaya) Tower, entrance to the Kremlin from Red Square, built in 1491.

The 170-foot memorial monument atop Mamayev Hill in Volgograd, site of bitterest fighting in the Battle of Stalingrad. (Size indicated by two maintenance men on right shoulder.)

Silhouetted statue of Saint Vladimir, whose baptism in 988 inaugurated the Christianity of Rus, on the heights above the Dnieper River at Kiev.

Russian Orthodox worshippers in prayer before an icon of the Theotokos (Mother of God) and the infant Jesus.

Evening worship and music at the Moscow Baptist Church.

General Secretary Alexei Bichkov of the All-Union Council of Evangelical Christians-Baptists (left) and the author.

desperate concern of Soviet leaders that Americans should save the Nixon presidency. Nixon, the anti-communist careerist, had become a familiar and negotiable adversary, at least on some issues. I recall attending a conference in Berlin in April 1974 and being implored at length by two Russian leaders to do everything I possibly could to prevent Nixon's downfall. (It can now be revealed that I failed, and was disinclined, to save Nixon.)

Nixon did fall that August. Gerald Ford went to Vladivostok and met Leonid Brezhnev in November 1974. There they worked out basic principles and equal limits for a SALT II Treaty limiting offensive nuclear weapons. Negotiations stalled during 1975 as the Ford administration foundered over disputes between the State and Defense departments and attacks by congressional hardliners. The fall of South Vietnam to Hanoi in April 1975 and Soviet-Cuban involvement in Angola subjected the administration to a fresh round of anti-Soviet alarmism. With conspicuous diffidence, Ford traveled to Helsinki in late July to sign the Final Act of the Conference on Security and Cooperation in Europe (CSCE), originally a Soviet initiative to stabilize boundaries, promote détente, and lower East-West trade barriers. Western insistence on strong humanitarian and human rights provisions was reluctantly accommodated by the Soviets. The Helsinki Final Act was welcomed by most Europeans, West and East, as a decisive step toward détente and continental wholeness. Many Americans fixed only on its human rights articles, particularly as weapons of anti-Soviet attack.

Secretary Kissinger nearly completed a SALT II agreement in Moscow in January 1976—but the consummating negotiations were called off by the Ford White House because, in that election year, the popular Ronald Reagan was running against Gerald Ford by attacking détente and arms control. Kissinger urged Ford to rebut Reagan head-on, but Richard B. Cheney (then White House Chief of Staff, later Secretary of Defense in the Bush administration) strongly advised against it. As Reagan stepped up his primary rhetoric, Ford pointedly announced in March, "We are going to forget the word détente." Thus détente was dropped from the official vocabulary and virtually from public discourse. It had lost its legitimacy in America. SALT was put on the shelf.[32]

Ten years of fairly steady deterioration of U.S.-Soviet relations followed that Reagan primary campaign of 1976 that nearly captured the Republican nomination. Reagan's turnabout toward the U.S.S.R. and the INF Treaty late in his own presidency cannot efface the fact that he contributed more than any other person to the forsaking of détente and a decade of regression to the harshest of Cold War hostilities. The political, economic, and human costs of that regression can never be adequately measured.

Carter and the Russians

Jimmy Carter raised new hopes for détente by emphasizing nuclear disarmament and reduced defense spending— at least in his 1976 campaign and his 1977 inaugural. But by the spring of 1978, Carter's collapse in public opinion polls and an increasingly aggressive opposition led his advisers to get Carter to "talk tough" to the Russians and deemphasize disarmament. As National Security Adviser Zbigniew Brzezinski increasingly gained the ear and the mind of President Carter, to the exclusion of other foreign policy advisers, the U.S. line hardened further. A White House colleague remarked that Brzezinski enjoyed being "the first Pole in 300 years in a position to really stick it to the Russians."[33] Brzezinski "played the China card" in May 1978, going off to Peking to share SALT secrets and talk about "common strategic interests," thus undoing the scrupulous correctness with which Nixon and Kissinger, to their credit, had balanced the U.S.-Soviet-Chinese triangle.

In May 1979, just weeks before the SALT II Treaty was signed in Vienna after seven long years of tedious negotiations, Carter sought to buy conservative support for the treaty by approving the MX missile, of all things. The Senate Foreign Relations Committee's summer 1979 hearings on the treaty became more of a platform for promoting increased military spending than for détente. While the administration's own testimony revealed that the Soviets under Brezhnev had made the major concessions in treaty negotiations, the public never quite discovered that fact. The truth was that the U.S.S.R. agreed to exclude "forward-based systems" (U.S. and other NATO bombers and missiles based in Europe) from both SALT I and SALT II limits; to allow very large numbers (20-28) of cruise missiles on U.S. bombers; to limit drastically the number of warheads on Soviet heavy missiles (down to 10 from a potential of 30 or more); and to scrap more than 250 intercontinental missiles, while the U.S. was not obliged to scrap any. On these very favorable terms, the Joint Chiefs of Staff supported the treaty, not only during the Carter administration but well into the Reagan administration— only to find their civilian chiefs, Reagan and Defense Secretary Caspar Weinberger, insisting that the treaty was "fatally flawed." The fact that these concessions were made during the Brezhnev years needs to be remembered in the Gorbachev years. There has been more continuity in Soviet arms control policies before and since 1985 than even some normally well-informed commentators now suppose.[34]

In September 1979 there was an absolutely capricious flap over a single, long-standing Soviet brigade in Cuba, which further poisoned the political atmosphere surrounding the "centerpiece of détente," the SALT II Treaty. The Iranian hostage crisis, from November 4 on, was so all-absorbing that it tended to preclude diplomatic progress on superpower issues. Then, without any significant public debate in the U.S. or most other NATO countries, NATO foreign ministers on December 12 gave the go-ahead to the development of Pershing II rockets and ground-launched cruise missiles for Europe. By that time, both administration and congressional leaders, along with the press, indicated that the SALT II Treaty was probably dead in the Senate.

All these things occurred before the Soviet invasion of Afghanistan December 27, 1979, which Carter with great hyperbole greeted as "the most serious crisis since World War II." At Carter's request, the SALT II Treaty was

131

removed from the Senate calendar. That the invasion was a barbarous assault on the Afghan people cannot be doubted; that it was the primary reason for the non-ratification of SALT II is very much to be doubted.

Reagan and the Evil Empire

For six years the Reagan administration was too tempted by ambitions for nuclear superiority and too stalemated by internal bureaucratic pressures to make any real progress toward disarmament. Its extremely anti-Soviet rhetoric and dubious charges of treaty violations hardly created a climate for agreement. Its Geneva proposals, whether for strategic arms cuts or Euromissiles, were so designedly one-sided as to be non-negotiable, thanks largely to the intellectual and bureaucratic talents of one man, Assistant Secretary of Defense Richard Perle, widely known in Washington circles as "The Prince of Darkness." Strobe Talbott's scrupulous account of Reagan's first-term arms control policies concluded that administration officials believed "the U.S. would do best with gambits at the negotiating table that would lead to diplomatic stalemate" while keeping up "the appearance of playing the old arms-control game."[35]

Reagan's Strategic Defense Initiative ("Star Wars") risked destroying the most vital bilateral accord, the ABM Treaty, even while it obstructed negotiations on offensive weapons, spurred the pursuit of new offensive technologies, multiplied U.S. nuclear tests, and threatened to cost a trillion dollars or more. His opposition to a comprehensive test ban frustrated the consummation of two decades of progress in negotiations under five previous administrations. His regional policies in Central America, Africa, and Asia tended to turn every indigenous or North-South conflict into an East-West confrontation. His ideological hostility, hectoring on human rights, and "rearmament" program led to five years of defensive Soviet conduct, including the reduction of Jewish emigration to near zero. His foreign policies altogether did more to generate an array of peace and anti-nuclear movements, albeit by way of reaction, than had any administration since the 1960s.

Things began to change in 1985. The pressure of the new movements in both America and Europe, the engagement of church leaders and other professions, the resistance of a Democratic Congress, enormous budget deficits, embarrassment in becoming the first administration in three decades to fail to negotiate a single arms agreement, and, most especially, the advent and disarmament initiatives of Mikhail Gorbachev, all combined to persuade Reagan to make some kind of peace with the Russians before he retired.

There were four summits (a record for any president), in Geneva, Reykjavik, Washington, and Moscow. There was a treaty to eliminate an entire category of nuclear weapons for the first time: intermediate nuclear forces (INF), missiles with ranges between 300 and 3,000 miles, most of which were deployed in Europe. The treaty did not affect the strategic nuclear arsenals of the superpowers, which kept growing all during the Reagan years, but were the topic of the START (Strategic Arms Reduction) Talks which might produce a treaty in the Bush administration.

The drama of reconciliation and friendship between Ronald Reagan and Mikhail Gorbachev led many observers to conclude that the Cold War had ended at last. The Cold War had seemed to end in 1959, and again in 1963, and again in 1972. Whether it was really over in 1989 as Reagan retired to his California ranch remained to be seen.

For most of the Bush administration's first year, the watchword was caution. There was a prolonged review of U.S. strategic policies, accompanied by indecision as to whether Gorbachev's reforms were genuine, doubts as to whether Gorbachev could survive, and a disposition to just sit tight and let Gorbachev's arms concessions keep coming. By the fall of 1989, George Bush apparently was persuaded that Gorbachev's leadership justified some U.S. commendation and accommodation. At a "pre-summit summit" in turbulent waters off Malta in early December, Presidents Bush and Gorbachev agreed to seek early accords on reductions in strategic arms (START), conventional forces in Europe (CFE), and chemical weapons, as well as on verification of continued nuclear testing within the limits of the still-unratified Threshold Test Ban (TTB) of 1974. Gorbachev appealed for "a common European home," Bush for "a Europe whole and free."

At the dawning of the last decade of the millennium, there was renewed talk of the end of the Cold War. Some Americans even joined in a quasi-apocalyptic celebration of "the end of history," the supposed triumph of Western democratic values, capitalist ideology, and nuclear deterrence. It was far from certain, however, that such triumphalism would ultimately prove to be a benign influence on the world's unending struggles for justice and peace.

CHAPTER 6

So Different, So Similar

You Russians and we Americans;—our countries so distant, so unlike at first glance—such a difference in social and political conditions and our respective methods of moral and practical development . . . and yet in certain features, and vastest ones, so resembling each other. The variety of stock-elements and tongues . . . the idea perennial through the ages that they both have their historic and divine mission . . . the grand expanse of territorial limits and boundaries—the unformed and nebulous state of many things . . . the deathless aspirations at the inmost centre of each great community . . . are certainly features you Russians and we Americans possess in common.

—Walt Whitman[1]
"Letter to Russia," 1881

Civilization is imperiled by . . . bureaucratized dogmatism, a spreading of mass myths that put entire peoples and continents under the power of cruel and treacherous demagogues.

—Andrei Sakharov[2]
Progress, Coexistence, and Intellectual Freedom

A generation ago, a witty Englishman produced an engaging portrait of the Russian people, highlighting the profound differences between them and his own com-

135

patriots. Because many Russians "look rather English," wrote Wright Miller, and

> have a similar sense of humour to the English, learn the same geometry and algebra, play the same hopscotch, prefer to be free from political police, would like more woolens and more nylons, wish little harm to their neighbours, would dash into the road to snatch a child from under a car—it does not follow that, with all this in common, they are so much like ourselves.[3]

The assessment of similarities and differences between two nations, especially two nations regarding each other as enemies, is an imperative of peacemaking. It may be that the differences between Americans and Russians are even greater than those between the English and the Russians—or, conversely, it may be that the similarities are really more profound. If the latter, the similarities may offer the potential bonds of reconciliation—or they may be precisely the factors that generate peculiarly intense rivalry and hostility.

There is a great paradox in comparing and contrasting the United States and the Soviet Union. The paradox is made the more stunning by the mutual ignorance of our two peoples. One side of the paradox is to discover how radically different are the historical experiences, cultural backgrounds, social patterns, and political systems of the two superpowers. The promise of détente more than once has been oversold because of an untutored appreciation of the enduring sources of estrangement and tension. The quick, hearty embraces with which some Americans celebrate fellow-feeling with some Russians can short-circuit authentic human encounter. Disillusionment, sometimes to despair, is the price to be paid for neglecting the realities of cultural chasms and mutual isolation.

But there is another side to the paradox. It is the surprising discovery that there are, after all, many parallels and affinities between the superpowers. That can be either a hopeful or a disheartening discovery; it is an arresting ambiguity. These similarities get projected into the affairs of many other peoples who may have good reason to view the world as dominated by a superpower condominium, albeit a competitive one.

First, there are indeed radical differences.

Freedom vs. Security

There is a conspicuous polarity between the two political cultures. For most Americans, the transcendent value and symbol has been *freedom*. Whether one thinks of the waves of immigrants fleeing Old World tyrannies, or the Declaration of Independence, or Franklin Roosevelt's Four Freedoms, or the powerful songs and rhetoric of the civil rights movement, there has been a deep-souled resonance to freedom. The freedom and independence of the nation have been variously enhanced by the world's oldest constitution, continental isolation, religious pluralism, economic abundance, and military might.

Security has been the passion and preoccupation of Russian history. All those invasions and conquests by Mongols, Swedes, Poles, French, Germans, and others have fortified the Russian determination to maintain a strong central state, whether tsarist or communist. The vastness of Russian territory means vulnerability in many directions, not just strength. The U.S.S.R. shares land borders with no fewer than twelve nations: Norway, Finland, Poland, Czechoslovakia, Hungary, Romania, Turkey, Iran, Afghanistan, China, Mongolia, and Korea— and also directly confronts Japan and the United States in the North Pacific. Russia has a conflicted history with every single one of these fourteen nations.

It is, of course, Nazi Germany's assault in the Great Patriotic War that has especially shaped the territorial imperatives felt by the Russians for the past half-century. A visit to Volgograd inevitably means viewing a film and a panorama of the Battle of Stalingrad: productions that dramatize the fierce power of hate to defeat Germany and the absolute determination to remain militarily strong. Goosestepping Young Pioneers at war monuments in all Soviet cities testify to this mix of bitter memory and resolute security.

137

There is a more domestic aspect of this preoccupation with security: a compound of the autocracy inherited from Mongol and tsarist times, with its obsession with secrecy and fear of anarchy, and the paternalistic socialism of the Soviet state. Notwithstanding consumer frustrations, Soviet citizens do share in a system of fundamental social security: a kind of social contract in which employment, health care, housing, and pensions are guaranteed, whatever their limitations.

The American-Russian polarity of freedom-security has been poignantly experienced by thousands of recent Russian immigrants to the United States. Seeking freedom, they have suffered the anxieties of insecurity concerning jobs, homes, health care, and urban violence. Some have returned to Mother Russia to reclaim their lost security.

Yet the freedom-security contrast is hardly absolute. While social security is an incomplete project in America, the welfare state has come a long way since 1935. And since 1947, *national security* has been the definitive concept of U.S. foreign policy—often to the impairment of freedom and other values. Its extreme anti-Soviet animus has often led to the danger Kennan warned against in his "Long Telegram" of 1946: that Americans "allow ourselves to become like those with whom we are coping."

On the other side, the Russians have inherited their own disparate traditions of freedom, which, to be sure, have yet to succeed in creating a liberal state. But it is a cruel disparagement of Russian spirit and genius over many generations not to recognize the currents of liberalization borne with great courage and suffering. Wright Miller has identified four of these traditions: (1) the tradition of peasant revolts against injustice; (2) the essentially Protestant tradition of the prophetic and ascetic monk, modeled in the fifteenth century by Nil of Sorsk, who preached a doctrine of justification by "prayer from the heart" as more important than liturgical observance and who protested against the use of state power or wealth for the Church; (3) the spirit of individual enterprise and trade among the peasants ("the rock on which every Soviet policy for complete collectivization of the land has split"); and (4) the tradition of the nineteenth century *intelligentsia* and its struggle against tyranny and reaction.[4]

Two other forces for potential liberalization of the Soviet state have been conspicuously responsive to opportunities created by Gorbachev's *glasnost* and *perestroika:* ethnic demands for autonomy in various republics and Orthodox renewal. The very survival of the Russian Orthodox Church more than seven decades and three generations after the imposition of a repressive atheist regime is a powerful sanction for intellectual pluralism, if not yet political opposition. In a May 1989 address to the European Ecumenical Assembly in Basel, Archbishop Kirill of Smolensk credited Orthodoxy's ecumenical and international associations with strengthening the intellectual vitality of the Church, whose very "existence, despite organized and powerful atheistic propaganda, made people think. . . . The voice of the Church returned to the country in a roundabout way . . . by means of resolutions and documents of ecumenical organizations, peacemaking conferences, reaching political and public circles."[5]

The Russian intelligentsia is a class that knows no precise parallel in America. It is not to be identified exclusively with academics, although professors and research scientists are included. Its leaders tend to be poets, novelists, artists, architects, actors, dancers, musicians, film and broadcast producers. Doctors, leading managers and technicians, and librarians also belong to this class which perhaps numbers 25 million persons out of a Soviet total of 290 million. The intelligentsia enjoyed special status in the first year of the Revolution, but Stalinist orthodoxies and purges decimated its most creative leadership. From the 1930s until the mid-1980s, there was a half-century of mutual mistrust between political rulers and intelligentsia—a mistrust only partially overcome during the brief "thaw" under Nikita Khrushchev in the late 1950s and early 1960s. It was the 1966 post-Khrushchev trial of Andrei Sinyavsky and Yuli Daniel, two writers sent to prison for publishing books abroad under pseudonyms, that provoked the rise of the "dissidents," along with *samizdat*, the self-published circulation of literary works and political protests. Years of action and reaction between official repression and freshets of dissidence followed.

One of the more spectacular aspects of *glasnost* is a degree of rapprochement between political leadership and the intelligentsia not seen since the 1920s. Gorbachev has reached out to the intelligentsia, much as he has reached out to the churches, soliciting spiritual and moral energy for *perestroika*. He freed Andrei Sakharov from exile, had a cordial meeting with that leading dissident, and permitted his election to the Soviet parliament; ended most forms of censorship, thus encouraging a resumption of de-Stalinization and filling in the "blank pages" of history; and permitted long-suppressed films and manuscripts to go public. Poet Yevgeni Yevtushenko, with a mixture of hope and caution, speaks of a "pre-renaissance" in literature and the arts, knowing that a political backlash could yet prevent the full flowering of Russian culture.

Individual and Community

Closely intertwined with the competing values of freedom and security are the credos of individualism and community. One credo is all-American. The other is very Russian.

Sociologist Robert Bellah and four collaborators have provided a thoroughly researched account of American individualism in their 1985 study, *Habits of the Heart: Individualism and Commitment in American Life*. Individualism, they report, "lies at the very core of American culture." While noting several different sources of this ethos, the authors claim that personal and national identity for all Americans is very much implicated in these affirmations:

> We believe in the dignity, indeed the sacredness, of the individual. Anything that would violate our right to think for ourselves, judge for ourselves, make our own decisions, live our lives as we see fit, is not only morally wrong, it is

sacrilegious. Our highest and noblest aspirations, not only for ourselves, but for those we care about, for our society and for the world, are closely linked to our individualism.[6]

Bellah et al. do not propose the abandonment of such a credo, but they do question whether it fosters genuine *individuality* if it doesn't view the individual "in relation to a larger whole, a community and a tradition."[7] They are ultimately concerned to nurture the common life, public life, as well as private life. In an inspired conclusion, *Habits of the Heart* declares:

> Perhaps enduring commitment to those we love and civic friendship toward our fellow citizens are preferable to restless competition and anxious self-defense. Perhaps common worship, in which we express our gratitude and wonder in the face of the mystery of being itself, is the most important thing of all. . . . We will need to remember that we did not create ourselves, that we owe what we are to the communities that formed us, and to what Paul Tillich called 'the structure of grace in history' that made such communities possible.[8]

Here perhaps are the deepest of human realities: that individuality and community are not really polar opposites but are inextricably bound up together. The drive of modern America—not least in the past decade—has been to atomize and abstract the individual from the public and nurturing community.

By contrast, the whole of Russian history has submerged the individual into the collectivity. It was so in Kievan Rus, in Mongol times, in all the tsarist centuries, and, with modern ideological warrants, in the Bolshevik decades.

In their psychic depths, Russians share a primordial sense of community. Wright Miller traces that sense to two ancient sources: the common life of village communities under the traditional order of the *Mir* or village assembly; and the communal liturgy of the Orthodox Church. Village life, in turn, was strongly cemented by intricately extensive kinship systems so that peasants were conscious of living in great families or clans. It has been the spirit of Orthodox Christianity to "help to breed in Russians their conviction that in the common sharing of an experience—divine in church worship, man-made in Communist achievement— they preserve a truer humanity than a Westerner can partake of in his over-cultivation of the individual."[9] Suzanne Massie suggests that family consciousness and Orthodox worship combined in early centuries to solidify the shared communitarian identity of the *sobornost*, not only at the village level but in the common bonds of nationhood:

> The whole Russian people once thought of themselves idealistically as a single, immense family, with the tsar as a father. Russian peasants, down through the centuries, addressed everyone, even strangers, in terms of kinship— father, mother, brother, sister. The individual life was only a fleeting moment in the life of this great clan. In their church, Russians found a full sense of this *sobornost*, or feeling of community. Orthodox worship was a family affair.[10]

This idealization of collectivism, of course, lent itself to the forced industrialization and collectivized farming of Stalin's "socialism in one country," as well as the hyper-nationalism and horrid scale of sacrifice in the Great Patriotic War. Stalin's first five-year plan proceeded by more than forced labor and mass murder: It inspired enthusiastic young people to travel in unheated freight trains to uninhabited wildernesses, and there to build great steel plants, to work evenings and double shifts and holidays without extra pay—and millions of peasants to abandon their villages and join the assembly lines of the vast new industries, typically working long days and having no place to sleep except in the streets or railroad stations.[11] There was an exhilarating sense of sharing in a dramatic crusade to lift poor and backward Russia out of the squalor and miseries of the past. Most of the people "retained the sense of belonging to one great Russian community," despite much oppression, privation, and personal suffering.[12]

A contemporary Russian writer greatly laments this

traditional devaluation of the individual for the sake of collective sacrifice:

> We have no history of respecting the individual person as the supreme value of society, we have simply never accepted that idea. Look at the war [World War II]—we wasted men, they didn't matter. The second thing is, we have no history of individual mobility in this country. People live the lives they were born to, in the places where they were born. This has started to change a little, but not very much. The third thing is the traditions of the Russian Orthodox Church. Russian Christians have always been taught not to expect too much on this earth—the greatest rewards are meant to come in the next life.[13]

This polarity of individualism versus community remains strong enough to account for a prime issue in the international debate on human rights. Western, and especially American, promoters of human rights tend to fix on the civil and political liberties of individuals, while socialist and Third World protagonists tend to be preoccupied with economic and social rights, not merely of individuals but of groups and nations. A frequent Cold War ritual has occurred whenever U.S. public criticism of Soviet repression has met with Soviet criticism of U.S. unemployment, homelessness, and racism.

East and West

The polarities between freedom and security, and between the individual and the community, partake of a profound historical estrangement between Russian culture and the West. It is commonplace to recognize that Russian isolation precluded any significant share in the Renaissance, the Reformation and Counter-Reformation, the Enlightenment, and the liberal revolutions of Europe—all of which formed the cultural heritage of the United States.

To label Russia as "Eastern" is therefore at least an important half-truth. It is to take seriously the centuries of Russian isolation from the West. It is to recall the fateful split between Eastern and Western Christianity that

143

developed over several centuries but became definitive in 1054. It is to remember the dual legacy of the Mongol conquests: the imposition of Asian patterns of autocracy and rigid separation from the West, nearly annihilating the European consciousness that had been nurtured during the flowering of Kievan Rus. It is to take account of the fall of Constantinople to the Turks in 1453, which not only encouraged Moscow's conceit as the Third Rome but interposed powerful Muslim barriers to communication with much of Europe. And it certainly means an awareness of the moral and ideological ostracism of the Soviet Union by the West after 1917, at times amounting to a virtual severance of political and cultural communication.

Russia before 1917 and after has been both a European and an Asian state. Perhaps fifty million citizens of the U.S.S.R. are ethnic Asians. Among ethnic Russians, however, there are deep anti-Asian sentiments. Russians in Siberia are perhaps the most Russian of all in their cultural consciousness. As the Soviet split with China widened in the 1960s, it became apparent that racist anti-Chinese attitudes underlay some of the ideological rhetoric. The Russian majority among Soviet peoples, barely 51 percent according to the 1989 census, will become a demographic minority in the 1990s.

Whatever the mix of Asian and European elements in Russian consciousness, there is a recurring struggle among Russians over the power and desirability of Western ways. Patriarch Nikon's seventeenth century ecclesiastical reforms invoked Western ideas that many priests regarded as treachery—and the Orthodox Church split. Peter the Great's importation of Western education, architecture, technology, and bureaucracy in the eighteenth century provoked a fierce nativist reaction. That reaction surged again when Catherine the Great established French as the language of royalty and French tutors spread Enlightenment culture among the Russian aristocracy.

It was among the emerging intelligentsia of the 1830s and 1840s that the Russian polarity between Westerners and Slavophiles was played out most dramatically. Both groups abhorred the repressive regime of Tsar Nicholas I: Westerners because the regime was closed to the democratic constitutionalism of the West, Slavophiles because the regime seemed an alien dynasty insensitive to the virtues of the peasant commune and the messianic national vision of the Orthodox Church. An aristocratic friend of Decembrist officers, Peter Tchaadayev, published *A Philosophic Letter* in 1836 that voiced the Westerners' dismay at the poverty of Russian heritage and the long cultural isolation from the West:

> Confined in our schism, nothing of what was happening in Europe reached us. We stood apart from the world's great venture. . . . While the whole world was building anew, we created nothing; we remained crouched in our hovels of log and thatch. In a word, we had no part in the new destinies of mankind. We were Christians, but the fruits of Christianity were not for us.[14]

Noted publicist Alexander Herzen, a Westerner in the 1830s, was converted by the Slavophiles by 1850 and celebrated the very isolation from Europe that Tchaadayev had so bitterly lamented:

> What a blessing it is for Russia that the rural commune has never been broken up, that private ownership has never replaced the property of the commune; how fortunate it is for the Russian people that they have remained outside all political movements, and, for that matter, outside European civilization.[15]

In the 1860s and 1870s, idealistic Slavophilism was overtaken by a new imperialistic and reactionary Pan-Slavism that projected Russian expansionism and inflamed traditional prejudices against Turks, Germans, and other non-Slavic peoples.

A more exalted, if less typical, expression of Russian destiny came in the later writings of Fyodor Dostoevsky: a messianic "Russian idea" of universal reconciliation through love and suffering in which a more Christ-like higher development of Russian culture would "redeem the errors of recent Western history."[16] Dostoevsky's ultimate conservatism, tending toward chauvinism, must also be recalled not merely for its critique of Western rationalism but for its prophetic anticipation of the Bolshevik Revolution decades later. The conspiratorial revolutionary of the 1870s, Sergei Nechayev (whose political philosophy so greatly influenced Lenin), was clearly the model for the revolutionary character, Peter Verkhovensky, in Dostoevsky's great political novel, *The Possessed*. Verkhovensky represents the nihilistic repudiation of both Christian heritage and moral scruples—and the antithesis of Dostoevsky's own "Russian idea."

There is, then, in Russian culture a profound sense of spiritual destiny that cannot accurately be denoted as either "Eastern" or "Western." Its content is unique and not easily accessible to American understanding. Its claim, however, is universal, as is the claim of the Russian Orthodox faith, which has nurtured that sense of destiny. So, too, is the claim of Bolshevik ideology, which sought to displace Orthodoxy but in many ways replicated it. Mikhail Gorbachev's "new thinking," however, is remarkable for its seeming abandonment of communist pretenses to universalism and its acceptance of cultural pluralism in the name of common humanity.

Wars Here and There

Perhaps nothing so divides Russian consciousness from American consciousness as this century's experience of two world wars, a violent revolution, and a civil war in the Russian homeland. Our American wars have all been fought "over there" in Europe or Korea or Vietnam: They have not devastated our cities and wasted our countryside. Not many of our public squares are dominated by towering memorials of World War II. There is no cemetery in the U.S. which quite parallels the Piskarevsky Cemetery in Leningrad where half a million victims of the 900-day siege are buried in mounds of 20,000 per mound and where family survivors come and stand for long periods, remembering and weeping. The domestic experience of world wars in the United States has been a boom time of economic recovery, occupational opportunity, and social mobility—so much so that the 1980s were marked by an older generation's nostalgia for "the good war" of the 1940s. The Russian remembrance of death and devastation in the 1940s remains a burning national trauma profoundly affecting politics, religion, and the arts. It is a trauma that equally underlies the Russian yearning for peace and the Russian determination to maintain military parity.

The Other Side of the Paradox

More than a century ago, an acute diplomatic observer of both American and Russian societies wrote that "the great republic of the New World and the vast empire of the North," despite being "surrounded by influences so opposite and antagonistic," shared many characteristics. To Albert F. Heard, the most "singular analogy" between the two peoples was their religious vitality, which had given rise to "extraordinary and extravagant ideas," "prophets and prophetesses of divers revelations," and a multiplicity of sects for whom "no doctrine has been too absurd, no creed too subversive of order or of morality, to find acceptance and gather adherents."[17]

If the range and depth of U.S.-Soviet differences compel our most consecrated efforts to understand them, an opposite inquiry is no less essential to understanding. The apprehension of an almost infinite array of striking similarities in the historical and cultural experiences of the superpowers is just as imperative. This other side of the paradox of understanding has already been anticipated by noting the lack of wisdom in drawing the contrasts too sharply.

After all, the U.S. and the U.S.S.R. are both great continental land powers breathing the burly mystique of bigness and invincibility. The Russian sense of bigness is documented by the world's largest land area, two and a half times that of the United States: an area that stretches over eleven time zones and nearly halfway around the world.

147

Some years ago, I had occasion to fly from Moscow across Siberia to Tokyo on a great northern route in the month of June. Leaving Moscow in the early evening as the sun was going down in the West, our Aeroflot plane never really lost sight of the sun over the top of the world during the night, until the same sun was finally rising in the East in the morning as we turned toward Vladivostok and Tokyo on our 5,000-mile ten-hour flight across eight time zones. Had we continued east over Soviet territory, we would have crossed three more time zones and then approached Alaska. We Americans like to say of our own land: "It's a big country!" The Russians have an even bigger one—much bigger.

We two superpowers both have heavy legacies of isolationism, which means recurring suspicion and paranoia toward the whole outside world. The legacy of isolation in both cases means that our two nations have vacillated between shutting out the outside world and intervening aggressively in it. There may be no logical consistency in that—but isolationism and interventionism share a psychic consistency.

We both have a mystical sense of destiny, of messianic identity in the dramas of history. Reinhold Niebuhr spoke of Americans' conceit as the "darlings of Divine Providence." This American "exceptionalism" derived in part from the puritan ethos and its sense of the American Commonwealth as the New Israel, a Chosen People, a new Promised Land. George Santayana affirmed that this nation was born with a "certain metaphysical passion." Ernest Tuveson has documented many texts that claim ours as a "redeemer nation."[18] Such claims have variously sanctioned territorial expansion, moralistic foreign policies, cultural imperialism, and unwarranted presumptions of innocence in world conflicts.

But we Americans are matched by our adversaries' mystique of belonging to Holy Mother Russia, a messianic identity nurtured by the Orthodox Church and by Slavophiles. That identity has proved stronger than economic ideology and for a long time reinforced Moscow's drive to monopolize authority over all other communist states. It was the image and identity powerfully invoked by Stalin to rouse the Russian people to the colossal sacrifices of the Great Patriotic War. Some of the world's hugest monuments are the great, sword-wielding mother-figures erected in many Soviet cities since World War II, such as the one on Mamayev Hill in Volgograd, the peak of bitterest fighting during the Battle of Stalingrad. That mother-monument is 170 feet tall, twenty feet taller than the Statue of Liberty. Russian nationalism, naturalism, and universalism are brought together in such images. In her recent study of *Mother Russia: The Feminine Myth in Russian Culture*, Joanna Hubbs suggests that the deepest religious feelings of the Russian people trace back to an ancient worship of Mother Earth. First as a pagan and then as a "Christianized goddess," that worship "embraced the growth, decay, and rebirth of all nature" and is a decisive clue to understanding Russian political and cultural development.[19]

Robert Kaiser, the *Washington Post*'s former Moscow correspondent, has testified that Russian patriotism is as strong as any human emotion anywhere. He confessed: "I am an American, I have lived in Britain and Asia and traveled throughout the world, but I have never seen anything to compare with Russian patriotism."[20] On second thought, however, Kaiser describes a parallel: Russians

> are patriotic on what might be called an American scale. They see no reason not to be proud of *everything* about their country. They compare it favorably with every other country on virtually every basis. This is a function of size, and of isolation from the outside—factors at work in America, too.[21]

We Americans and those Russians both have a distinctive revolutionary heritage, a national memory of overthrowing an old order. We have our sacred documents and our founding fathers (founding mothers, too, although they have yet to become national icons). Washington, Franklin, Adams, Jefferson, Madison—their names and words and deeds have been hallowed for generations. Towns, schools, and streets bear their names all over the United States.

There is no doubt that they were extraordinary men. But the rituals by which some Americans make contemporary issues subservient to the words or imagined minds of eighteenth century figures can become demagogic exercises that impair the liberties of today's citizens. Such rituals are especially pernicious in the forever-evolving field of constitutional law.

And then there is Lenin, who never wished to become a cult figure but who is worshiped as the perfect model of good Soviet behavior—for being (it is claimed) an exemplary child, a disciplined scholar, a brilliant thinker, a man of modest life-style, a courageous and compassionate leader. The darker aspects of his being, of course, get no mention by the cult. Stalin not only attempted to displace the Lenin cult for a time by developing his own megalomaniacal cult; he also robbed his compatriots of all the other luminaries who might be celebrated in the Soviet pantheon—men like Bukharin, Trotsky, Kamenev, and Zinoviev, all purge victims.

There is still a Stalin shrine in the square of his Georgian hometown of Gori. A pavilion covers the modest two-room cottage of his birth. In an adjacent exhibit hall, an extensive array of heroic photos, honors, and other mementos is on display. There is a darkened sanctuary at the center of which is a bust of Stalin reclining on a velvet bier, while memorial music plays softly.

The Lenin cult fully recovered after Stalin. Many cities and towns bear Lenin's name. His mausoleum in Red Square is the most sacred national shrine. His statue stands in the square of every city and town. His portrait hangs in every public hall and school room. Every party or government policy invokes his words and ideas. Whether Gorbachev's instruction to fill in the "blank pages" of history will eventually besmirch the icon of Lenin is a suspenseful question just now.

Both the U.S. and the U.S.S.R. profess ideologies of equality: ours in our very Declaration of Independence (at least for one gender), theirs in the Marxist vision of a classless society. Yet both countries perpetuate severe inequalities and have great moral difficulty rationalizing them. Not least of *glasnost*'s early achievements was to expose the extravagance and corruption of many Soviet elites—and that at a time when the economic and fiscal policies of the United States were simultaneously enhancing the riches of the wealthy and further depressing the poverty of a growing underclass.

We both struggle with our ethnic and racial pluralisms, with serious unresolved conflicts and with non-Caucasian peoples assuming larger and larger proportions of our total populations. There are some one hundred separate ethnic groups in the Soviet Union, with a myriad of races, religions, languages, and architectures. Soviets as well as Americans must cope with such issues as bilingualism, intermarriage, assimilation, and affirmative action. We are both nations of nations, with marvelous opportunities to manifest the blessings of harmony-in-diversity—but with great difficulties in doing so.

We both have federal governmental systems that constantly and bitterly struggle to strike a balance between central authority and local autonomy. That is very much the story of Gorbachev's attempts at restructuring the Soviet system, or *perestroika*. His encouragement of decentralization has been greeted by demands for independence from various Soviet republics (especially the Baltic states) that seemed to threaten to break up the Union—a prospect bound to provoke a conservative backlash.

Both nations nurture anti-governmental, anti-political attitudes. Ours is the prejudice of a business civilization that glorifies all the presumed virtues of private business while damning all the works of government—a prejudice sanctioned by the anti-political moralisms of bourgeois Protestantism. In pre-Revolutionary times, Russians tended to share "a natural opposition to the representatives of government," viewing public authorities as evils to be "tolerated only because of overriding necessity."[22] This traditional disposition has been somewhat reinforced by Marxist ideology that views the state as a temporary expedient that must wither away in the glorious communist

151

future. The oppressiveness of the Soviet state has hardly made for a more positive evaluation—and *glasnost* has loosed a torrent of political alienation from party bosses. Both political systems confront widespread public cynicism and a crisis of civic virtue.

Both societies have become grossly materialistic in our industrialized, technicized, urbanized, bureaucratized, managerial patterns of living and doing. Mahatma Gandhi more than a half century ago rightly understood capitalist and communist models not as opposites but as common Western modes of rationalizing economic production at the expense of human community, which underscored Gandhi's commitment to the preservation of village culture. The "village prose" of some contemporary Soviet writers makes much the same point. In Valentin Rasputin's *Farewell to Matyora,* there is a poignant conflict of values between technological modernization and the sanctity of traditional village community. A centuries-old village is to be destroyed for the sake of constructing a huge hydroelectric dam. The grieving of elderly peasants at the loss of their village and their ancient homes is depicted in passages of stunning and majestic sorrow.[23]

Both nations once professed an anti-militarist ideology. The United States long held to its pristine prejudice against peacetime standing armies as inimical to democratic liberties. The Soviet Revolution preached that militarism reflected tsarist decadence and the evils of capitalist imperialism. But for decades both nations have been crushing the elemental and spiritual needs of our own and other peoples by the ponderous weight of our militarized institutions.

This pretentious distinction of being called "superpowers" derives primarily from the fact that our two nations possess 95 percent of the world's nuclear weapons. We share the moral presumption that it is *good* for us to have them, and *bad* for others to have them. As a participant in nuclear Non-Proliferation Treaty Review Conferences in Geneva, I have been astonished by the solidarity of superpower partnership in that forum—a partnership that is galling to most governments that have renounced nuclear options for themselves. We two are the world's nuclear imperialists, as well as its prime interventionists.[24]

It has taken some time, and much trouble, for both superpowers to discover that the buildup of nuclear arsenals has been accompanied by an actual decline of political power and even of usable military power around the world. Russell Baker, the political wit of the *New York Times,* has colorfully portrayed this parallel decline of superpower power:

> Look at the Soviet Union and the United States. Superpowers, right? And who cares? Do they get any respect? They lurch around the mountains of Afghanistan and Central American jungles like a couple of gigantic, ham-handed Rodney Dangerfields muttering, 'I don't get no respect.' Where is the glory in being a superpower when illiterate mountain tribes won't do what you tell them? When a lot of Latinos install a government they know you're going to hate?[25]

This parallelism of the dark side of superpower experience struck me with special force as I listened to a radio news report from Afghanistan in early 1989, shortly before the Soviet withdrawal. A network correspondent in the besieged capital, Kabul, described an eerie nighttime scene in which Soviet and Afghan government forces were lighting up the sky with flares all around the perimeter of the city as Mujaheddin guerrillas no doubt prepared their after-dark raids. Twenty-two years before, I had sat one evening on a hotel rooftop in Saigon (now Ho Chi Minh City) and watched U.S. Army flares all around the perimeter of that embattled capital as Viet Cong guerrillas pressed their own night warfare. It was a weird and witching spectacle revisited in the news from Kabul. Russian and American interventions in Asian civil wars have been disastrous to both Asian peoples and themselves.

Both superpowers have persistently indulged in the perversion of truth as they have hyped their indignation against each other. For many years, anti-American propaganda in so much Soviet rhetoric and media (not least from "peace" groups) has been painful to hear and to read. But the problem of truthfulness is hardly one-sided. Kennan has noted the "primitivism" of American propaganda against the U.S.S.R.: its "endless series of distortions and oversimplifications," its "systematic dehumanization" of Soviet leadership, its "routine exaggeration" of Soviet military capabilities, its "monotonous misrepresentation" of the Soviet people, and its "reckless application of the double standard to the judgment of Soviet conduct and our own."[26]

In analyzing the failures of détente, Raymond Garthoff's authoritative study notes the many varieties of parallel conduct by the superpowers in the past two decades, including the invocation of double standards by both sides. Both have "sanctimoniously accused the other" of violating the code of conduct set forth in the Basic Principles agreed to in 1972. Both have been extremely myopic in underestimating the effects of their own provocations. Two examples barely a year apart: U.S. rapprochement with China in 1978 as a conspicuous tactic for intimidating the U.S.S.R. unleashed more furies in the Kremlin than Jimmy Carter could imagine; Soviet intervention in Afghanistan as a "defensive" effort against U.S.-Chinese encirclement provoked a more alarmist response from Carter than Leonid Brezhnev could imagine. Both have been "reluctant to acknowledge, even to recognize, failures of their own political systems," and only "too ready to project responsibility onto the other side." Examples: Soviet charges of U.S. responsibility for internal opposition in Poland, and U.S. charges of Soviet responsibility for revolution in Central America.[27] Both projections slight indigenous realities in regions the superpowers regard as within their own "back yards."

So, the similarities of American and Soviet conduct are not necessarily auspicious for the making of peace between the superpowers. But there are common experiences, common hopes for peace, and even common religious faiths that may yet provide the bonds of mutual respect and peaceable relationships. It is to the religious life and institutions of the Soviet Union, an intermittent topic in all preceding chapters, that we now turn directly.

CHAPTER 7

THE LARGEST CHRISTIAN COUNTRY

*Orthodox Christianity created the first distinctively Russian culture
and provided the basic forms of artistic expression and the framework
of belief for modern Russia. The Orthodox Church also played a key
role in infecting Russia with the essentially Byzantine idea that there
is a special dignity and destiny for an Orthodox society and but one
true answer to controversies arising within it.*

—James Billington[1]
The Icon and the Axe

*Moscow stands for the unsurpassed beauty and glory of worship.
She believes that the whole of life is the sphere of the operation of
divine Grace and is primarily concerned with the application of
Christianity to communal life. Her Church represents the most
devotional and the most artistic of all Christian traditions.*

—Nicolas Zernov[2]
The Russians and Their Church

Two indispensable propositions have guided this study
of Christianity and the superpowers.

One: There is *no non-political way* to understand religious
life in the Soviet Union.

And two: There is *no non-religious way* to understand
Soviet politics, history, and culture.

155

The second proposition would have seemed literally incredible to most Americans before 1980, so fixed was the image of the Soviet Union as an atheist state that had reduced the persecuted and pitiable remnants of religion to archaism and irrelevance. It may still seem preposterous to claim that the Soviet Union is the largest Christian country in the world. However, that is not a value judgment: it is the recognition that nothing today or in the past has been so definitive of Russian ways of thinking and feeling, of folkways and art and literature, as the Christian heritage of the U.S.S.R. It was Orthodox Christianity that largely defined Russian nationhood and has been the prime bearer of Russian heritage. The Russian Orthodox Church remains the largest national church in the world, the largest member church in the World Council of Churches, and larger than the total membership of all thirty-two member communions of the National Council of Churches U.S.A.

There are perhaps 75 million Christians altogether in the U.S.S.R. in a total population of 290 million. That is thus about one-fourth the Soviet total, but four times the membership of the Communist Party (18 million). While precise counts are unavailable and estimates vary, the Russian Orthodox Church embraces perhaps 50-60 million members in 8,000 or more congregations. The approximate size of other communions:

*Georgian Orthodox Church: 3 million, 200 congregations.
*Armenian Apostolic Church: 2 million, 500 congregations.
*"Old Believers" (a "fundamentalist" remnant of the seventeenth-century schism): 1 million.
*Roman Catholic Church (both Latin and Eastern Rite): 5 million, 1,325 congregations.
*Baptists (All-Union Council of Evangelical Christians-Baptists, plus a minority of unregistered "Reform Baptists"): 2 million, 6,000 congregations.
*Lutherans: 600,000 (primarily in Estonia and Latvia), 350 congregations.
*Pentecostals: 100,000.
*Seventh-Day Adventists: 40,000.

*Mennonites: 40,000.
*Methodists: 10,000 (primarily in Estonia where one church in Tallinn has more than 1,000 members), 17 congregations.

A higher percentage of the Soviet population regularly attends Christian worship than is the case in most West European countries.[3]

While the 75 million Christians altogether comprise a majority of the religious believers in the U.S.S.R., there may be as many as 60 million other religious folk. Altogether, nearly half the Soviet population may be religious believers.

There may be almost as many Muslims as there are Russian Orthodox: perhaps 50 million, concentrated in the "Muslim Crescent" that stretches from Azerbaijan to the five republics of Soviet Central Asia: Turkestan, Kazakhstan, Uzbekistan, Kirghizia, and Tadzhik. Communists and Christians alike share a growing anxiety about the rapid growth of these Islamic peoples and their possible susceptibility to the Islamic fundamentalism of southwest Asia. There was an extraordinary, and to Soviet church leaders a very embarrassing, moment in the summer of 1980 at a meeting of U.S. and Soviet Christians in Geneva. It was the summer after the Soviet invasion of Afghanistan. Following a statement by a Russian Orthodox hierarch justifying that invasion on the official line that a fraternal socialist state had requested intervention, an Armenian hierarch blurted out a rather different explanation: "I thank God that the Soviet government has acted to protect us from the Islamic hordes!"

Estimates of Buddhist population range from 50,000 to more than a million, concentrated in the regions of Tuva, Irkutsk, Buryat, and Chita close to the borders with Mongolia.

There are perhaps 2 million Jews. Here one must distinguish between ethnic Jews, officially regarded by the state as a nationality, and religiously practicing Jews—perhaps only one-tenth of the total Jewish population, or about 200,000. There may be as many as 300,000 ethnic Jews who belong to the privileged Communist Party—so there are ironic complications in understanding the harsh predicament of some Jews. (The problematical survival of Jewish religious and cultural institutions and the issues of Jewish emigration will be discussed in the next two chapters.)

Orthodox Origins

Nestor, the eleventh-century Christian monk who chronicled the conversion of Prince Vladimir and the baptism of Rus the century before in 988, is the perhaps fanciful source for those nation-defining events. According to Nestor, Vladimir had been a mighty warrior and a very violent and lusty man. He had erected giant statues to pagan gods, especially to Perun, the god of thunder and lightning. In seeking to consolidate his political and military power, Vladimir sought both a diplomatic marriage and religious counsel. The princess he wished to marry was the sister of the emperor of Constantinople and a Christian. A delegation of his countrymen had visited the great church of Saint Sophia in Constantinople. There they had seen priests arrayed in gorgeous robes. They had heard marvelous choirs sing antiphonally across a vast sanctuary. They had been overwhelmed by the majestic liturgy. They returned to Kiev and told the prince about these things:

> We knew not whether we were in heaven or on earth. We cannot forget that beauty. . . . The only thing we know is that there God dwells among the people. . . . Having tasted something sweet, we do not want anything bitter.[4]

So then all things seemed to work together for Prince Vladimir: love and beauty and piety and power. The prince got himself baptized. He married Princess Anna. He expanded his domains. He tore down the colossal statue of Perun, the god of thunder and lightning, from its summit above the Dnieper River, and had it hurled down into that river. And he summoned all the thousands of inhabitants of his capital to a mass baptism in the Dnieper.

These were the storied events celebrated during the Russian Christian Millennium in 1988.

For three centuries, the bishops of Rus were Greek. As an extension of Byzantine Christianity, the Church of Rus shared (and shares) the main characteristics of Eastern Orthodoxy: (1) *Fidelity* to the Seven Ecumenical Councils between the fourth and eighth centuries. (2) *Collegiality* among Orthodox bishops, including the Ecumenical Patriarch of Constantinople (which means: no Orthodox pope. The Bishop of Rome, the Roman Catholic Pope, is honored in principle but not as authority). (3) *Unity* in faith and sacraments among all Orthodox communions (agreement in all matters of doctrine and full sacramental communion).

Three of the Seven Ecumenical Councils are especially important for understanding Orthodox theology.

The Council of Nicea in 325 formulated the Nicene Creed, affirming the Incarnation of Jesus Christ as one with the Godhead: *Homoousios*, or "consubstantial" with God, one in essence. It was the amendment of the Nicene Creed by Pope Sergius IV in 1014 that did much to provoke the fateful East-West split in the Christian world. In truth, the Orthodox remain faithful to the original creed, while Roman Catholics and Protestants employ the amendment.

The Council of Ephesus in 431 affirmed Mary theologically as "Mother of God," the *Theotokos*, and not simply as mother of Christ. Unlike Roman Catholics, however, the Orthodox have never made dogmas of either the Immaculate Conception or the Bodily Assumption of Mary. Nevertheless, belief in the Assumption of the *Theotokos* is affirmed in hymns sung on the Feast of the Dormition (or "falling asleep") on August 15. The largest of cathedrals in the Kremlin is Assumption Cathedral. The veneration of Mary and the rich feminine images of Holy Mother Russia have powerfully blended together in the depths of Russian consciousness.

The Second Council of Nicea in 787 proclaimed the veneration of icons in the midst of a 120-year controversy during which Iconoclasts had proclaimed that any religious art is idolatrous. For another half-century after Nicea II, the resistance to religious art persisted. In 843, Empress Theodora of Constantinople vindicated the Holy Images by decreeing support of Nicea II and all other councils—a decree that continues to be celebrated as "The Triumph of Orthodoxy."

Ecclesiastical Cold War

The East-West schism is traditionally fixed at the year 1054 when a papal delegation to Constantinople delivered the Bull of Excommunication on the altar of Saint Sophia Cathedral. That decisive act has been followed by more than nine centuries of ecclesiastical cold war. It was preceded, however, by a growing process of estrangement, which began as early as the fifth century. Barbarian invasions shattered the political unity of the Latin West with the Greek East. The rise of Islam in the seventh and eighth centuries brought most of the Mediterranean world under Arab rule and thereby made East-West communication precarious. The creation of the Holy Roman Empire in the West, with Pope Leo III's coronation of Charlemagne on Christmas Day 800, found Byzantium, the New Rome, still conceiving itself as the center of the Roman Empire—and the political division within Christendom sharpened. With the breakdown of imperial unity, the Roman papacy became increasingly autocratic, to the consternation of Eastern bishops. With passing generations and diminished communication, most theologians ceased to be bilingual, further compounding the difficulties of East-West relations. And a pattern of priestly celibacy became fixed in the West, while Eastern priests (except bishops) continued to marry.

All these developing tendencies toward separation over a period of seven centuries helped set the stage for the dramatic schism of the eleventh century. Two divisive and related issues, one political and one creedal, forced the drama to its bitter climax: the power of the papacy and the amendment of the Nicene Creed. Papal authority had evolved into an absolute politico-religious monarchy that was intolerable to the Eastern insistence on consultation and collegiality. In 1014, Pope Sergius IV decreed a dogmatic insertion that the Eastern bishops rejected as usurping the authority of Nicea and destroying the balance of the Trinity. Those words, "and from the Son" and known by the Latin *filioque,* had originated in Spanish practice in the sixth century and were sanctioned by Charlemagne in 809. The original language of Nicea had professed belief in the Holy Spirit, "who proceeds from the Father, who with the Father and the Son together is worshipped and together glorified." In amended form, it became "who proceeds from the Father and from the Son . . ."[5]

The inability of Eastern and Western churches to resolve these issues of papal authority and the *filioque* led to their mutual excommunication in 1054.

To the particular sources of Russian estrangement from the West after 1054—the Mongol Yoke, the fall of Constantinople to the Turks in 1453, the autocracy of the tsars, the emergence of anti-Western Slavophiles, the ideological hostility of the Bolsheviks, the tyranny and paranoia of Stalin—we must add this even earlier history of seven centuries of East-West alienation before 1054. That is a necessary reminder of the ecumenical gulf between Western Protestants and Catholics, on one hand, and the Russian Orthodox Church, on the other.

Orthodox Gifts

Some years ago, in one of my first visits to a Russian Orthodox church, I confronted convincing evidence of the power of the liturgy. I had expected to see many *babushki* (grandmothers) and they were indeed there. I had wondered how many younger persons, especially families, would be there. They were there, too, in large numbers. But what struck me most was the reverence and endurance of very young children, standing through a two-hour liturgy. There were two girls standing near me, obviously sisters, one about eight years old, the other maybe six, who caught my eye repeatedly. They stood patiently, without fidgeting, and with radiant faces throughout the services. They obviously knew the liturgy and responded appropriately to it. They were joyously involved in an event that was tremendously important to them. A whimsical thought slipped through my wandering mind: those two little girls may not be KGB agents! And I also mused, as a mere Methodist, that any church so capable of captivating the consciousness of such young children with its liturgy is surely a powerful institution.

At the end of a more recent (but pre-Gorbachev and pre-Millennium) ecumenical exchange in the Soviet Union, a Russian theologian asked me how I evaluated the experience. I made some very positive comments—but expressed some disappointment that we had not encountered more of the Church's life beyond the liturgy. He held up his hands and said, with much feeling: "Please, Al! The liturgy is all we have!" That statement reflected both the political constraints upon the churches and the multiplicity of functions served by the liturgy: sacramental, educational, musical, artistic, moral, memorial, national, and counter-cultural. Since 1988, the Church has been permitted fields of service beyond the liturgy. But the centrality of the liturgy remains expressive of the eucharistic consciousness of Orthodoxy in both Church and society. John Meyendorff puts it thus:

> Both as a memorial and as an anticipation of the world to come, the Eucharist is the place where the Church identifies itself with the Kingdom of God. . . . The liturgical life forms the very basis of Orthodox piety. It is the realization and expression of the mystery of the divine presence in the Church and proclaims the truths of the faith. It also governs to a large extent the moral behavior of the faithful, sometimes inviting them to do penance and fast, at other times summoning them to glorify the Creator and share in the messianic banquet.[6]

The spiritual gifts that non-Orthodox Americans may receive today from the heritage of Russian Orthodoxy were celebrated by the United Methodist Council of Bishops in their 1986 Pastoral Letter and Foundation Document, *In Defense of Creation: The Nuclear Crisis and a Just Peace:*

*A "whole world theology" in which there is no boundary between nature and grace, for God's presence is throughout all Creation and revelation is everywhere.

*A firm grasp of the Incarnation of Jesus Christ, rich in the mystical power of transcendence, but rich also in physical embodiments to be seen, felt, kissed, like ikons, which are really concrete symbols of relations among all generations and whose visible focus makes them centers of prayers.
*A lively sense of brotherhood and sisterhood with all fellow Christians.
*A vibrant Resurrection faith among a people who have known massive suffering and death, so that Easter is anticipated each year with fasting and all-night vigils, then celebrated with an explosive "Christ is risen! Alleluia! Alleluia! Alleluia"
*An indomitable belief that both suffering and joy are the essential marks of Christian discipleship.[7]

As part of the Washington Cathedral's ecumenical celebration of the 1988 Millennium, James Billington (Librarian of Congress) noted four features of Russian Orthodox spirituality—all tending to reflect the tension between hierarchy and individual spirituality in the Church: (1) A mystical emphasis on individual prayer and inner renewal. (2) A "multi-media liturgy" which is more audio-visual than verbal, with brilliant icon screens, great choirs, and glittering processions. (3) A tradition of voluntary and redemptive suffering, vivified by the canonizing of Prince Vladimir's sons, Boris and Gleb, who declined to resist their murders by elder brother Svyato-polk. (4) A cult of the Virgin which emphasizes the *Theotokos*, the Mother of God, and the spirituality of women more than the claim of virginity.[8]

To these particular traditions and gifts we may add *the power of tradition itself:* the communal identity of a deep-rooted historical consciousness that transcends all present troubles, remembers the struggles and suffering of all past generations, celebrates the saints as contem-poraries, and counsels infinite patience. It is this power of tradition that is represented by the icons of Russian Orthodox faith, not only in churches and museums but in the homes of most Russian families, even families that do not profess the faith. For Russian Christians, icons are reverenced as living symbols, as deliberately unnatural screens of transcendence, as windows opening the spiritual world, as acts of prayer and devotion, as sources of healing, as teachers, as the special saints for whom believers are named, even as personal friends.

Icons should not, however, be viewed as representations of spirituality apart from the very sensual, physical world that, Orthodox Christians fervently believe, also manifests the grace and beauty of God. Anthony Ugolnik, an American Orthodox scholar who winsomely interprets Russian Christianity to Protestant compatriots in his recent book, *The Illuminating Icon*, writes:

> The theology of the icon, which seeks to 'illumine' the senses and thereby the imagination, can also prepare the believer to look outward, even into the secular world, to find the image of the Creator. This claim on the imagination will allow the very act of interpretation, the structures of meaning that the Christian assigns to the world and experience, to transfigure the culture of his or her people. Russia's church may seem weak indeed to the Western Christian because its external mission has been severely limited by the state under which it has lived. But its developed theology, with the primacy it gives to the image, has allowed the Russian Orthodox Church to exert a tremendous power over the Russian imagination.[9]

Romans and Russians

There is a particularly strained history of Roman Catholicism in and with the Soviet Union. Its bitterness has three major roots: (1) the centuries of Catholic-Orthodox antipathies since the East-West split of 1054; (2) the fact that most Roman Catholics are not ethnic Russians and belong to nations that have lost their independence; and (3) the militant anti-communism of the Vatican until the papacy of John XXIII (and somewhat revisited under John Paul II).

The majority of Roman Catholics in the U.S.S.R. live in the Baltic states, the Ukraine, and former Polish territories: all regions burdened with historic grievances against

Russian authorities. Lithuania is the most Catholic of the fifteen republics with six dioceses, perhaps 600 parishes, 700 priests, and a seminary in Kaunas. Soviet authorities officially closed the Catholic monasteries and convents many years ago, although some have continued a precarious secret life. The Catholic Church serves as a vehicle for assertive Lithuanian nationalism, both in Lithuania itself and in emigre communities in the U.S. and elsewhere. It is this compound of religion and ethnicity in Lithuania that has not only provoked severe Soviet measures but also complicated Vatican-U.S.S.R. relations.

Few if any Christian churches have had a more tangled history than Eastern Rite (Ukrainian) Catholics, also known as Uniates (a term which some reject as a slur). They have been caught for four centuries in the conflict between the Russian Orthodox Church and the papacy. It was in 1596 that these originally Orthodox folk in Ukrainian territory then ruled by Poland were pressured to break with Orthodoxy and accept the authority of Rome. Some of the Ukrainian bishops yielded to this pressure on the basis of a series of special accommodations: they were permitted to retain Orthodox liturgy, language, and canon law, as well as a married priesthood. In all the centuries since, the Russian Orthodox Church has fought to reclaim these churches, mostly in the Ukraine. Official Soviet sanctions were imposed in 1946 when the Eastern Rite was outlawed. A serious complication was the alleged pro-Nazi complicity of Eastern Rite clergy in the 1930s and 1940s, many of whom were executed or incarcerated. Several million members continued to maintain an underground and exile church, which nurtures Ukrainian nationalism and anti-Soviet grievances. In L'vov in 1989, tens of thousands of Ukrainian Catholics publicly demonstrated for their legitimacy. There were reports of Soviet government conversations with both Russian Orthodox and Eastern Rite clergy concerning the possibility of ending legal bars against the latter. On December 1, 1989, President Gorbachev visited Pope John Paul II in the Vatican (an historic first for any top Soviet leader), apparently having agreed to the ultimate legalization of the Ukrainian Catholic Church.

The Inclusive Baptists

Spread throughout almost all the fifteen Soviet republics are the two million Christians loosely called "Baptists," most of whom are properly identified as belonging to the All-Union Council of Evangelical Christians-Baptists. That council is a merger of evangelical communities required by state authorities in 1944. It includes groups with Mennonite, Presbyterian, Pentecostal, and other sectarian origins, primarily from German agricultural settlements and British evangelists in the nineteenth century. On my visit to a Baptist church in Tashkent, Uzbekistan, the local pastor took me aside and whispered somewhat mischievously: "I'm really a Presbyterian!" (There is a much older Protestant heritage in the Lutheran churches of Baltic peoples dating to the sixteenth century.)

Most Baptist churches are rather plain, unadorned structures called "houses of prayer." Some are set away from the street in the interior of city blocks (as if to avoid being a public nuisance). Many houses of prayer conduct not only multiple Sunday services but evening services throughout the week. The services themselves tend to be as long as Orthodox liturgies and with a similar multiplicity of functions: two hours or more, with three or four sermons by different preachers (which may be more like Bible lessons), half a dozen or more anthems by large well-drilled choirs, and fervent prayers offered by laypersons from their seats or standpoints. (Often there are many standees.)

I was invited to undertake a preaching mission to Soviet Baptist churches in 1984. My itinerary began at the 5,000-member Moscow Baptist Church and proceeded to congregations in the Ukrainian, Georgian, and Armenian republics. The Baptists I met were, for the most part, very warmhearted, hospitable fundamentalists. They were full of goodwill toward Americans—and also full of exaggerated notions as to the supernatural powers of American preachers, whether to heal the dying or to transform the policies of governments. I was advised by one of my hosts to take their biblicism seriously: "If you will remember to raise your Bible every so often during your sermons," he suggested, "you can say just about anything!" I did—and I did. I was also repeatedly confronted with Baptist seriousness about "the heresy of infant baptism." (As a mere Methodist, I had to confess my heretical views.) This preoccupation with proper baptism is one of the defining boundaries separating Baptists from the much larger Orthodox Church in which the sacraments of both baptism and communion may include infants from birth.

A diminishing minority of Baptists remains outside the All-Union Council, having refused to register with state authorities and to accept the severe restrictions on evangelistic activities decreed by the Khrushchev regime in 1960. In 1965, after the fall of Khrushchev, some of these unregistered "Reform Baptists" organized their own council and eventually were imprisoned or went underground. One of their leaders, Georgi Vins, was sentenced to five years in a Siberian labor camp in 1974—then released to the U.S. in 1979 in exchange for a Soviet spy. The courage and martyrdom of many Baptists, registered and unregistered, are among the most compelling witnesses of modern Christianity. Some such cases, however, are problematical in being used to inflame the most incendiary anti-Soviet and anti-ecumenical sentiments with shrill propaganda and occasionally with disruptive tactics in worship services in both the U.S. and U.S.S.R.

The music in many Baptist churches is as powerful in its genre as the liturgical music of the Orthodox. Baptist choirs also serve vital social functions in lieu of the group activities that the law has prohibited. In Odessa, I met a large choir of pensioners whose director was eighty-seven years-old. In the nearby town of Shevchenko, there is a youth choir of forty members, some of whom also participate in the service with poetry readings and guitar duets. Not only the services but the frequent choir rehearsals become occasions for a more rounded church life and fellowship.

One memorable evening with a Baptist congregation in Tbilisi, capital of the republic of Georgia, especially revealed to me that not all is grim and bitter in the churches. It was a multilingual congregation, which meant that my sermon

167

had to be translated, sentence by sentence, into Russian, then Georgian, then Ossetian. About five minutes of preaching stretched out over twenty or twenty-five. There were anthems in various languages, sung magnificently. Then, to my delight, a beautiful young chorister, with a bit of mischief in her eyes, fixed squarely on me, began to sing in English: "Swing low, sweet chariot . . ." The service ended, a large group of pastors and parishioners moved to the backyard of a home in the heights above Tbilisi for a dinner of hot-hot-hot Georgian food, much lively discussion, and good humor. Inside the home my host, with an ambivalent mix of pride and embarrassment, showed me his teen-age son's studio of recently painted nudes. At evening's end, with some ceremony, I was presented with a bag of eight huge cucumbers. (I can't recall what became of them.) Sometime past midnight, I was driven to the train station in a car with four men, all exuberantly singing Christmas carols to me in Russian and Georgian, then demanding that I sing carols to them in English—which, of course, I did, very loudly, on a very hot summer night in Soviet Georgia.

CHAPTER **8**

THE HARSH SYMPHONIA

The Church is separate from the state. . . . The school shall be separate from the Church. The teaching of religion is prohibited in all state, municipal, or private educational institutions where a general education is given. . . . No ecclesiastical or religious association shall have the right to own property. Such associations shall not enjoy the right of legal entity. All property belonging to churches and religious associations existing in Russia shall become public property.

—Soviet *Decree on Separation of Church from State and of School from Church*
January 23, 1918[1]

It is a hard time that the Holy Church of Christ is now going through in the Russian land. Both the open and secret enemies of the truth of Christ persecute this truth and aim at destroying the work of Christ, and, instead of Christian love, sow everywhere the seeds of evil, of hatred, and of fratricidal struggle.

—Patriarch Tikhon's
Decree Excommunicating the Communists,
January 27, 1918[2]

If the pattern of church-state relations throughout the thousand years of Russian history had actually been

169

determined by the political theology of Eastern Christianity, there might never have been a communist revolution or persecution of the Church or a Cold War. That political theology partook of Greek philosophy and its characteristic emphasis on universal harmony. Church-state relations were to be guided by the harmonious concept of *symphonia:* cooperation rather than separation or confrontation. Priests and princes were to share in the divine commission to lead the nation to holiness of all life.

In practice, however, both Constantinople and Rus used the idea of *symphonia* to subordinate the Church to the state and to manipulate religion for the aggrandizement of empire.

Any present discussion of religious liberty in the Soviet Union must recall both the rationale of *symphonia* and the historical reality of ecclesial subservience. Then add the centuries of Russian isolation from the liberating epochs of the West—the Renaissance, the Reformation, and the Enlightenment. The subordination of the Orthodox Church became official with Peter the Great's abolition of the Patriarchate in 1721 and the reduction of the hierarchy to the status of imperial functionaries. The church itself became scandalously implicated in ostentatious wealth and political oppression. It was that subservience and corruption of some of the clergy, notwithstanding the profound spirituality and fidelity of most priests and laity, that inclined Russian revolutionaries toward acceptance of the harsh Marxist critique of religion. That critique, in ways far beyond anything Marx himself would have justified, became the warrant for the Bolshevik repression of religious liberty. The initial resistance to the Revolution in 1918–20 by a just-reestablished Patriarchate and by armed clerics intensified the church-state conflict. In the decades that followed, the ancient ideal of *symphonia* would be totally forsaken and faithful Christians would become martyrs by the millions.

Marx on Religion

Before tracing the pattern of Russian church-state relations since 1917, a brief review of what Karl Marx actually had to say about religion is offered as a corrective to simplistic notions of his critique. Such notions have been repeatedly asserted to repudiate all possibility of Christian-Marxist dialogue and unwittingly to endorse Soviet pretenses that "Marxism-Leninism" is a unified and coherent body of thought.

The most well-known Marxist phrase, that religion is "the opium of the people," does indeed reflect Marx's judgment on the historical relations between religious institutions and economic institutions as oppressive and dehumanizing. Both sets of institutions were viewed as sources of alienation: of unfulfilled human possibilities, and of lost personal freedom and autonomy. But that "opium" phrase is too seldom recalled in the context of Marx's whole paragraph in his *Critique of Hegel's Philosophy of Right*. Preceding that phrase are five strikingly positive notes about the power and functions of religious experience—notes that almost call for a theology of liberation:

> Religious distress is at the same time the expression of real distress and the protest against real distress. Religion is the sigh of the oppressed creature, the heart of a heartless world, just as it is the spirit of the spiritless situation.[3]

It is only then that Marx speaks of "opium."

In *Das Capital*, moreover, Marx frequently quotes Martin Luther in developing his critique of economic oppression. In seven different places, Marx cites Luther's rejection of usury, calling particular attention to Luther's condemnation of the usurer as the greatest "enemy of man" who strives to be "God over all men."[4]

It is this moral earnestness of Marx that links him to the biblical prophets and their protests against oppression of the poor and religion-without-justice. Marxism and Christianity, at their normative core, share some vital characteristics: (1) moral passion, (2) communitarian values, (3) transnational perspectives, (4) a purposive view of history, and (5) commitment to social change to make human life fully human. John Bennett's writings on Christianity and communism, ever since the 1940s, have emphasized the emergence of communism as a consequence of "the failure of Christians, and of Christian churches, to be true to the revolutionary implications of their own faith."[5]

Orthodoxy and Revolution

Bennett's lament echoes the confession of Russian Orthodox theologian-philosopher Nicholas Berdyaev who renounced his youthful Marxism and was expelled from the Soviet Union in 1922, spending his later years in Berlin and Paris. In *The Russian Idea,* first published in England in 1947, Berdyaev wrote,

> The militant godlessness of the communist Revolution is to be explained not only by the state of mind of the communists, . . . but also by the historical sins of Ortho-doxy which had failed to carry out its mission for the transfiguration of life, which had been a support of an order which was based upon wrong and oppression. Christians must recognize their guilt and not be content to accuse the adversaries of Christianity and consign them to perdi-tion. . . . The official Church occupied a conservative position . . . and was slavishly subject to the old regime.[6]

At the turn of this century, there were many impulses toward reform in the Russian Orthodox Church, even as there were profound political and social rumbles. The early years of World War I complicated the tasks of church reform—but in the brief opening of Russian society after the February Revolution of 1917, the Church's bishops felt free to reestablish the Patriarchate for the first time since 1721, presumably hoping to restore substantial Church auton-omy. Metropolitan Tikhon of Moscow became the new Patriarch. But the scene changed dramatically for the worse with Lenin's October Revolution and its militant atheism.

Lenin on Religion

Lenin fully shared Marx's critique of religion, especially the depiction of religion as a tool of oppression by the ruling classes. He was particularly vehement in his contempt for

172

the Orthodox Church, which, he charged, had "plundered and corrupted the people." Lenin was more sympathetic to the Protestant sects because he viewed them as victims of official and class oppression. Intellectually, he was even more of an aggressive atheist than was Marx. Lenin wrote,

> Every religious idea, every idea of God, even flirting with the idea of God, is unutterable vileness, . . . vileness of the most dangerous kind, 'contagion' of the most abominable kind. Millions of filthy deeds, acts of violence and physical contagions are far less dangerous than the subtle, spiritual idea of a God decked out in the smartest 'ideological' costumes.[7]

Lenin's pronouncements and policies on religion were more expedient than consistent. Prior to the October Revolution, he advocated a distinction between state neutrality toward religion as a private affair and Communist party militancy in promoting atheism. That distinction tended to dissolve in the chaos of civil strife after the revolution. On January 23, 1918, the new government issued its Decree on Separation of Church from State, which also proclaimed the separation of education from the Church, the abolition of religious property and legal status, and the authority of government to decide which places of worship might be made available to religious associations.

Patriarch Tikhon urged resistance to the Bolsheviks and pronounced anathema against anyone attacking the Church. He apparently hoped and believed the Bolshevik Revolution would fail, and thereby became identified with the losing side in the Civil War.

Nevertheless, Lenin sought to enlist religious support and urged a cautious policy that would avoid offending believers. The emphasis for a time was on state tolerance combined with antireligious propaganda by the party. In 1921, as the civil war ended, the state intensified pressure on the Church for political loyalty—but bitter and even violent resistance continued. Perhaps 1,000 or more priests, 28 bishops, and thousands of laity lost their lives. Others, along with nuns and monks, were imprisoned or deported.

173

In the famine of 1920–21, the government seized many Church valuables for the purchase of food. The still-resisting Patriarch Tikhon was arrested, then imprisoned in 1922—only to be released in 1923 when he recanted his opposition.

The legacy of Lenin's personal views and official policies in the 1917–24 period is therefore highly ambiguous. That legacy may be invoked for either repression (and that in varying degrees) or a more permissive or even respectful policy. In 1988, Mikhail Gorbachev claimed Lenin's authority for a permissive and even solicitous approach to the churches.

Stalin: Persecution and Restoration

The immediate aftermath of Lenin's rule was one of increasing severity and much suffering. Stalin's antipathy to religion dated to his youth. As a student and would-be priest at the Orthodox seminary in Tbilisi, he was repelled by both the indoctrination and the censorship. After repeated infractions of seminary rules regarding reading and outside activities (he had joined a Marxist study group), he was expelled at the age of nineteen. Later he testified that the seminary made him a revolutionary instead of a priest:

> The place was a hotbed of espionage and chicanery. At nine in the morning we assembled for tea, and when we returned to our bedrooms all the drawers had been rifled. And just as they daily went through our papers, they daily went through our souls. I could not stand it; everything infuriated me.[8]

One of the most extraordinary facts about communist leadership in the Soviet Union is that Lenin, Stalin, Khrushchev, and Gorbachev had all grown up in devout Orthodox homes.

In 1925 the League of Militant Atheists was formed. In that same year, the Patriarchate was forcibly vacated. From 1927 to 1943, administration of Orthodox affairs was left in the hands of Metropolitan Sergei who, upon his own release from prison, issued a pastoral letter affirming the Church's loyalty to the Soviet state.

In 1929 Stalin's harsh Law on Religious Associations was promulgated. That law, with periodic amendments, continued for nearly sixty years to provide the norms for Soviet policy. The law required local registration of all religious groups and a minimum of twenty members each. Forbidden were all group activities for children, youth, and women, as well as for education, excursions, libraries, health, hobbies, or any other purpose except worship. Severe as these prohibitions were, they were not nearly as cruel as the actual conduct of Stalinist government over the next decade. There were sweeping persecutions and the closing or demolition of most churches, monasteries, and seminaries. Many bishops and priests were executed or imprisoned on charges of resisting Stalin's forced collectivization of agriculture. And there sprang up once again an underground church with its hermits and wandering monks.

There had been 50,000 Russian Orthodox clergy and 54,000 churches in 1914. By 1939, there were fewer than 1,000 clergy and fewer than 1,000 churches.

There had been over 1,000 monasteries and convents. By 1939 there were none.

There had been 57 seminaries. By 1939 there were none.

There had been 37,000 parochial schools; 34,000 parish libraries; 1,000 church homes for the aged; 291 church hospitals. By 1939 there were none of these.[9]

It was in the midst of the immeasurable horror of World War II that Stalin, appealing for the defense of Holy Mother Russia, relented and thousands of churches were reopened. The Patriarchate was reactivated under Metropolitan Sergei after an abrupt summons to the Kremlin to meet Stalin. Church headquarters moved from a rude log cabin on a dirt road to the palatial former German embassy in Moscow.

In the Days of Khrushchev and Brezhnev

Nikita Khrushchev's memoirs testify to a very pious childhood:

> My mother was very religious. . . . When I think back to my childhood, I can remember vividly the saints on the icons against the wall of our wooden hut, their faces darkened by fumes from the oil lamps. I remember being taught to kneel and pray in front of the icons with the grown-ups in church. When we were taught to read, we read the scriptures.

It was an atheist village school teacher who "set me on a path which took me away from all that."[10]

After Khrushchev's denunciation of Stalin at the Twentieth Congress of the Communist Party in 1956, thousands of religious prisoners were released from labor camps. That proved to be a false signal concerning prospects for religious liberty in the years just ahead.

Today's Russian Christians are painfully ambivalent in comparing Stalin and Khrushchev. They remember that Stalin reopened the churches—18,000 by 1950, along with 60 monasteries and convents and eight seminaries. But they also remember that Khrushchev, in many ways a reformer, instituted a harsh new wave of religious persecution in the early 1960s. It was not a bloody wave, by Stalin's early standards, but a very severe one—perhaps as a tactic, the churches were sacrificed to placate ideological conservatives while liberalization proceeded in other sectors. Half the churches were closed again, as were half or more of the monasteries, convents, and seminaries. Longtime efforts to alienate children and youth from the churches were now given the force of law: their membership and even participation in religious institutions, as well as religious instruction by pastors, were officially forbidden. In practice, the laws were unevenly and inconsistently enforced. Some clergy were subjected to arbitrary pressures through laws unrelated to religion, such as an "anti-parasite" law ostensibly aimed at prostitutes and others not engaged in productive labor. Church membership continued to be a liability in education and employment. In hundreds, perhaps thousands of cases, dissident Christians were sentenced to prison, labor camps, psychiatric hospitals, or Siberian exile.

Two Moscow priests, Nikolai Eshliman and Gleb

Yakunin, addressed critical letters in late 1965 to both Patriarch Alexei and Soviet Presidium Chairman Nikolai Podgorny, protesting the government's "systematic and destructive intervention in ecclesiastical life" during Khrushchev's rule (which ended in 1964). The letter to the Patriarch was simultaneously reverent and scathing:

> We stand with respect before the mystery and grandeur of the episcopal rank, we have the fear of God in our hearts, we recognize our own human unworthiness. Nevertheless, moved by the intractable demands of Christian conscience, we feel it is our duty to say that such a situation in the Church could occur only with the connivance of the supreme ecclesiastical authorities, who have deviated from their sacred duty before Christ and the Church and have already violated the apostolic command by 'compromising with the world.'[11]

In May 1966, the offended Patriarch suspended Fathers Eshliman and Yakunin until they should fully repent. A decade later, following the Helsinki Final Act with its human rights provisions, Father Yakunin was instrumental in organizing a Christian Committee for the Defense of Believers' Rights, which disseminated hundreds of reports on the status of church-state relations and individual cases of oppression to groups in Western countries. In 1979, the brave and unyielding Father Gleb published a very candid and lengthy report on "The Present State of the Russian Orthodox Church and the Prospects for Religious Revival in Russia," severely castigating the Patriarch (now Pimen) and various bishops by name for their subservience to government and rebuking the clergy generally for the "Pharisaism, indifference, laziness, hypocrisy, and informing that are so prevalent in the parishes of the Moscow Patriarchate."[12] Gleb Yakunin was convicted of "anti-Soviet agitation and propaganda" in August 1980 and sentenced to prison for five years. In 1987, following release from prison, Father Yakunin was restored to his priestly office.

In 1965, a government Council for Religious Affairs (CRA) had replaced two separate organs Stalin had created in 1944 (one for Orthodoxy, the other for non-Orthodox bodies). That council made a show of defending believers' rights and curbing arbitrary local harassment of churches. But the CRA (and the religious affairs section of the KGB) continued the intrusive monitoring and manipulation of the churches inherited from tsarist centuries: the churches were compelled to separate themselves from the state and from politics (except for statements supporting government policy)—yet the state remained very much engaged in constraints upon the churches. The constitutional separation of church and state remained a one-way street.

In a famous "Lenten Letter" to Patriarch Pimen in 1972, Nobel Prizewinner Alexander Solzhenitsyn wrote:

> We have lost the radiant ethical atmosphere of Christianity in which for a millennium our morals were grounded. . . . We are losing the last features and marks of a Christian people—can this really not be the *principal* concern of the Russian Patriarch? . . . The Church is ruled dictatorially by atheists—a sight never before seen in two millennia! . . . By what reasoning is it possible to convince oneself that the planned *destruction* of the spirit and body of the Church under the guidance of atheists is the best way of *preserving* it? Preserving it for whom? Certainly not for Christ.[13]

The Patriarch declined to reply. Solzhenitsyn's continuing barrage of religious and political dissents led to his expulsion in early 1974. The Church had indeed compromised for the sake of its own preservation—and in hopes that a more open future lay ahead.

The 1977 Constitution of the U.S.S.R., the third since 1917, provided a slightly liberalized guarantee of religious freedom by affirming the right to "profess" a religion as well as to conduct worship. Article 52 of the constitution reads:

> Citizens of the U.S.S.R. are guaranteed freedom of conscience, that is, the right to profess or not to profess any religion, and to conduct religious worship or atheistic propaganda. Incitement of hostility or hatred on religious grounds is prohibited. In the U.S.S.R., the church is separated from the state and the school from the church.

The 1970s witnessed a conspicuous growth in church attendance and membership, as well as a more assertive religious dissidence. There was even talk of a "religious renaissance," although hundreds of prisoners of conscience remained incarcerated. A symbol of both youthful hopes and unending persecution in the 1970s is the Christian Seminar on Problems of Religious Renaissance, founded in Moscow in 1974 by recently baptized Orthodox young people. Dissatisfied with the limits of liturgy and official church publications, this "religio-philosophical" discussion group soon found its meetings harassed by the KGB. Arrests began in 1978. Founder Alexander Ogorodnikov was convicted of "parasitism" and sentenced to prison for a year, after which he was dispatched to a camp and internal exile for "anti-Soviet agitation and propaganda." Other members of the Christian Seminar were also imprisoned or interned in psychiatric hospitals—but the Seminar continued to meet in several cities.[14]

A source of great confusion and dismay among Russian Christians has been a series of arrests of leading religious dissidents, followed by their public "recantations" and "confessions." The most notable "recantation" was broadcast on Soviet television in 1980 by an immensely popular Orthodox priest, Dimitri Dudko. Father Dimitri's question-and-answer sessions following Saturday evening services in his churches had attracted huge crowds from great distances to hear his simple and straightforward expositions of Christian faith. His parish newsletter, however, offered increasingly candid comments on current events—which led to his arrest, provoking worldwide protests. Following five months' incarceration, Father Dimitri was forced to sign and broadcast a "confession" that, while making use of his own words, was primarily composed by the KGB. His return to his parish in Grebnevo, northeast of Moscow, was marked by conspicuous disorientation and loneliness.[15]

During the 1970s, a curious contradiction became more and more apparent. In principle, Christianity and communism are mutually exclusive: party members cannot be Christian, church members cannot belong to the party. In practice, however, there is a fuzzy gray region of indeterminate boundaries in which Christian heritage and political identity meet and mix for millions of Soviet citizens. A majority of children, including the children of many party members, are baptized. Young women who do not admit to church membership wear crosses on chains around their necks. Most homes display icons. Soviet diplomats of my acquaintance have spoken freely of their Christian parents and their own baptism. Churches that long ago became museums attract more and more visitors who could nurture their spirits without formally joining active churches. Young people and an increasing number of academics and other professionals are drawn to the churches seeking a counter-culture to the sterile and fading credos of "Marxist-Leninist" ideology. Soviet writers freely and popularly address religious themes.

Leonid Brezhnev, as he lay close to death in 1982 and perhaps contemplated the mysteries of eternity, signaled a new day for the Russian Orthodox Church. In what may have been his last decision, he directed that the great Danilov Monastery in Moscow, lost to the Church for decades, be returned to the Church. No longer would it be profaned as an umbrella factory, a refrigerator plant, or a jail: It was to become grandly refurbished as the site for a new headquarters for the Moscow Patriarchate, with several new churches, conference halls, and even a hotel—just in time for the thousandth anniversary of the Russian Orthodox Church.

CHAPTER 9

GLASNOST AND THE MILLENNIUM

For all the contradictions of the present-day world, for all the diversity of social and political systems in it, and for all the different choices made by the nations in different times, this world is nevertheless one whole. We are all passengers aboard one ship, the Earth, and we must not allow it to be wrecked. There will be no second Noah's Ark.

—Mikhail S. Gorbachev[1]
Perestroika

The great event of the Baptism of Russia happened in 988. . . . The acceptance of Christianity by Prince Vladimir had a significant meaning for the ancient Russian state, for it gave the basis for unity of a multinational state, helped to strengthen it and widen the relationships with many other ancient states. The Baptism of Russia laid the foundation of the Russian Orthodox Church which was to become a major component in the evolution of Russian history.

—Nina Bobrova[2]
"The Celebration of the Millennium
of Christianity in Russia"

Seldom have two ostensibly different historical dramas interacted so spectacularly as the conjunction of the *glasnost* of Mikhail Gorbachev with the Millennium of Russian Christianity in the late 1980s. Of course, there were those who attributed the conjunction to Divine Providence, as did General Secretary Arie Brouwer of the National Council of Churches U.S.A. in remarks at the Bolshoi Theater's Millennial celebrations on June 10, 1988. Moreover, given the intensive interaction of politics and religion throughout Russian history, it would be difficult to prove that these simultaneous happenings were purely coincidental. Both the advent of Gorbachev and the Millennial events had been preceded by the widespread revival that some Christians had dared to call a "religious renaissance" since the mid-1970s.

Gorbachev's first reported remarks on religion did not offer any hope that the churches might participate significantly in *glasnost*. In a November 1986 speech in Uzbekistan, he called for "a decisive and uncompromising struggle against manifestations of religion" and also for a strengthening of "atheistic propaganda."[3] It seemed reminiscent of Khrushchev's dualistic approach twenty-five years before: broad cultural reform but religious repression. Perhaps Gorbachev would mobilize hardline ideological support for *glasnost* and *perestroika* by renewing the Bolshevik assault on the churches.

But that apprehension was increasingly allayed as ambitious plans for the Millennium proceeded with visible government support. Three academic conferences on the historical significance of the Millennium—in Kiev (1986), Moscow (1987), and Leningrad (1988)—staged an unprecedented and cordial collaboration between theologians and secular Soviet scholars. At one of these conferences, a historian from the Soviet Academy of Sciences prefaced his paper by saying: "The Church can surely exist without us non-religious scholars—but we cannot exist without the Church!"[4]

A new Soviet State Councillor for Religious Affairs, career diplomat Konstantin M. Kharchev, visited the United States in 1986 and 1987 and repeatedly acknowledged historic Soviet "mistakes" in abusing the churches. He promised new legislation that would permit churches to own property and he reported that church leaders were appearing on Soviet television. While reaffirming the ideological expectation that "religious consciousness will disappear with the coming of pure Communism," Kharchev allowed that such a state might not be achieved for a thousand years and that, in the meantime, churches could play a positive role in society. He offered himself as a personal case of changed attitudes: "I used to treat believers in the old way. I was accustomed to thinking of them as riff-raff, backward types on a level with criminals. I had to develop a new mentality."[5] In a January 1988 article in *Izvestia*, Kharchev was even more forthcoming. Candidly referring to the "negative phenomena of the thirties" (under Stalin), he listed

massive and unjustifiable closing of prayer buildings, tyranny in respect to clergy, and neglect of the legal rights of believers and their religious feelings. Today it is impossible to recall these things without grief. In the years of stagnation [i.e., under Brezhnev] there was a gap between the real religious situation and the lacquered public depiction of it.[6]

More than any of his predecessors at the Council of Religious Affairs, Kharchev seemed determined to honor the Council's claims to defend believers' rights.

The dramas of political reform and religious renewal were most visibly joined on April 29, 1988 when Mikhail Gorbachev warmly received Patriarch Pimen and a delegation of five Orthodox metropolitans and enlisted the churches in the moral and spiritual tasks of *perestroika*. It had been forty-five years since the leader of the Communist Party had met with church leaders—Stalin's wartime summons to Metropolitan Sergei and other bishops. Acknowledging the "mistakes" of earlier times and repudiating the narrowness of Stalinist restrictions, Gorbachev declared: "The Church cannot distance itself from the complex problems that disturb humanity or from the changes taking place in society." He promised, as had

Kharchev, a more liberal law implementing the constitutional guarantee of freedom of conscience. He added:

> The believers are Soviet people, workers, patriots and they have the full right to express their conviction with dignity. *Perestroika*, democratization, and *glasnost* concern them as well—in full measure and without any restrictions. This is especially true of ethics and morals, a domain where universal norms and customs come in so helpful for our common cause.[7]

According to Bishop Basil Rodzianko (retired) of the Orthodox Church in America and grandson of the last Speaker in the pre-Revolutionary Russian parliament, Gorbachev also disclosed his own religious nurture to church leaders. From ages two through seven, Mikhail Sergeevich

> came under the influence of a very religious family. His mother is still a devout member of the Russian Orthodox Church. He, himself, spoke quite openly that he knew the dangers of keeping and safeguarding that which was a treasure for the spiritual life of the family and was secretly used when he described how his grandparents had concealed the icons of Jesus and Mary under the portraits of Lenin and Stalin. His own baptism, apparently, happened when he was seven.[8]

The month of June 1988 witnessed the most stunning profusion of Millennial events, prefaced by the amiable Reagan-Gorbachev summit in Moscow and Reagan's visit to the Danilov Monastery. At Zagorsk's Holy Trinity Monastery, the Russian Orthodox Church held its first *Sobor* (Council) in seventeen years, reported 30 million baptisms since 1971, drafted new statutes democratizing parish governance, and canonized nine saints including "Golden Age" iconographer Andrei Rublev. Ground was broken for the first new church in Moscow since the Revolution, with Patriarch Pimen, other hierarchs, and a vast ecumenical and international throng present to hear State Councillor Kharchev declare that the new church "will be a fine embodiment" of the fact that "believers and non-believers in our Soviet country have but one history, one Motherland and one common future."[9]

At the Bolshoi Theater June 10, with Raisa Gorbachev seated between Metropolitan Filaret of Minsk and Councillor Kharchev, there were five hours of Millennial messages from world religious leaders. Raisa herself publicly affirmed her husband's commitment to partnership with the churches in the struggle for moral and spiritual reform. That evening, also at the Bolshoi, there were three hours of choral music, including offerings by a choir from the Theological Academy in Zagorsk—the first time a religious group had performed at the Bolshoi—all of which was broadcast over nationwide state television. The Moscow celebrations were echoed in cities and towns throughout the U.S.S.R.

Night after night that month, Soviet TV presented a ninety-minute documentary, "Church," with candid films of the Stalinist campaign against the churches, showing the dynamiting of Moscow's Saviour Cathedral, the smashing of bells, and the burning of icons—and also presenting the testimonies of believers, including a young woman who declared: "You have to believe in God. Without God you are dead. Religious faith is life itself." Another TV documentary featured the ministry of a young priest who criticized the lack of moral dimensions in his secular education, abandoned his job as a technician, and found fulfillment in serving others through his priesthood.

Mikhail Gorbachev took the occasion of the extraordinary Communist Party Conference that same month to make his most substantial public statement about religious freedom:

> I want to deal with the important question of freedom of conscience. Attention to this matter is currently at a high point because of the millennial anniversary of the introduction of Christianity into Rus. We do not hide our opinion that the religious worldview is nonmaterialistic and nonscientific. But this is no reason to show disrespect for the spiritual world of believing people, and it certainly is no

185

> justification for the use of any kind of administrative pressure in order to confirm materialistic views. . . .
>
> All believers, irrespective of their religious denomination, are citizens of the U.S.S.R. with full rights. The overwhelming majority of them participated actively in our economic and social life and in performing the tasks of perestroika. The draft of the law on freedom of conscience which is now being prepared will be based on Leninist principles and will take into account the realities of the present.[10]

Gorbachev, typically, did not specify which Leninist principles would form the basis of the new law. In mid-1989 it was disclosed that the new Soviet Law on Freedom of Conscience would restore the right of "juridical personality" to the churches for the first time since 1918. The churches would once again have legal status. It would also prohibit discrimination on religious grounds and provide for religious education, the publication of religious literature, and social ministries—while omitting many of the detailed restrictions in Stalin's 1929 Law on Religious Associations.

The momentum of *glasnost*-Millennial action in 1988 and 1989 produced these other developments:

*1,610 new congregations were registered in 1988 (compared with only 104 in 1987), including 1,244 Russian Orthodox, 72 Georgian Orthodox, 71 Roman Catholic, 48 mosques, and 36 Baptist.

*937 churches and church buildings were returned to communities of believers in 1988.

*Several additional monasteries, including the Kievan Monastery of the Caves (the first monastic community), have been returned to the Russian Orthodox Church.

*Orthodox seminaries have been permitted substantial increases in enrollment and new seminaries are planned.

*Soviet authorities have at last approved the establishment of a new Moscow seminary for the All-Union Council of Evangelical Christians-Baptists, which had previously been limited to correspondence schools for pastors. Additional evangelical seminaries are projected for Kiev, Riga, Tallinn, Alma Ata, and Novosibirsk.

*More than 1,250,000 Bibles were imported from the West in 1988, compared with only 20,000 in the previous three years.

*The history of religion has been included in general Russian history courses in many state schools throughout the U.S.S.R. Nearly 300 high school students in Tbilisi were enrolled in an experimental history of religion class "because Christianity helped to preserve the character and soul of the Georgian nationality," explained the director of the Pedagogical Research Institute.

*A Protestant pastor has been permitted to conduct optional Bible classes in state high schools in Riga.

*The churches have been invited to send volunteers into Soviet hospitals where they have been well-received by staff. The city of Leningrad has turned over a hospital to the Russian Orthodox Church.

*In early 1989, the U.S. State Department confirmed that all religious prisoners in the U.S.S.R. had been released. There had been 265 persons classified as religious prisoners in 1987, of whom 116 were Baptists.

*3,400 Baptists and Pentecostals were permitted to emigrate in 1988.

*An Episcopal priest from the U.S. who had specially ministered to Vietnam veterans was invited to help Soviet clergy minister to veterans of the Afghan War.

*Special restrictions on Jehovah's Witnesses and Seventh-Day Adventists were lifted. (In 1987, Adventists had been permitted to open a seminary.)

*A council of churches was established in Estonia and other new ecumenical ventures were undertaken in Leningrad and other cities.

*Religious leaders were included in the Soviet government's 1988 delegation to the United Nations Human Rights Commission in Geneva.

*In April 1989, four church leaders were elected to the new Soviet Congress of People's Deputies: Patriarch Pimen, Metropolitan Alexei of Leningrad and Novgorod, Metropolitan Pitirim of Volokolamsk, and Catholicos Vasken I of the Armenian Apostolic Church.[11]

In an emotional personal testimony to the significance of all these developments, Father Vitaly Borovoy of the Russian Orthodox Church told the European Ecumenical Assembly in Basel in 1989:

> For me this is dream come true. All my life I dream of day when my Church—Orthodox Church—is free and my country is leader for peace. And now is happening! It is always my dream and now is happening!

Was it the political initiatives of an atheist, Mikhail Gorbachev's *glasnost* and *perestroika*, that generated all these remarkable happenings? Or was it the irresistible power of Russian remembrance of its Christian heritage in its Millennial celebrations? Or was it both, in some immeasurable combination? Would these new possibilities for Christian witness and service endure and expand beyond the Millennial afterglow, and be secured in Soviet law, and such law itself be justly executed? The answers to all such questions lay somewhere in the ineffable *symphonia* of Russian religion and politics.

Glasnost and the Jews

Like most reform movements, *glasnost* has proved to be a mixed blessing. One of the distressing ironies of *glasnost* is that it has unleashed a freshet of blatant anti-Semitism. There has been a very deep and persistent strain of hatred toward Jews throughout Russian history, brutally manifested in the pogroms of the late nineteenth and early twentieth centuries and in Stalin's pathological persecutions.

In Nikita Khrushchev's memoirs, there is a remarkably detailed ten-page account of the anti-Semitism that "grew like a growth in Stalin's own brain." According to Khrushchev, Stalin viewed many Jewish leaders as "agents of American Zionism and imperialism" and contrived barbaric ways to liquidate them. One such victim was Solomon Mikhoels, the "greatest actor of the Yiddish theater" and the brother of one of the Kremlin doctors falsely accused of attempting to poison Stalin. Khrushchev remembered:

> They killed him like beasts. They killed him secretly. . . . It was announced that Mikhoels had fallen in front of a truck. Actually he was thrown in front of a truck. . . . And who did it? Stalin did it, or at least it was done on his instructions.[12]

On February 12, 1989, the Solomon Mikhoels Cultural Center was opened in Moscow and was hailed by the World Jewish Congress as "testimony of the Soviet Government's rehabilitation of Jewish martyrs killed in the black years of Stalin's rule." Nobel Prizewinner Elie Wiesel, surrounded by rabbis and other Jewish leaders from many countries, described the opening as "the start of a marvelous dream."[13]

The most conspicuous current eruption of anti-Semitism comes from a boisterous, xenophobic, ultra-nationalist society known as Pamyat (Memory). There are Pamyat groups in a number of cities, holding street rallies, disrupting liberal gatherings, hurling the epithet "Jew-lover" at reformers and dissidents. In March 1989, Pamyat attracted a crowd of more than 3,000 in the center of Moscow to honor the memory of Stalin on the thirty-sixth anniversary of his death. In its more violent forms, recent bursts of anti-Semitism have led to the smashing of Jewish tombstones and synagogue windows.

Transcending the ugliness of the Pamyat phenomenon, *glasnost* has produced several very positive developments concerning Jews: the release of all Jewish prisoners of conscience; the establishment of hitherto-forbidden Jewish cultural centers and clubs in many cities; a sudden proliferation of Jewish music and drama groups and dance troupes; and a substantial increase in Jewish emigration to Israel, the United States, and other countries. That increase accelerated from 914 in 1986 to 8,155 in 1987 and about 20,000 in 1988. Early in 1989, the Israeli government estimated the total for 1989 would reach 40,000; by mid-year it appeared that the total would be significantly higher. Soviet authorities have promised reform of emigration regulations that, among other onerous provisions, have limited the right to apply to those having first degree relatives abroad and also required affidavits of consent from family members remaining in the U.S.S.R. The enforcement of these restrictions has been waived in many cases. Public demonstrations by *refuseniks* (persons denied visas to emigrate) have been less subject to police intervention and arrest. Recently, there have been the most constructive conversations between Soviet and Israeli government representatives since 1967, raising hopes for the eventual resumption of diplomatic relations.

American Jewish leaders estimated in 1988 that 400,000 Soviet Jews (out of about 2,000,000) wished to emigrate. Nearly 300,000 had already emigrated from 1968 to 1988. Whether *glasnost's* exhilarating new opportunities to reconstruct Jewish institutions in the U.S.S.R. will reduce the number of persons wishing to emigrate will surely depend on the confidence that the Soviet Union will remain an increasingly open society.

There is an unfortunate contradiction in the pattern of U.S. human rights policy since the early 1970s: a policy that has focused substantially on this issue of Jewish emigration from the U.S.S.R. External U.S. pressure, especially pressure linked to arms control and trade issues, has clearly boomeranged. In the most promising period of détente, in 1973, just after the SALT I agreements, 35,000 Jews were permitted to emigrate. In 1974, Senator Henry M. Jackson (Democrat of Washington), an opponent of détente with strong political support in the American Jewish community, sponsored the Jackson-Vanik Amendment to deny trade advantages to the U.S.S.R. until Jewish emigration increased to 60,0000 a year. The result was that emigration *decreased* steadily for five years. Only with the signing of the SALT II Treaty in 1979 (which renewed hopes for détente) did Jewish emigration rise again—to a record 51,320 in 1979. But then came a new administration opposed to SALT II and pursuing a shrill anti-Soviet policy, especially on human rights issues. By 1981, Jewish emigration dropped below 10,000 for the year. In 1982, the total was only

2,688—then 1,314 in 1983, 896 in 1984, 1,140 in 1985, and 914 in 1986.[14] It was only with the renewal of summit diplomacy, the tempering of Ronald Reagan's rhetoric, and the INF Treaty that emigration began to increase significantly. In February 1989, the American Jewish Congress voted to seek at least a temporary suspension of the Jackson-Vanik Amendment in recognition of the dramatic upward trend. On May 12, 1989, President Bush announced his intention to "work with Congress" to achieve such a waiver.

There seem to be several hard lessons in this experience. The mustering of moral indignation by the United States in order to shame and pressure the Soviet Union to liberalize its civil policies is likely to hurt precisely those the indignation pretends to help. As important as increased trade with the U.S. may be to Soviet leaders, they are likely to be more heavily influenced by considerations of national pride and prestige. And the development of a more democratic society in the Soviet Union is aided more by peaceable relations with the United States than by U.S. hostility, self-righteousness, and attempts at external coercion.

CHAPTER 10

ECUMENISM AND THE SUPERPOWERS

As opposed to Protestantism and Roman Catholicism, the Orthodox Church claims to be the true Church of Christ from which Western Christians have separated. Its claims are as exclusive and categorical as those of Rome, but they are put forth in the name of a different conception of the Church. . . . the Church as a Body . . . is totally present everywhere that the Eucharist is celebrated, in every local church, and no authority, apart from that of the Spirit, can possibly impose itself on the people of God united in Jesus Christ.

—John Meyendorff[1]
The Orthodox Church

We make this appeal as servants of Christ gathered from among the churches of the U.S.A. and the U.S.S.R. We have been drawn together across the differences of language and culture by our common Christian calling to foster life in the midst of a race towards death. We affirm our unity in confessing Christ as Lord and Saviour.

—"Choose Life," Statement of U.S.S.R.
and U.S. Church Representatives,
March 1979 in Geneva[2]

If the full meaning of the word *oikoumene*—the whole family of Earth—is taken seriously, the relationships between American and Russian Christians take on a significance far beyond their official ecclesiastical connections. The conflict between their respective nations remains perilous for all nations and has already been terribly costly for virtually every nation. Their churches are called to partnership in the ministry of reconciliation, a ministry of engagement in the struggle for "justice, peace, and integrity of Creation"—the phrase crafted by the Vancouver Assembly of the World Council of Churches in 1983.

In the landmark ecumenical conferences of the 1920s and 1930s—Stockholm Life and Work (1925), Lausanne Faith and Order (1927), Oxford Church, Community, and State (1937)—the very few Russian participants were exiles from Stalinism. A Moscow Consultation of Orthodox Churches in July 1948 rejected membership in the new World Council of Churches, which would officially come into being the very next month in Amsterdam. That rejection came during one of the most ominous periods early in the Cold War, shortly after the communist coup in Czechoslovakia and during the Soviet-imposed Berlin Blockade. (A decade later, in an address at the Moscow Theological Academy, Metropolitan Nikolai acknowledged that there were non-theological factors in Russian Orthodoxy's initial rejection of the WCC: "For certain historical reasons, the Russian Church has long been unable to help the Christians of the West in their quest for church unity.")[3] However, the objections to the WCC in 1948 were stated in purely theological terms. A resolution adopted at the Moscow Consultation lamented the alleged neglect of "spiritual" priorities in the nascent World Council:

> The direction of the efforts of the ecumenical movement into the channels of social and political life, and towards the creation of an 'Ecumenical Church' as an influential international force, appears to us to be a falling into the temptation rejected by Christ in the wilderness. . . . the contemporary ecumenical movement no longer attempts to secure the reunion of the Churches by spiritual ways and means.[4]

Strangely enough, that lamentation anticipated the complaints of American Protestant conservatives in later years. The apprehension of some Western Christians that the Russian Orthodox Church would be a revolutionary political force was thus countered in 1948 and long afterward by the Russians' very conservative insistence on the precedence of doctrinal unity over practical cooperation.

The Amsterdam Assembly of 1948 was largely a Western European-North American affair with no Russian and little Eastern European representation. Its deliberations, however, were deeply conscious of the Cold War and sought to lift theology above identification with the West and with either capitalism or communism. The Assembly also met in only the earliest stages of post-war decolonization that by the 1960s would transform the makeup of both the United Nations and the World Council of Churches. The Moscow Patriarchate also declined to participate in WCC's Second Assembly in Evanston in 1954, not only because of doctrinal priorities but also because the WCC was alleged to be anti-Soviet. The Council had supported the U.S.-UN "police action" against the North Korean invasion of the South in 1950. The WCC's Commission of the Churches on International Affairs was chaired by an Englishman, Sir Kenneth Grubb, and its two top staff executives were Americans, O. Frederick Nolde and Richard M. Fagley.

It was in March 1956, once more a time of intense Cold War animosities, that the National Council of the Churches of Christ in the U.S.A. sent a deputation to U.S.S.R. churches as a "first step" toward continuing communication and other exchange programs. Headed by NCC president Eugene Carson Blake, then Stated Clerk of the Presbyterian Church U.S.A., the nine-member delegation worshipped in Orthodox and Baptist churches, met with Soviet government officials dealing with religious affairs, and discussed a wide range of church-state, theological, and international issues. That visit was reciprocated the following June when eight leaders of four Soviet communions visited Protestant churches in six U.S. cities, as well as the NCC General Board meeting in Toledo.

WCC Membership and Controversies

The entry of the Russian Orthodox Church into full membership of the World Council of Churches at the New Delhi Assembly in 1961 followed three years of visitations by Russian observers at various WCC meetings and programs. The timing was paradoxical; this ecumenical opening to the East came just as the Khrushchev regime was closing down thousands of Orthodox churches and institutions.

In all succeeding WCC assemblies, difficult issues affecting U.S.-Soviet relations have been debated. The lack of freedom for Russian delegates to dissent publicly from Soviet foreign policy without fear of reprisals has regularly contrasted with the candor of American delegates often critical of U.S. policy (as on Vietnam, the arms race, and Central America). There has been a pastoral concern in the WCC that Soviet church leaders be able to return home without having to confront government retribution. Consequently, there has sometimes been an apparent double standard in the way WCC bodies deliberate and decide on political issues. In some cases, WCC leaders have resorted to extensive private conversations and correspondence to seek redress of human rights abuses, believing that public condemnation would help neither the victims nor the churches closest to them. The 1980 Melbourne Conference of the WCC Commission on World Mission and Evangelism acknowledged such an apparent double standard:

> Some countries and people we dare not identify for the simple reason that such a specific public identification by the conference may endanger the position—even the lives—of many of our brothers and sisters. . . . We therefore confess our inability to be as prophetic as we ought to be as that may, in some instances, entail imposing martyrdom on our fellow believers in those countries—something we dare not do from a safe distance.[5]

At the Uppsala Assembly in July 1968, there were ominous signs of Soviet pressure on the reformist government of Alexander Dubcek and his "socialism with a human face" in Czechoslovakia. Czech theologian Josef Hromádka, a member of the WCC Central Committee (1947–68) and a sometime visiting professor at Princeton Seminary in the 1940s, pleaded with Assembly delegates not to aggravate the situation by censuring Soviet conduct. After some debate, the Assembly heeded the plea. But a month later, on August 21, 1968, Soviet troops and those of four Warsaw Pact states invaded Czechoslovakia. That invasion was sharply protested by the officers of WCC's Central Committee:

> We deplore the military intervention into the affairs of Czechoslovakia . . . by the governments of the U.S.S.R., Poland, East Germany, Hungary, and Bulgaria. . . . We appeal to the government of the U.S.S.R. to reconsider the policy which dictated the military intervention, to remove all its troops from Czechoslovakia at the earliest possible moment, and to renounce the use of force or its threat upon its allies. . . . We express to the churches and the people of Czechoslovakia our concord and sympathy in their ordeal. We support their peaceful resistance to the reimposition of spiritual and social controls unacceptable to a brave and courageous nation.[6]

The political and religious reverberations of the Soviet attack were kaleidoscopic. NATO abandoned plans for mutual force reductions in Europe. The Pentagon seized the moment to announce a go-ahead decision on deployment of the $5.5 billion Sentinel ABM system. The State Department curtailed cultural exchange programs with the U.S.S.R. The SALT Talks were postponed indefinitely. The governing Democratic Party, meeting the very next week in its Chicago convention, was made more vulnerable to the hardline presidential campaign of Richard Nixon, who narrowly defeated Hubert Humphrey in the 1968 election by a 500,0000-vote margin out of 75,000,000 votes cast. And it would be the Nixon administration that would proceed with the deployment of MIRVs in 1970, thus forsaking the original intent of the SALT Talks: the prevention of a new offensive arms race. Seldom have the iniquities of one great power so quickly compounded the perversities of its adversary.

The 1975 Nairobi Assembly of the World Council of Churches was unexpectedly confronted with a long letter from Russian Orthodox priest Gleb Yakunin and layman Lev Regelson in Moscow, appealing for ecumenical help in protesting religious persecution in the U.S.S.R. The letter invoked the human rights provisions of the just-concluded Helsinki accords on Security and Cooperation in Europe. The defensiveness of Russian delegates (and their implied threat to withdraw from the Council), concern for their welfare, and a simultaneous determination to respond to the urgency of the Yakunin-Regelson appeal made for an intensely emotional debate widely reported in the world press. Rather than specifically condemning the U.S.S.R., the Assembly finally adopted a resolution that requested "the General Secretary to see to it that questions of religious liberty be the subject of intense consultations with the member churches of the signatory states of the Helsinki Agreement" and called for a report to be presented to the WCC Central Committee a year later.[7] Subsequently, the WCC established a Human Rights Advisory Group and held a number of consultations on religious liberty.

The Soviet invasion of Afghanistan in December 1979 was reproved in February 1980 by the WCC Executive Committee for "the latest direct, armed intervention in one country by another" which heightened world tensions and was a "threat to peace." At the next WCC Assembly in Vancouver, in July 1983, the continued Soviet warfare in Afghanistan was the topic of extended debate. The resolution adopted by the Assembly focused on efforts by the UN Secretary General to end the conflict, including "withdrawal of Soviet troops from Afghanistan in the context of an overall political settlement, including agreement between Afghanistan and the U.S.S.R." Some delegates sought sharper language condemning Soviet aggression and demanding the unconditional withdrawal of Soviet troops—but were turned down in favor of UN initiatives.[8] Archbishop Kirill of the Russian Orthodox Church, in an implicit rebuke to Soviet policy, supported both Executive Committee and Vancouver resolutions on Afghanistan.

Bilateral Ecumenism

During a meeting of the WCC Central Committee in Jamaica in January 1979, conversations took place between U.S. and Soviet members that were to lead to a profound reorientation in their ecumenical relations. It was the winter of climactic negotiations for a SALT II Treaty, long regarded by both superpowers as the measure that would do most to ratify détente and set them on the path toward a genuinely peaceable relationship. A decision was taken in Jamaica to convene, on short notice, a consultation in Geneva March 27-29, 1979, bringing together major leaders of the churches of both countries. Perhaps nobody in Jamaica—or at the Geneva Consultation, for that matter—could have anticipated the long-range consequences of that decision.

At the Ecumenical Centre, headquarters for the WCC and other international bodies, ten delegates from the National Council of Churches confronted ten delegates from Soviet churches for three days of difficult discussions. Differences of language and theological style were not the only obstacles to agreement. There were serious political and ideological tensions over numerous military, regional, and human rights issues.

That meeting in Geneva, afterward known as the "Choose Life Consultation," finally succeeded in creating the very first joint theological statement by U.S. and U.S.S.R. church leaders.[9] While the statement concluded with a "call to action" on SALT II and other disarmament issues, it was the theological and ecclesial portions that made "Choose Life" the charter of bilateral ecumenism for years to come. The title reflected the statement's opening text from Deuteronomy 30:19: "I call heaven and earth to witness against you this day, that I have set before you life

199

and death, blessing and curse. Therefore, choose life, that you and your descendants may live."

"Choose Life" won immediate and widespread approval in both countries. The NCC Governing Board, the United Methodist Council of Bishops, and other church bodies speedily endorsed it. The full text of this Christian theological statement was published in the official Soviet government paper, *Izvestia,* a most unusual departure, which gave an enormous lift to the churches of the U.S.S.R.

Even more important in the long run was the determination to institutionalize this developing bilateral relationship. Accordingly, similar delegations met at Geneva's John Knox House in 1980 to project a series of exchanges and educational and media programs. The NCC created a U.S.-U.S.S.R. Church Relations Program and proceeded to plan an ambitious schedule of ecumenical seminars in the U.S.S.R. NBC-TV produced two one-hour documentaries on "The Church of the Russians," narrated by Professor V. Bruce Rigdon of McCormick Seminary. In 1983 Don Nead, chaplain at Purdue University, founded the John T. Conner Center for U.S.-U.S.S.R. Reconciliation, named for a recently deceased campus minister who had promoted peace studies in higher education. The Conner Center has offered special summer schools at Purdue and has given leadership to travel seminars in the U.S.S.R. The first in a series of exchanges by Russian Orthodox theological faculty and students toured U.S. seminaries in 1986.

Both prior and subsequent to the Choose Life Consultation of 1979, the periodic visitations by church leaders begun in 1956 continued both in the U.S.S.R. (1962, 1974, 1984), and in the U.S.A. (1963, 1975, 1981, 1984). There was wider ecumenical sponsorship of an October 1969 consultation in St. Louis on "Christian Concern for the Limitation and Reduction of Arms." The NCC and the U.S. Catholic Conference jointly convened that consultation in which eight prominent Russian participants were joined by ten U.S. Roman Catholics (including four bishops) and seven U.S. Protestants. (For some reason, NCC-Roman Catholic cooperation in such matters has languished in subsequent years.) The commitment to disarmament was manifested in joint U.S.-U.S.S.R. prayer vigils at the sites of the Reagan-Gorbachev summits in Geneva, Washington, and Moscow.

Perhaps the greatest impact of this bilateral activity on the U.S. churches has come from the NCC-sponsored seminars in the Soviet Union. About fifteen hundred Americans have participated in these seminars and have greatly multiplied their influence through many thousands of followup programs in U.S. communities and the media coverage generated thereby.

Dominoes Woes

Not all the media coverage of NCC's U.S.-U.S.S.R. program has been positive. A particularly hurtful pattern of media misrepresentation and vilification occurred at the end of the NCC's largest-ever ecumenical exchange in 1984 in which 266 Americans visited the Soviet Union. Participants undertook an ambitious preparatory reading program, including Trevor Beeson's sober account of the hard life of martyred Soviet churches in his definitive study, *Discretion and Valour.* A four-day orientation in New York included presentations by a tough-minded Kremlinologist from the Library of Congress, a former director of Soviet affairs in the State Department, a renowned specialist in Soviet law and human rights from Harvard Law School, Russian Orthodox and Jewish leaders concerned about continuing Soviet repression. Almost everywhere the seminar and its ten subgroups traveled in the U.S.S.R., the issues of war and peace, human rights, and dissent were discussed. At times the Soviet views were uncomfortably harsh, propagandistic, and one-sided. But the hard issues were not evaded.

Two unfortunate, anecdotal, and rather sensational newspaper accounts by Moscow correspondents for the *New York Times* and the *Los Angeles Times* conveyed a contrary story: that NCC leaders were ill-informed, naive about Soviet church life, insensitive to repression, and coopted by communist propaganda. At the Moscow Baptist

Church, a service and concert of sacred music, at which seminar participants were special guests, was disrupted by several unregistered Baptists whose large signs reported numbers of imprisoned pastors. Seminar leaders declined to insinuate themselves into this incident and were thereupon portrayed by the press as unsympathetic to the prisoners.

These unfortunate press stories quickly set in motion a whole train of media misrepresentation throughout the United States and other countries. The *Washington Post* pontificated editorially against the NCC under the sarcastic head, "In the Soviet Paradise." (An embarrassed *Post* later published letters from two prominent Washingtonians who had participated in the seminar, chiding the paper for its unprofessional conduct in accepting the *New York Times* report without further investigation. To its credit, the *Post* then published its own rather full and fair account of the seminar.) The *Wall Street Journal* joined the assault on the NCC, also accepting the *Times* account, and editorially scorned the "Deferential Reverends." Then came *Time* magazine with still another sarcastic head: "See and Hear No Evil." NBC-TV in New York broadcast two scathing editorials charging that the seminar had been "hood-winked." And then came the syndicated editorials of the Scripps-Howard newspapers all around the country, calling NCC leaders "apologists for the totalitarian left." There was no way the National Council of Churches could obtain equal time and space to respond to all these assaults on its religious integrity and moral credibility.

This entire episode is a case study in the damage that "pack journalism" can do. It illustrates the domino effect that often activates American media: an erroneous or spurious story rapidly spreads throughout the papers, the magazines, and the air waves, escalating the rhetoric and generating unfair and sometimes vicious misjudgments. At its worst in the area of U.S.-Soviet relations, such media misconduct contributed to a kind of neo-McCarthyism in the 1970s and 1980s.[10]

The Orthodox Within

The National Council of Churches embraces within its own "community of communions" nine Orthodox member churches, based primarily in ethnic communities with roots and continuing links in Eastern Europe and the Near East. They are therefore bearers of historical perspectives and particular grievances that are indispensable to U.S.-U.S.S.R. ecumenical dialogue. Four of these communions have roots among the peoples of the Soviet Union: The Orthodox Church in America (440 churches, 1 million members); The Patriarchal Parishes of the Russian Orthodox Church (38 churches, 10,000 members); The Ukrainian Orthodox Church in America (27 churches, 5,000 members); The Diocese of The Armenian Church of America (66 churches, 450,000 members).[11]

Until recently, the Orthodox presence in the NCC has tended to be rather marginal to the mainline Protestant denominations in terms of policy, program, and staff. Similarly, Orthodox parishes in many American cities have tended to be marginal to local ecumenical and civic life. The Russian Orthodox Millennium in 1988 provided an unprecedented occasion for non-Orthodox churches throughout the United States to study Russian church history and theology, share in Orthodox liturgies, overcome estrangement from Orthodox clergy and congregations, and confront issues of U.S.-U.S.S.R. relations with new perspectives. The NCC's Friendship Press made "The Peoples and Churches of the Soviet Union" its study priority for 1987–88 and published several works focused on the Millennium. The Washington Cathedral hosted an exhibition of icons, a week of lectures and music, and, together with St. Nicholas Orthodox Cathedral, two major ecumenical festival services for the Millennium.

Two marks of ecumenical progress were the recent election of Father Leonid Kishkovsky of The Orthodox Church in America to the presidency of the National Council, and Deacon Michael Roshak, also of the OCA, as the first director of the NCC's new Europe/U.S.S.R. Office.

CPC and CAREE

In 1958, Professor Josef Hromádka of Czechoslovakia, a theologian committed to a ministry of critical coexistence with his country's communist government, founded an organization based in the Eastern European churches but open to Christians from any country. Called the Christian Peace Conference, its primary purpose was to seek an end to the Cold War. In the 1960s there was a flurry of Christian-Marxist dialogues in Czechoslovakia and elsewhere in which some CPC leaders (but not Russians) invested great hopes. Professor Hromádka's personal integrity and courage assured at least a limited degree of autonomy and diversity in CPC's meetings and studies, although CPC pronouncements and publications clearly tilted toward Soviet policy. The 1968 CPC Assembly coincided with the Prague Spring in April and was marked by the enthusiasms of Czech liberalization, substantial American participation, and the freest discussions in CPC's history.

Just four months later, when Soviet troops invaded his country, CPC President Hromádka (then 79 years old) protested bitterly in a letter personally delivered to the Soviet ambassador in Prague. The invasion had provoked feelings of "disappointment, regret, and shame. In my long life I do not know a greater tragedy. . . . The Soviet government could not have committed a more tragic error." To his CPC colleagues meeting in Paris six weeks later, Hromádka wrote:

> I am not able to express the depth of our disappointment, our grief, our feelings of outrage, and even betrayal. . . . In my mind 21 August is written in much darker colours than 15 March 1939. The Nazis were our chief enemies and always declared quite openly their intentions towards us and the whole of Eastern Europe. But on 21 August our friends and allies invaded our country.[12]

That November, CPC General Secretary Jaroslav Ondra was purged. The organization's autonomy was destroyed.

Hromádka resigned as president. Not many months later, he died a brokenhearted man. Christian-Marxist dialogues also died.

Those Americans who had known Dr. Hromádka and respected him for his courage, even when he doubted their own, could hardly continue in the same relationship to the movement he founded and then abandoned in despair. Some Western European regional CPC committees simply dissolved in protest, never to return. An autonomous U.S. Committee for the CPC struggled for two years to find a formula that would permit some liaison with the subdued CPC (then presided over by Metropolitan Nikodim of the Russian Orthodox Church) but would also provide a base for criticizing CPC and Soviet policy—and also for pursuing topics not tolerated by CPC's new regime, such as Christian-Marxist dialogue and relations with China. The formula finally developed was to regroup as CAREE: "Christians Associated for Relations with Eastern Europe." CAREE pointedly declined to participate officially in the CPC Assembly of 1972. Subsequently CAREE became officially related to the National Council of Churches with representation on NCC's Europe Committee and International Affairs Commission.

The dramatic death of Metropolitan Nikodim in the arms of Pope John Paul I at the Vatican in 1978 (not many days before that brief papacy itself ended in death) was followed by the election of (now-Bishop) Karoly Toth of the Hungarian Reformed Church to the CPC presidency. Toth had previously served as CPC general secretary in Prague. In both capacities, Toth made special efforts to encourage open and candid participation of Western and Third World Christians, gaining the confidence of many U.S. church leaders.

After the U.S.S.R. invaded Afghanistan in December 1979, and CPC officers issued a statement lamely conforming to Soviet rationalizations for the invasion, CAREE's General Committee addressed a strong protest to CPC, declaring,

> we must strongly deplore the intervention by the Soviet
> Union in Afghanistan . . . and the fact of intolerable
> suffering and destruction caused by the presence of Soviet
> power in Afghanistan. . . . Villages are being destroyed by
> air and tank attacks. . . . The economy of the country is
> being undermined by this strife so that poverty and
> starvation become worse. Furthermore the movement of
> Soviet troops into Afghanistan has heightened fear and
> suspicion throughout the world. It is in itself a powerful
> contributor to the breakdown of détente and arms control.[13]

Similar protests came from many other groups. President Toth
decided to convene a consultation in Budapest (not Prague)
August 25-26, 1980, to discuss these protests—apparently in
the face of Russian resistance. It fell to me to present CAREE's
case in Budapest against the Soviet invasion and the CPC
statement. I was then roundly attacked by Russian and Czech
officials of the CPC—but just as roundly supported by persons
from India, Sri Lanka, England, France, and the World Council
of Churches. The consultation ended with approval of
recommendations that the CPC *Bulletin* publish the critical
WCC statement, as well as a story containing statements both
critical and supportive of the CPC position. (To my knowledge,
the *Bulletin* never complied.)

CAREE's own work continues with two particularly
significant projects: a journal published since 1981, *Occasional Papers on Religion in Eastern Europe* (OPREE), and an
Institute on Peace and Understanding for East-West
academic dialogues. CAREE has also helped to facilitate the
occasional "Karlovy Vary meetings," seven of which have
been held since a 1962 consultation in Karlovy Vary,
Czechoslovakia. These have been off-the-record discussions between top U.S. and Eastern European church
leaders, alternating between Czech and American sites.
While including Russian participants, these sessions have
provided more substantial space for non-Russian leaders
than have other East-West ecumenical circles.

Between the KGB and the FBI

Most U.S. leaders in the WCC, NCC, and CAREE who
have been intensively engaged in relationships with Soviet

churches have long known that these relationships do not take place in a political vacuum. Both the U.S. and Soviet governments have been oppressively involved in them. To put it very plainly: Christian relations between these two nations proceed on a hazardous course between the KGB and the FBI. Americans engaged in any gathering with Soviet groups have had to assume that some person or persons on the Soviet side would monitor and report to authorities. Such an assumption is not so much a matter of paranoia as it is a kindness to the Soviet partners and an appreciation of pressures upon them.

American participants in these encounters have also had to confront the mixture of intrusiveness, incompetence, and malevolence in some of their own government's shenanigans. In April 1985, the State Department hosted and co-sponsored an "International Conference on Religious Liberty" with the Institute on Religion and Democracy. While both President Reagan and Secretary Shultz addressed the 200 attendees, it was basically an IRD show that misappropriated the names of ecumenical and denominational leaders and provided a platform for bashing the National Council of Churches and its relationships with the Russian Orthodox Church. This coopting of the State Department for right wing religious propaganda was a bizarre abuse of religious liberty in the name of religious liberty.

More serious was the congressional release in December 1987 of a scurrilous FBI report on "Soviet Active Measures in the United States, 1986–87," which simultaneously managed to defame the Russian Orthodox Millennium as a "facade" for repression, Russian Baptists as propagandists, CAREE as a "Soviet front organization," and the National Council of Churches for its "increasing contacts" with CAREE. Whether willful or ignorant, that report purveys more than injurious and intimidating misinformation: it reveals a crude insensitivity to the ambiguities of Christian life in the Soviet Union and of the ecumenical imperatives of American churches.[14]

Congressional hearings in June 1989 disclosed extensive FBI interception of private correspondence between U.S. citizens and persons in the Soviet Union and Eastern Europe—intrusions defended by FBI Director William S. Sessions as matters of "overriding national interest." Increasing communication between U.S. and U.S.S.R. churches faces intimidating surveillance.

Genuine religious liberty is far from being fully realized in the land of the KGB—but it also remains threatened by the conduct of the United States government.

A Theological Postscript

The pages of this volume have been heavy with the burdens of history. It is a prime task of Christian theology to interpret the burdens of history in the light of God's love abounding in grace, mercy, and peace. That means articulating a hopeful faith in full apprehension of the violence and treachery and suffering which surely must have blighted God's own hopes for our creatureliness. And that means offering a vista on our lives and our world from the vantage of the life and death and eternal power of Jesus Christ.

One of the special strengths of ecumenical theology—that is, theology formed by the ecclesial encounters of Christians with other Christians from diverse traditions and cultures—is precisely that it bears the historical burdens and gifts of a multiplicity of peoples. These concluding paragraphs present an account of some of the salient themes that have emerged since 1979 as ecumenical relationships between U.S. and U.S.S.R. church leaders have been transformed from casual contact to sustained partnership. These are also themes that serve to enrich a theology of peacemaking by transcending traditional Western discussions about war and peace, such as arguments between just war theory and pacifism—for they are themes that reflect the radical seriousness of the whole Earth's precarious future, the intolerability of enmity, and the imperative to say what we really mean now by God and Christ and Spirit and Creation and the End-time.

There is emerging between the American and Russian churches a *confluent theology*, a special testimony formed by the coming together of radically different streams of Christian history and experience into a common reservoir of conviction and spirituality. The primary sources of confluent theology in U.S.-U.S.S.R. church relations continue to be the bilateral Geneva consultations of 1979 and 1980. Again and again over the past decade, the themes and the texts from those events have been recalled, not only by the very limited circle of participants but by congregations, assemblies, and media in many places.

Seven topics lifted out of the terse text of the "Choose Life" statement of 1979 (and somewhat rearranged) provide the major themes of this confluent theology: (1) Creation and New Creation; (2) radical responsibility for history; (3) security in shalom; (4) the idolatry of nuclear arms; (5) overcoming principalities and powers; (6) Christ, the Conqueror of Death; and (7) our unity in Christ.

These themes have helped to inaugurate a new exaltation of peacemaking in the mission of the churches, not only in the United States and the Soviet Union but in the worldwide circle of the *oikoumene*. Peacemaking has acquired a new transcendence in two senses: (1) It has become at last an institutional priority in the churches. And (2) it has been lifted up to the most serious levels of theological discussion.

(1) Creation and New Creation

In 1979, "Choose Life" proclaimed peacemaking to be the very character of God as Creator—and rejected the violence of nations and the wasting of nature as profanations of God's New Creation in Jesus Christ:

> We bear witness that the Lord our God is a God of peace who wills the well-being of the whole of His Creation. . . . The gifts of God given to His people for the service of the New

Creation in Christ are everywhere diverted to the destruction of peace and order.

This recovery of a theology of Creation in response to nuclear and environmental crises is one of the most striking and most positive developments in recent Christian thought. That development is manifest in the conciliar study process launched by the WCC's Vancouver Assembly in 1983 on the theme "Justice, Peace, and Integrity of Creation." It is conspicuous in the United Methodist Council of Bishops' 1986 Pastoral Letter, *In Defense of Creation: The Nuclear Crisis and a Just Peace*. It is central to the reconstructive theologies of some individual theologians, such as Jürgen Moltmann's *God in Creation* and Sallie McFague's *Models of God: Theology for an Ecological, Nuclear Age*.[1] It was beautifully and magisterially proclaimed in a plenary address by French Cardinal Roger Etchegaray at the European Ecumenical Assembly in Basel in May 1989, on the topic "Peace with Justice for the Whole Creation."

Some American conservatives have scorned this renewal of creation theology as somehow too geocentric, too pretentious concerning the place of Planet Earth in God's cosmos. That fatuous complaint, however, too readily becomes an excuse for not doing everything humanly possible to preserve and defend that precious God-given portion of Creation over which human beings have a special and imperative trusteeship. The fact that astronomers now project the probable distention and death of the sun some billions of years from now is hardly a reason to discount the sacred worth of Earthlings and of all the good things that nourish and sustain human life. A serious theology of Creation will celebrate the harmony of humanity with nature and empower a new family loyalty to the whole community of Earth. Such a conception of the harmony of Creation owes much to the symphonic style of Eastern Orthodox tradition. At the Basel Assembly, Archbishop Kirill of Smolensk (A "Choose Life" participant a decade earlier) proclaimed a theocentric ethic based on God as Creator, which teaches "wholeness, interconnectedness and the value of the whole creation" and which establishes

211

"the real balance between humankind and nature, stressing the fact that all creation has one purpose—the glorification of the Creator."[2]

(2) Radical Responsibility for History

"Choose Life" was indeed presumptuous, and appropriately so, regarding the progress of the nations in developing weapons of annihilation. The 1979 consultation took seriously the possibility that military technology could make the Earth a wasteland and thereby terminate human history. This is to claim a kind of human partnership in eschatology: a capacity to create the End-time for all the generations of God's children while presuming on God's promises of eternal life thereafter. "Choose Life" noted that

> only twenty years separate us from the moment when we will be called upon to mark prayerfully the bi-millenary anniversary of the coming to the world of our Lord and Saviour, Jesus Christ, the Prince of Peace. How shall we meet that day!? In what state shall we present our planet to the Creator: shall it be a blooming garden or a lifeless, burnt out, devastated land!?

It was then that the statement went on to Deuteronomy's "therefore choose life that you and your descendants may live."

Most of that language about the bimillennium of Jesus Christ and its implications for our stewardship of history and of Planet Earth came directly from a theological paper presented by Metropolitan Juvenaly, then chairman of the External Relations Department of the Moscow Patriarchate. This demonstrates that Russian Orthodox hierarchs and American Protestants could agree on the radicality of human freedom and responsibility in history—and affirm that radicality as both God's great gift and God's great risk. To choose life or death for succeeding generations is a human choice. God will not manipulate that choice.

There are several alternative eschatologies that severely discount this claim of human responsibility. One particularly grotesque vision (see Hal Lindsey, *Late, Great Planet Earth*) is to welcome a holocaust as hastening "the Rapture" and the Reign of Christ. A more benign but no less problematical opinion (offered by Billy Graham in a recent sermon at the Washington Cathedral) is to profess the confidence that God will somehow intervene to prevent a war of annihilation—that our apparent freedom is really within a supernatural fail-safe system that will protect us from self-destruction. Still another diversion from responsibility (that of Stanley Hauerwas in a Fall 1986 article in *The Asbury Theological Journal*) is to assert that this very concern to preserve the future for coming generations is the sin of "survivalism" and a failure to leave the future to God.

To all such escapisms, must we not respond that faith in the Incarnation of Jesus Christ means taking God-given humanity and history with utmost seriousness—and that whatever redemption may mean in some extra-historical infinity, we are bidden by Christ to know it here and now in our earthly soul-and-body finitude?

(3) The Security of Shalom

There has been a chronic disposition among most people, Christians included, to regard peace as an unattainable ideal but security as a real-world strategy; to view the welfare of other nations as desirable if they are allies but contrary to "the national interest" if they are adversaries; and, especially for Americans, to presume that national sovereignty means the actual power to control our own destiny.

The advent of nuclear weapons and other totalitarian threats to the biosphere has paradoxically impelled Christians toward recalling the wholeness of our own prophetic tradition. Which is to say that the decisive intrusion of the most fateful physical perils into our consciousness has commanded the recovery of our spiritual heritage in the Scriptures. "Choose Life" declared that God

> has granted us and all His people a vision of *shalom* for the present time and for the ages to come in which all peoples and nations will dwell together in security.

It is the disjoining of security from *shalom* that has become most dangerous in our generation because

> the very longing for security on the part of nations is often used to justify . . . an escalation of terror rather than the establishment of full security.

Security is a legitimate concern, even a promise of the prophets—but only in the context of *shalom*, that well-being of the whole community in which peace and justice are inseparable. Security is indivisible when the whole Earth is threatened. The security and well-being of other nations, even and especially of "enemies," are essential to the well-being and security of our own nation. "Choose Life" anticipated the Palme Commission's core concept of "common security."[3] *Shalom* is neither a simple greeting nor a sentimental feeling. It is the purpose and the moral law of God grounded in God's good Creation. Jesus Christ is the incarnation of *shalom* and the hope of all Creation.

(4) The Idolatry of Nuclear Arms

The disjuncture of security from *shalom* is most blatant and most profane in the sacralizing of nuclear weapons, particularly in the doctrine of nuclear deterrence, which for four decades has been the fixation, the absolute sanction, of national security. That is an ultimately absurd and contradictory doctrine of peace through terror, a scandal to the Christ who casts out fear.

"Choose Life" viewed such a concept of security as both illusory and blasphemous:

> We confessed that seeking our security through [nuclear] arms is in fact a false and idolatrous hope and that true security can be found only in relationships of trust.

Thus nuclear issues are not just a matter for cost-benefit analysis, or only to be weighed in the calculus of proportionality and discrimination according to the traditional just war theory. They must be seen as ultimately constituting *theological issues*. The United Methodist Bishops further developed this ultimately theological concern in *In Defense of Creation:*

> Deterrence has too long been reverenced as the unquestioned idol of national security. It has become an ideology of conformity too frequently invoked to disparage dissent and to dismiss any alternative foreign policy proposals. In its most idolatrous forms, it has blinded its proponents to the many-sided requirements of genuine security.

The Bishops appealed to an "ethic of reciprocity . . . shaped by an acceptance of mutual vulnerability, a vision of common security, and the escalation of mutual trust rather than mutual terror."[4] Such an ethic may be especially difficult for great powers accustomed to imposing their will on smaller nations, but it has become the prerequisite to the survival and well-being of the great powers themselves, for they are precisely the prime targets of weapons of mass destruction and they are also increasingly vulnerable to terrorism and the proliferation of weapons technologies.

(5) Overcoming Principalities and Powers

"Choose Life" was not at all naive about the cumulative power of evil and its threat to diminish the possibility of ever achieving security among the nations:

> We recognize that we ourselves and the peoples of our two nations, and indeed, every man, woman and child in all the world, are caught in this spiral of terror. We perceived that the threat of this escalation is slipping beyond human control . . . for 'we wrestle, not against flesh and blood, but against principalities, against powers.' (Ephesians 6:12)

The discussion of "principalities and powers" focused not only on the dynamics between the superpowers but on the domestic institutions within both nations that have frustrated freedom and justice for their peoples.

It would be a serious mistake to identify "principalities

and powers" simply with governments and not to note the darker perversions of human consciousness that abuse the powers of government. As the just ordering of our common life, government is rightly grounded in God's good Creation. Its work of justice includes the restraint of those who sinfully abuse the common life or the sanctity of individual persons. In the United States, a short list of "principalities and powers" might include the aggressive pursuit of corporate profits at the expense of the public interest, the personal lust for power among industrialists and politicians, the technocratic mystique of weapons development, the bureaucratic momentum of military technology, and the self-righteous absolutism of anti-communism, anti-Sovietism, and even anti-socialism. There are doubtless parallels on the Soviet side, as our historical sketches suggest.

Yet "Choose Life" did not despair about prospects for achieving "relationships of trust," for "Christ has overcome the principalities and powers (Colossians 2:15). JESUS IS LORD! That passage might have been rendered in even more appropriate language if it had used the wording of the Revised Standard Version: Christ "disarmed the principalities and powers, . . . triumphing over them in him."

(6) Christ, the Conqueror of Death

This is the paradox of a radically incarnational view of history: we are to take history itself with utmost seriousness, but always to be conscious of the pilgrimage of the generations, always remembering our continuity with the Communion of the Saints who have preceded us and whom, in the mercies of God, we shall embrace in the time to come.

The second paragraph of "Choose Life" drew on the core belief of Russian Christians, whether Orthodox or Baptist or other: the power of Christ to overcome the powers of death. While such language touched the personal lives of Americans who shared in the drafting, it evoked the constant remembrance of the enormity of suffering and death in Russian experience:

Gathered in Geneva during the season of Lent we have been especially conscious of the sufferings of our Lord who offered Himself that we might have life and have it abundantly (John 10:10). From our faith in Christ, the All Powerful, the Conqueror of Death, we have drawn strength to choose life in spite of the spreading power of death.

This is not a passive affirmation of faith in the Resurrection, resigned to the powers of death in human affairs but ultimately confident of immortality. Rather it is a very pro-active, empowering commission to resist the forces that have caused and may yet cause numberless unnatural deaths through the enmities of nations. All the images of Christ in "Choose Life" are images of power and action.

(7) Our Unity in Christ

There have been astonishing transfigurations of Christian spirituality in recent years as thousands of Americans and Russians have discovered each other to be sisters and brothers in Christ. To share each other's liturgies and prayers and hymns, to worship in new ways together, to develop emotional bonds of deep and trusting friendship, to form covenants between specific American congregations and specific Russian congregations, to believe without doubt in the other's commitment to peace, and to know that you really do share one Lord, one faith, one baptism with multitudes among your "enemies" is to make hostilities between you particularly intolerable. The very first paragraph of "Choose Life" appeals to a new sense of oneness in Christ:

> We have been drawn together across the differences of language and culture by our common Christian calling to foster life in the midst of a race towards death. We affirm our unity in confessing Christ as Lord and Saviour.

Here again, we must testify that the witness of Christian unity is much more than doctrinal agreement or ecclesiastical collaboration. It is to disclose to the world that ecumenism means peacemaking among all the peoples of Earth.

The follow-up Geneva Consultation of 1980 was captivated by a text from the second chapter of Paul's Letter to the Ephesians:

> Now in Christ Jesus you who once were far off have been brought near in the blood of Christ. For he is our peace, who has made us both one, and has broken down the dividing wall of hostility, . . . that he might create . . . one new humanity instead of two, so making peace, and might reconcile us both to God in one body through the cross, thereby bringing the hostility to an end. . . . So then you are no longer strangers, . . . but you are fellow citizens with the saints and members of the household of God. . . . (Ephesians 2:13-16, 19).

That familiar text now speaks to us in a powerful new way in the context of U.S.-Soviet relations. It means facing the reality of our hostility and of the walls that have divided us—and it speaks to the central work of Christ as reconciler and peacemaker. It means developing a *theology of the other side* of the walls, seeing the humanity on the other side, then seeing the face of Christ in that humanity.

A theology of the other side might well begin in *identification with the suffering* on the other side: with the assurance that God suffers everywhere God's children suffer, across every boundary of nation, race, credo, or manifesto.

Such a theology is also a *theology of ambiguity:* a theology that knows that there is a mixture of justice and injustice, of compassion and cruelty, on both sides of almost any enduring conflict. That is not to claim a capacity to measure guilt with arithmetical exactness on either side (or to claim "moral equivalence"). That would pretend to a power of ultimate judgment we have no right to and no capacity for. This intentional cultivation of ambiguity is to guard against the blindness and all-too-frequent brutality of self-righteousness. It is also to seek out the diversity of others on the other side: both the majority and minorities, the powerful and the powerless, the guardians of institutions and the victims of institutions. And it is to keep searching for alternative vantage points from which to view the conflict.

More often than we want to know, a theology of ambiguity will point to our own need of repentance and to what ought to be a basic article of our faith: *repentance is usually the precondition of reconciliation.* The transformation of a bitter relationship requires a conversion of the spirit.

A theology of the other side demands *an openness to both the gifts and the grievances* of those other people. Nothing is more precious in the recent surge of American Christian interest in Soviet Christians than the discovery that those Christians over there have priceless treasures of faith and culture and experience to share with us.

A theology of the other side will remind us again and again of the prophetic heritage which knows that God's judgment may be worked on us through the very enemies we are tempted to hate—whether by their harshness and hate toward us, or by their surprising acts of conciliation and even love.

This, then, is the icon of Christ in the confluent theology shared today by some Russians and some Americans: the Christ of the New Creation, the Christ who is the Incarnation of *shalom* and of the very heart of God, the Christ who casts down idols and casts out terror, the Christ who is disarming principalities and powers, who is conquering death, who is breaking down the dividing walls of hostility and making us one new humanity, the Christ whose face and whose suffering body are always over there on the other side of the wall and not this side only, the Christ who is our peace.

NOTES

CHAPTER 1. THE CHALLENGE OF SOVIETOLOGY

1. Harold J. Berman, "The Devil and Soviet Russia," in Samuel Hendel, ed., *The Soviet Crucible: The Soviet System in Theory and Practice*, Second Ed. (New York: D. VanNostrand Company, 1963), p. 5.
2. Georgi Arbatov and Willem Oltmans, *The Soviet Viewpoint* (New York: Dodd, Mead and Company, 1983), p. 10.
3. George Shultz, *Vienna Meeting: Commitment, Cooperation, and the Challenge of Compliance*, Current Policy No. 1145 (Washington: U.S. Department of State, 1989), p. 3.
4. *Soviet Perceptions of the U.S.: Results of a Surrogate Interview Project* (Washington: U.S. International Communication Agency, 1980), p. 2.
5. George F. Kennan, *The Nuclear Delusion: Soviet-American Relations in the Atomic Age* (New York: Pantheon Books, 1982), p. xxii.
6. James Leonard, comment in conference at the University of Texas, proceedings published in Alan F. Neidle, ed., *Nuclear Negotiations: Reassessing Arms Control Goals in U.S.-Soviet Relations* (Austin: Lyndon B. Johnson School of Public Affairs, 1982), p. 105.
7. Stephen F. Cohen, *Rethinking the Soviet Experience: Politics and History Since 1917* (New York: Oxford University Press, 1985), pp. 8-27.
8. Edmund W. Robb and Julia Robb, *The Betrayal of the Church: Apostasy and Renewal in the Mainline Denominations* (Westchester, Ill.: Crossway Books, 1986), pp. 13, 17-18, 22, 38, 193, 207.

CHAPTER 2. THE RUSSIAN STORY

1. Nicolas Zernov, *The Russians and Their Church*, Third Ed. (Crestwood, N.Y.: St. Vladimir's Seminary Press, 1976), p. 176.
2. Vladimir I. Lenin, "The Principal Task of Our Time," 1918 essay quoted in Robert Payne, *The Life and Death of Lenin* (New York: Simon and Schuster, 1964), p. 457.
3. Yuri Trifonov, *Literaturnoe obozrenie*, No. 4, 1977, 101, quoted in Stephen F. Cohen, *Rethinking the Soviet Experience: Politics and History Since 1917* (New York: Oxford University Press, 1985), p. x.
4. Louis Halle, *The Cold War as History* (New York: Harper & Row, 1967), p. 11.
5. James Billington, *The Icon and the Axe: An Interpretive History of Russian Culture* (New York: Random House, Vintage Books, 1970), p. 18.
6. Alexander Ulyanov testimony quoted in Robert Payne, *The Life and Death of Lenin*, pp. 71-72.
7. Michael Harrington, *Socialism* (New York: Saturday Review Press, 1972). See especially chapter 4, "The Unknown Karl Marx."
8. Leo Tolstoy, *War and Peace*, Edmund Fuller Ed. (New York: Dell Publishing Company, 1955), pp. 366-67.
9. Alan Moorehead, *The Russian Revolution* (New York: Harper and Brothers, 1958), pp. 94-95.
10. W. Bruce Lincoln, *Passage Through Armageddon: The Russians in War and Revolution 1914–1918* (New York: Simon and Schuster, 1986), p. 510.
11. D. F. Fleming, *The Cold War and its Origins*, vol. I, *1917–1950* (Garden City, N.Y.: Doubleday, 1961), pp. 19-20.
12. Harrison Salisbury, *The 900 Days: The Siege of Leningrad* (New York: Harper & Row, 1969), pp. 513-16.
13. Ibid., pp. 506, 513, 515.
14. Ibid., p. 579.
15. Nicolas Zernov, *The Russians and Their Church*, pp. 178-79.
16. Suzanne Massie, *Land of the Firebird: The Beauty of Old Russia* (New York: Simon and Schuster, 1980), pp. 14-15.
17. Chingiz Aitmatov, *The Day Lasts More Than a Hundred Years*, tr. John French (Bloomington: Indiana University Press, 1983), pp. 99-103.

CHAPTER 3. BETWEEN THE REVOLUTIONS

1. Thomas Jefferson's 1807 letter to William Duane quoted in Dumas Malone, *Jefferson and His Time*, vol. 5, *Jefferson the*

President: Second Term 1807–1809 (Boston: Little, Brown and Company, 1974), p. 440.

2. Nicholas Berdyaev, *The Russian Idea,* tr. R. M. French (Boston: Beacon Press, 1962), p. 2.

3. Tsar Alexander I's 1824 letter to Russian Minister Tuyll quoted in Dexter Perkins, *Hands Off: A History of the Monroe Doctrine* (Boston: Little, Brown and Company, 1946), p. 57. The full text of Monroe's message of December 2, 1823 is contained in Perkins, pp. 390-92.

4. Alexis de Tocqueville, *Democracy in America,* vol. 1, Phillips Bradley Edition (New York: Vintage Books, 1956), p. 452.

5. Henry Winter Davis, *The War of Ormuzd and Ahriman in the Nineteenth Century,* quoted in Robert V. Daniels, *Russia: The Roots of Confrontation* (Cambridge: Harvard University Press, 1985), p. 68.

6. Valentin Pikul, "The Flight of the Bumble-Bee Over the Atlantic," *Soviet Life,* No. 8 (359), August 1986, p. 63.

7. Thomas Jefferson's 1805 letter to Tsar Alexander I quoted in Dumas Malone, *Jefferson the President,* Volume 5, pp. 442-44.

8. *Writings of John Quincy Adams* quoted in Dexter Perkins, *Hands Off,* p. 24.

9. John Quincy Adams, *Memoirs,* VI, 163, quoted in Thomas A. Bailey, *A Diplomatic History of the American People,* Fourth Edition (New York: Appleton-Century-Crofts, 1950), p. 182.

10. Chilean writer Bilbao quoted in Dexter Perkins, *Hands Off,* pp. 104-5.

11. Thomas A. Bailey, *A Diplomatic History,* pp. 298-300.

12. Valentin Pikul, "The Flight of the Bumble-Bee," pp. 63-64.

13. Ibid.

14. Oliver Wendell Holmes, *The Complete Poetical Works of Oliver Wendell Holmes,* Cambridge Ed. (Boston: Houghton Mifflin, 1975), p. 198.

15. Ibid., p. 199.

16. Thomas A. Bailey, *A Diplomatic History,* pp. 398-99.

17. Alexander DeConde, *A History of American Foreign Policy* (New York: Charles Scribner's Sons, 1963), pp. 273-74. Ten years of military misrule by the U.S. Army (1867–77), without any civilian government, were marked by lawlessness, violent incidents, the soldiers' degrading of native women, and the alienation of the population.

18. Anthony Ugolnik, *The Illuminating Icon* (Grand Rapids: William B. Eerdmans Publishing Company, 1989), p. 233.

19. Thomas A. Bailey, *A Diplomatic History,* p. 532.

20. Alexander DeConde, *A History of American Foreign Policy,* p. 364.

21. Ibid.

22. Ivan Bloch, *The Future of War, in Its Technical, Political and Economic Relations,* quoted in Walter Millis and James Real, *The*

    Abolition of War (New York: The Macmillan Company, 1963), pp. 33-5.

23. Ibid., p. 36-37.
24. Mikhail S. Gorbachev, *Perestroika: New Thinking for Our Country and the World* (New York: Harper & Row, 1987), pp. 129-30, 132.
25. Finley Peter Dunne, *Mr. Dooley Says* (New York: Charles Scribner's Sons, 1910), p. 208.
26. Robert V. Daniels, *Russia: The Roots of Confrontation*, pp. 71-72.
27. Ibid.
28. Woodrow Wilson's April 2, 1917 address to Congress in *Papers Relating to the Foreign Relations of the United States, 1917*, Supplement 1, *The World War* (Washington: U.S. Government Printing Office, 1931), 200, quoted in George F. Kennan, *Russia Leaves the War: Soviet-American Relations, 1917–1920* (Princeton: Princeton University Press, 1956), p. 18.
29. George F. Kennan, *Russia and the West Under Lenin and Stalin* (Boston: Little, Brown and Company, 1960), pp. 47-48.

CHAPTER 4. BETWEEN THE WARS

1. George F. Kennan, *Russia and the West Under Lenin and Stalin* (Boston: Little, Brown and Company, 1960), p. 369.
2. Joseph V. Stalin's speech on the 1936 Constitution, November 25, 1936, in Samuel Hendel, ed., *The Soviet Crucible: The Soviet System in Theory and Practice*, Second Ed. (New York: D. VanNostrand Company, 1963), pp. 308, 311.
3. Frederick L. Schuman, *Russia Since 1917* (New York: Alfred A. Knopf, 1957), p. 117.
4. *Pravda*, September 15, 1957, quoted in George F. Kennan, *Russia and the West*, p. 65.
5. Woodrow Wilson quoted in Robert V. Daniels, *Russia: The Roots of Confrontation* (Cambridge: Harvard University Press, 1985), p. 138.
6. Frederick L. Schuman, *Russia Since 1917*, p. 119.
7. General William Graves quoted in Robert V. Daniels, *Russia: The Roots of Confrontation*, pp. 138-39.
8. George F. Kennan, *Russia and the West*, p. 117.
9. Thomas A. Bailey, *Woodrow Wilson and the Lost Peace* (Chicago: Quadrangle Books, 1963), pp. 22-23.
10. Woodrow Wilson quoted in George F. Kennan, *Russia Leaves the War: Soviet-American Relations, 1917–1920* (Princeton: Princeton University Press, 1956), p. 257.
11. Thomas A. Bailey, *Woodrow Wilson and the Lost Peace*, pp. 311-12.

12. George F. Kennan, *Russia and the West*, pp. 130-35.
13. Ibid., pp. 137-42.
14. Robert V. Daniels, *Russia: The Roots of Confrontation*, p. 194.
15. George F. Kennan, *Russia and the West*, p. 203.
16. Ibid., p. 206.
17. Richard F. Rosser, *An Introduction to Soviet Foreign Policy* (Englewood Cliffs, New Jersey: Prentice-Hall, 1969), p. 144.
18. Ibid., p. 206.
19. Ted Morgan, *FDR: A Biography* (New York: Simon and Schuster, 1985), pp. 397-98.
20. Robert V. Daniels, *Russia: The Roots of Confrontation*, pp. 198-99.
21. George F. Kennan, *Russia and the West*, p. 290.
22. Ibid., pp. 310-11.
23. Pope Pius XII message to Franco quoted in Paul Blanshard, *American Freedom and Catholic Power* (Boston: Beacon Press, 1949), pp. 237-38.
24. Reinhold Niebuhr quoted in Richard Fox, *Reinhold Niebuhr: A Biography* (New York: Pantheon Books, 1985), p. 190.

CHAPTER 5. THE PERPETUAL POST-WAR NON-PEACE

1. Herbert Butterfield, *Christianity, Diplomacy, and War* (New York: Abingdon-Cokesbury Press, n.d.), p. 43.
2. Adlai E. Stevenson, *Friends and Enemies* (New York: Harper and Brothers, 1959), p. 101.
3. Louis Halle, *The Cold War as History* (New York: Harper & Row, 1967), p. xiii.
4. D. F. Fleming, *The Cold War and Its Origins*, vol. I, *1917–1950* (Garden City, New York: Doubleday and Company, 1961), p. 141.
5. James MacGregor Burns, *Roosevelt: The Soldier of Freedom, 1940–1945* (New York: Harcourt Brace Jovanovich, 1970), p. 152.
6. Ibid.
7. Ibid., p. 248.
8. Eric Larrabee, *Commander in Chief: Franklin Delano Roosevelt, His Lieutenants, and Their War* (New York: Harper and Row, 1987), p. 187.
9. Fleming, *The Cold War and Its Origins*, Vol. 1, pp. 140-41.
10. Ibid., pp. 332-33.
11. Halle, *The Cold War as History*, pp. 32-37.
12. Eberhard Bethge, tr. Erich Mosbacher et al., *Dietrich Bonhoeffer: Man of Vision, Man of Courage* (New York: Harper and Row, 1970), pp. 626-76.

13. Halle, *The Cold War as History*, p. 38.
14. Winston S. Churchill, *The Second World War: Triumph and Tragedy* (New York: Bantam Books, 1962), p. 197.
15. Ted Morgan, *FDR: A Biography* (New York: Simon and Schuster, 1985), p. 760.
16. James MacGregor Burns, *Roosevelt: The Soldier of Freedom*, pp. 584-87.
17. Fleming, *The Cold War and Its Origins*, vol. 1, pp. 216-17.
18. Robert V. Daniels, *Russia: The Roots of Confrontation* (Cambridge: Harvard University Press, 1985), p. 221.
19. Fleming, *The Cold War and its Origins*, vol. I, p. 293.
20. Harry S. Truman, *Memoirs: Year of Decisions* (New York: Doubleday and Company, 1955), p. 228.
21. Halle, *The Cold War as History*, p. 163.
22. McGeorge Bundy, *Danger and Survival: Choices About the Bomb in the First Fifty Years* (New York: Random House, 1988), pp. 88, 650-51. See also Gar Alperovitz, *Atomic Diplomacy: Hiroshima and Potsdam*, Expanded and Updated Ed. (New York: Penguin Books, 1985); Martin J. Sherwin, *A World Destroyed: The Atomic Bomb and the Grand Alliance* (New York: Alfred A. Knopf, 1975); and Peter Wyden, *Day One: Before Hiroshima and After* (New York: Simon and Schuster, 1984).
23. Alperovitz, *Atomic Diplomacy*, p. 44.
24. Ibid., p. 8.
25. George Kennan's "Long Telegram" quoted in Halle, *The Cold War as History*, p. 106.
26. "Mr. X" (George F. Kennan), "The Sources of Soviet Conduct," *Foreign Affairs*, XXV, No. 4 (July 1947), pp. 566-82.
27. George F. Kennan, *Memoirs: 1950–1963* (Boston: Little, Brown and Company, 1972), pp. 39-53.
28. Truman, *Memoirs*, p. 412.
29. Halle, *The Cold War as History*, p. 190.
30. Walter LaFeber, *America, Russia, and the Cold War: 1945–1984*, Fifth Edition (New York: Alfred A. Knopf, 1985), pp. 96-97.
31. Raymond Garthoff, *Détente and Confrontation: American-Soviet Relations from Nixon to Reagan* (Washington: The Brookings Institution, 1985), pp. 136-39.
32. Ibid., pp. 547-48, 1083-84.
33. LaFeber, *America, Russia, and the Cold War*, p. 285.
34. A more comprehensive account of the SALT II negotiations is offered in Alan Geyer, *The Idea of Disarmament! Rethinking the Unthinkable*, Revised Ed. (Elgin, Illinois: Brethren Press, 1986), pp. 109-19. Soviet concessions are detailed on pages 117-18.
35. Strobe Talbott, *Deadly Gambits: The Reagan Administration and the Stalemate in Nuclear Arms Control* (New York: Alfred A. Knopf, 1984), p. xii.

CHAPTER 6. SO DIFFERENT, SO SIMILAR

1. Clifton Joseph Furness, ed., *Walt Whitman's Workshop* (New York: Russell and Russell, 1964), pp. 251-52. Whitman's "Letter to Russia" was written as a preface to an expected Russian translation of his *Leaves of Grass*—but the translation was never completed.
2. Andrei Sakharov, *Progress, Coexistence, and Intellectual Freedom* (New York: W. W. Norton Company, 1968), p. 27.
3. Wright Miller, *Russians as People* (New York: E. P. Dutton, 1961), pp. 9-10.
4. Ibid., pp. 121-23.
5. Archbishop Kirill of Smolensk, "Reconciliation in Europe—Heritage and Vision: The Ecology of the Spirit," address at European Ecumenical Assembly, Basel, May 15, 1989 (unpublished manuscript), p. 4.
6. Robert Bellah et al., *Habits of the Heart: Individualism and Commitment in American Life* (New York: Harper & Row, 1985), p. 142.
7. Ibid., p. 143.
8. Ibid., p. 295.
9. Miller, *Russians as People*, p. 103.
10. Suzanne Massie, *Land of the Firebird: The Beauty of Old Russia* (New York: Simon and Schuster, 1980), p. 26.
11. Miller, *Russians as People*, p. 103.
12. Ibid., p. 186.
13. Quoted in Robert G. Kaiser, *Russia: The People and the Power* (New York: Pocket Books, 1976), pp. 20-21.
14. Peter Tchaadayev, *A Philosophic Letter*, quoted in Lionel Kochan, *The Making of Modern Russia* (Baltimore: Penguin Books, 1963), p. 153.
15. Alexander Herzen quoted in Kochan, *The Making of Modern Russia*, p. 154.
16. James Billington, *The Icon and the Axe: An Interpretive History of Russian Culture* (New York: Random House, Vintage Books, 1970), p. 424.
17. Albert F. Heard, *The Russian Church and Russian Dissent* (New York: Harper and Brothers, 1887), p. 206.
18. Ernest Lee Tuveson, *Redeemer Nation: The Idea of America's Millennial Role* (Chicago: University of Chicago Press, 1968).
19. Joanna Hubbs, *Mother Russia: The Feminine Myth in Russian Culture* (Bloomington: Indiana University Press, 1988), p. 123.
20. Robert G. Kaiser, *Russia: The People and the Power*, p. 204.
21. Ibid., p. 290.
22. Wright Miller, *Russians as People*, pp. 114-15.
23. Valentin Resputin, *Farewell to Matyora* (New York: Macmillan, 1979).

24. Alan Geyer, *The Idea of Disarmament! Rethinking the Unthinkable* Rev. Ed. (Elgin, Ill.: Brethren Press, 1986), pp. 132-38.
25. Russell Baker, "A Little Respect, Please," *New York Times*, April 11, 1984, p. A27.
26. George F. Kennan, *The Nuclear Delusion: Soviet-American Relations in the Atomic Age* (New York: Pantheon Books, 1983), p. 197.
27. Raymond Garthoff, *Détente and Confrontation: American-Soviet Relations from Nixon to Reagan* (Washington: The Brookings Institution, 1985), pp. 1080-83.

CHAPTER 7. THE LARGEST CHRISTIAN COUNTRY

1. James Billington, *The Icon and the Axe: An Interpretive History of Russian Culture* (New York: Random House, Vintage Books, 1966), p. x.
2. Nicolas Zernov, *The Russians and Their Church* (Crestwood, New York: St. Vladimir's Seminary Press, 1978), p. 180.
3. Statistical data on religious membership are problematical at best. Sources vary widely in their estimates. Figures here are based on Trevor Beeson, *Discretion and Valour: Religious Conditions in Russia and Eastern Europe*, Rev. Ed. (Philadelphia: Fortress Press, 1982); Paul D. Steeves, *Keeping the Faiths: Religion and Ideology in the Soviet Union* (New York: Holmes and Meier, 1989); recent press reports and personal interviews.
4. J. Martin Bailey, *One Thousand Years: Stories from the History of Christianity in the U.S.S.R.* (New York: Friendship Press, 1987), p. 15.
5. The preceding few paragraphs owe much to the authoritative and lucid exposition by Timothy Ware, *The Orthodox Church*, Revised Ed. (New York: Penguin Books, 1983), pp. 51-67.
6. John Meyendorff, *The Orthodox Church*, Third Revised Ed. (Crestwood, New York: St. Vladimir's Seminary Press, 1981), pp. 70, 75.
7. The United Methodist Council of Bishops, *In Defense of Creation: The Nuclear Crisis and a Just Peace* (Nashville: Graded Press, 1986), p. 68.
8. James Billington lecture at Washington Cathedral, May 13, 1988. Author's personal notes.
9. Anthony Ugolnik, *The Illuminating Icon* (Grand Rapids: William B. Eerdmans Publishing Company, 1989), p. 61.

CHAPTER 8. THE HARSH SYMPHONIA

1. *Decree on Separation of Church from State* quoted in Trevor Beeson, *Discretion and Valour: Religious Conditions in Russia and*

Eastern Europe, Rev. Ed. (Philadelphia: Fortress Press, 1982), pp. 34-35.

2. Patriarch Tikhon's *Decree Excommunicating the Communists* quoted in William C. Fletcher, *The Russian Orthodox Church Underground 1917–1970* (London: Oxford University Press, 1971), p. 20.

3. Karl Marx and Friedrich Engels, *On Religion* (New York: Schocken Books, 1964), p. 42.

4. Max Josef Suda, "The Critique of Religion in Karl Marx's *Capital*," in Paul Mojzes, ed., *Varieties of Christian-Marxist Dialogue* (Philadelphia: The Ecumenical Press, 1978), p. 26.

5. John C. Bennett, *Christianity and Communism Today* (New York: Association Press, 1962), pp. 77-80.

6. Nicholas Berdyaev, *The Russian Idea*, trans. R. M. French (Boston: Beacon Press, 1962), pp. 247-48.

7. Vladimir I. Lenin, *Works*, Fourth Edition (Moscow: Marx-Engels-Lenin Institute, 1941–50), Vol. 35, pp, 89-90, 93, quoted in David K. Shipler, *Russia: Broken Idols, Solemn Dreams* (New York: Times Books, 1983), p. 271.

8. Joseph V. Stalin quoted in Jerome Davis, *Behind Soviet Power: Stalin and the Russians* (New York: The Readers Press, 1946), p. 15.

9. Trevor Beeson, *Discretion and Valour*, p. 58.

10. Nikita S. Khrushchev, *Khrushchev Remembers*, trans. and ed. Strobe Talbott (Boston: Little, Brown and Company, 1970), p. 22.

11. Nikolai I. Eshliman and Gleb P. Yakunin letter quoted in Beeson, *Discretion and Valour*, p. 76.

12. The full text of the 1979 Yakunin Report is contained in Sergei Pushkarev, Vladimir Rusak, and Gleb Yakunin, *Christianity and Government in Russia and the Soviet Union: Reflections on the Millennium* (Boulder, Colorado: Westview Press, 1989), pp. 107-45.

13. Alexander Solzhenitsyn's "Lenten Letter" quoted in Beeson, *Discretion and Valour*, pp. 77-78.

14. Trevor Beeson, *Discretion and Valour*, pp. 82-83.

15. A substantial account of Orthodox dissent from the 1960s to the early 1980s is provided by Jane Ellis, *The Russian Orthodox Church: A Contemporary History* (London: Croom Helm, 1986).

CHAPTER 9. GLASNOST AND THE MILLENNIUM

1. Mikhail S. Gorbachev, *Perestroika: New Thinking for Our Country and the World* (New York: Harper and Row, 1987), p. 12.

2. Nina Bobrova, "The Celebration of the Millennium of Christianity in Russia," *Rapprochement*, The Newsletter of the John T. Conner Center for U.S.-U.S.S.R. Reconciliation, June 1988, pp. 1-2.

3. Mikhail S. Gorbachev quoted in Paul D. Steeves, *Keeping the Faiths: Religion and Ideology in the Soviet Union* (New York: Holmes and Meier, 1989), p. 171.

4. Interview with Father Dmitry Grigorieff of Washington's St. Nicholas Orthodox Cathedral, a participant in all three Millennial seminars, April 7, 1988.

5. Konstantin M. Kharchev interview by William Teska, reported in "Glasnost and Religion," *Rapprochement*, June 1988, p. 7.

6. Konstantin M. Kharchev, *Izvestia*, January 27, 1986, p. 3, quoted in Paul D. Steeves, *Keeping the Faiths*, pp. 176-77.

7. Mikhail S. Gorbachev, April 29, 1988, quoted in Ninan Koshy, *Perestroika: Some Preliminary Comments* (Geneva: World Council of Churches, 1988), p. 17.

8. Bishop Basil Rodzianko, "Glasnost: A Voice Crying Out," *Report from the Capital*, February 1989, p. 7.

9. Konstantin M. Kharchev's remarks at dedication, *Journal of the Moscow Patriarchate*, quoted in *Rapprochement*, December 1988, p. 2.

10. Mikhail S. Gorbachev, *Izvestia*, June 29, 1988, p. 4, quoted in Paul D. Steeves, *Keeping the Faiths*, p. 172.

11. This list of recent developments in Soviet church life is compiled from personal interviews, news reports, and oral and written church reports.

12. Nikita S. Khrushchev, *Khrushchev Remembers*, trans. and ed. Strobe Talbott (Boston: Little, Brown and Company, 1970), pp. 261-62.

13. David Remnick, "Jewish Center Opens in Moscow," *The Washington Post*, February 13, 1989, p. B-1.

14. *Wrap-up Leadership Report*, National Conference on Soviet Jewry, March 1987, p. 3.

CHAPTER 10. ECUMENISM AND THE SUPER-POWERS

1. John Meyendorff, *The Orthodox Church*, Third Rev. Ed. (Crestwood, New York: St. Vladimir's Seminary Press, 1981), p. 225.

2. "Choose Life," Statement of U.S.S.R. and U.S. Church Representatives, Geneva, March 1979. Text published in Alan Geyer, *The Idea of Disarmament! Rethinking the Unthinkable*, Rev. Ed. (Elgin, Ill.: Brethren Press, 1986), pp. 219-23.

3. J. A. Hebly, *The Russians and the World Council of Churches* (Belfast: Christian Journals Limited, 1978), p. 35.
4. Ruth Rouse and Stephen Charles Neill, *A History of the Ecumenical Movement, 1517–1948* (Philadelphia: Westminster Press, 1954), p. 667.
5. Leon Howell, *Acting in Faith: The World Council of Churches Since 1975* (Geneva: World Council of Churches, 1982), p. 43.
6. "World Council Deplores Soviet Intervention," *The Christian Century*, Vol. LXXXV, No. 38, September 18, 1968, p. 1161.
7. Jane Ellis, *The Russian Orthodox Church: A Contemporary History* (London: Croom Helm, 1986), p. 359.
8. David Gill, ed., *Gathered for Life: Official Report VI Assembly, World Council of Churches* (Geneva: World Council of Churches, 1983), pp. 161-62.
9. "Choose Life," pp. 219-23.
10. A more detailed account of media responses to the NCC's 1984 seminar is found in Alan Geyer, "The NCC Takes Another Beating: The Media and the Russians," *Christianity and Crisis*, Vol. 44, No. 15, October 1, 1984, pp. 349-52. The author was a participant in the seminar.
11. Constance H. Jacquet, Jr., ed., *Yearbook of the American and Canadian Churches 1988* (Nashville: Abingdon Press, 1988), pp. 246-53.
12. Trevor Beeson, *Discretion and Valour: Religious Conditions in Russia and Eastern Europe*, Rev. Ed. (Philadelphia: Fortress Press, 1982), p. 244.
13. General Committee of CAREE, "A Response to the Statement of the Leadership of the Christian Peace Conference (January 22, 1980) Concerning the Military Intervention of the Soviet Union in Afghanistan," June 13, 1980 letter to the Christian Peace Conference.
14. Federal Bureau of Investigation, *Soviet Active Measures in the United States, 1986–7*, declassified text published in *The Congressional Record*, December 9, 1987, pp. E4720-21.

A THEOLOGICAL POSTSCRIPT

1. Jürgen Moltmann, *God in Creation* (San Francisco: Harper & Row, 1985); Sallie McFague, *Models of God: Theology for an Ecological, Nuclear Age* (Philadelphia: Fortress Press, 1987).
2. Archbishop Kirill of Smolensk, "Reconciliation in Europe—Heritage and Vision: The Ecology of the Spirit," address at European Ecumenical Assembly, Basel, May 15, 1989.
3. The Independent Commission on Disarmament and Security Issues, *Common Security: A Blueprint for Survival* (New York:

Simon and Schuster, 1982), p. 139: "States can no longer seek security at each other's expense: it can be attained only through cooperative undertakings. Security in the nuclear age means common security. Even ideological opponents and political rivals have a shared interest in survival. There must be partnership in the struggle against war itself. The search for arms control and disarmament is the pursuit of common gains, not unilateral advantage. *A doctrine of common security must replace the present expedient of deterrence through armaments. International peace must rest on a commitment to joint survival rather than a threat of national destruction.*"

4. The United Methodist Council of Bishops, *In Defense of `Creation: The Nuclear Crisis and a Just Peace* (Nashville: Graded Press, 1986), pp. 46, 48.

INDEX

ABM Treaty, 127-28, 132
Acheson, Dean, 11, 124
Adams, John Quincy, 66-67
Afghanistan, Soviet invasion
    of, 153-54
  and CAREE and CPC, 205-6
  and SALT II Treaty, 131-32
  and World Council of
    Churches, 198-99
Aitmatov, Chingiz, 24, 58-60
Alaska, 62-64, 67, 71-73
Alexander I, 43, 61, 63-67
Alexander II, 44
Alexander III, 44-45, 79
Arbatov, Georgi, 15, 20
Avvakum, Archpriest, 51

Baker, Russell, 153
Baptist Churches in U.S.S.R.,
    156, 166-68, 186-87
Baruch Plan, 120-21
Bell, Bishop George, 113-14
Bellah, Robert, 140-41
Bennett, John C., 171-72
Berdyaev, Nicholas, 61, 172
Berlin Blockade, 123-24
Berlin Wall, 119
Berman, Harold J., 15
Billington, James, 155, 163
Bloch, Ivan S., 76-77, 81

Bobrova, Nina, 181
Bonhoeffer, Dietrich, 113-14
Borovoy, Vitaly, 188
Boxer Rebellion, 75
Brandt, Willy, 127
Brest-Litovsk, Treaty of, 47, 84,
    86, 89
Brezhnev, Leonid, 129, 154, 180
Brzezinski, Zbigniew, 130
Bukharin, Nikolai, 79
Bullitt, William C., 91-92, 98
Bundy, McGeorge, 120
Bush, George, 18, 133-34
Butterfield, Herbert, 105
Byrnes, James F., 120

CAREE, 204-7
Carnegie, Andrew, 78
Carter, Jimmy, 130-32, 154
Catherine the Great, 42-43, 51,
    65, 144
Cheney, Richard B., 129
China
  and Jimmy Carter, 154
  Cold War in Asia, 124-25
  and Richard Nixon, 127
  U.S. Open Door Policy, 73-75
"Choose Life" Consultation,
    193, 199-200, 210-18

Christian Peace Conference, 32, 204-7
Churchill, Winston
  Big Three Conferences, 109
  British Minister of War, 86
  at Casablanca, 111
  and Eastern Europe, 116
  Iron Curtain speech, 108
  Paris Peace Conference, 90-91
Civil War, Russian, 48, 53-54, 83-89
Civil War, U.S., 68-70
Clemenceau, Georges, 86, 89-92
Colby, Bainbridge, 96
Comintern, 84, 100
Crimean War, 68-69
Cuban Missile Crisis, 126-27
Cyril, Saint, 38-39
Czechoslovakia
  and CAREE, 204-6
  and CPC, 204-6
  Czech Legion, 86-87
  and Marshall Plan, 123
  Munich crisis, 102
  Soviet invasion of, 123, 127, 197, 204-6
  Soviet Pact with (1935), 86-87, 100, 102

Davis, Henry Winter, 64-65
Decembrists, 43
Dostoevsky, Fyodor, 145-46
Dubceck, Alexander, 197
Dudko, Dimitri, 179
Dulles, John Foster, 30, 120, 122

Ecumenical Councils, Seven, 159-60
Eisenhower, Dwight D., 112, 126, 127
European Ecumenical Assembly, 139, 211-12

FBI, 206-8
Ford, Gerald, 129-30

France, 100-103
Franco, Francisco, 100-102

Gandhi, Mahatma, 152
Garthoff, Raymond, 154
Genoa Conference on Economic Recovery, 95-96
Germany
  Berlin Blockade and NATO, 123
  Berlin Wall, 119
  Genoa Conference, 95-96
  Ostpolitik of Willy Brandt, 127
  Paris Peace Conference, 89, 92
  Treaty of Brest-Litovsk, 47, 84, 86, 89
  Weimar Republic, 98-100
  and World War I, 47-48, 84, 86
  and World War II, 98-104, 106, 110-15, 117, 119, 137. *See also* Hitler, Adolf
Glasnost, 16, 20, 139, 151
Godunov, Boris, 50-51
Gorbachev, Mikhail S.
  on the arms race, 77
  and churches, 17, 39, 165, 174, 181-88
  disarmament initiatives of, 133
  and glasnost, 16, 139, 181-88. *See also* perestroika
  political leadership of, 18, 49
  and Pope John Paul II, 165
Gorchakov, Prince Alexander, 70
Graham, Billy, 30, 213
Graves, General William, 88
Gromyko, Andrei, 120-21

Halle, Louis
  on the Cold War, 107, 115
  on Russian behavior, 36
  on unconditional surrender, 112
  on U.S. Asian policy, 125

Hammer, Armand, 94
Harriman, W. Averell, 118
Harrington, Michael, 46
Hay, John, 74-75
Helsinki Final Act, 129
Herman, Saint, 73
Herzen, Alexander, 145
Hiroshima, 112-13, 119-20
Hitler, Adolf, 96, 99-104, 113-14
Hitler-Soviet Pact, 32, 96, 103
Holmes, Oliver Wendell, 70-71
Hoover, Herbert, 92-94, 97
Hromádka, Josef, 197, 204-205
Hubbs, Joanna, 149

Icons, 163-64
INF Treaty, 16, 130, 133
Institute on Religion and De-
    mocracy, 28, 29, 30, 207
Ivan III (the Great), 41
Ivan IV (the Terrible), 41-42, 50

Jackson, Henry M., 190
Jackson-Vanik Amendment,
    190-91
Japan, 73-76, 97, 112, 116
Jefferson, Thomas, 61, 65,
Jews
    anti-Soviet attitudes of, 31-32
    emigration, 78-79, 132, 189-
        91
    and glasnost, 188-91
    and the Holocaust, 50, 90
    pogroms against, 52, 78-79
    population in U.S.S.R., 157-
        58
John XXIII, Pope, 31
John Paul II, Pope, 165
Johnson, Lyndon B., 127

Kaiser, Robert, 149
Kennan, George F.
    on anti-Soviet attitudes, 25,
        83, 153-54
    and containment, 121-22
    foreign service training of, 26
    and Korean War, 124

and Long Telegram, 121, 138
and Marshall Plan, 122
on NSC-68, 126
on Russian Civil War, 88-89
on Weimar Republic, 100
on World War I, 80-81
Kennedy, John F., 106, 127
Kerensky, Alexander, 47, 53,
    84, 87
KGB, 206-8
Kharechev, Konstantin M.,
    182-85
Khrushchev, Nikita S.
    on anti-Semitism, 188-89
    cultural "thaw" of, 139
    death of first wife, 54
    and religion, 175-77, 182, 196
    U.S. visit of, 127
    U-2 and Paris Summit, 126
Kiev, 37-41
King, Admiral Ernest J., 110
Kirill, Archbishop, 139, 199,
    211-12
Kishkovsky, Leonid, 203
Kissinger, Henry, 128-30
Kolchak, Admiral, 86-87
Korean War, 124-25

League of Nations, 22, 93, 100,
    102
Lend-Lease Aid, 109-11, 118
Lenin, V. I.
    and William C. Bullitt, 91
    as cult figure, 150
    Decree on Peace, 80
    New Economic Policy, 48, 94
    Paris Peace Conference, 90
    on religion, 172-74
    as revolutionary, 45-49, 54,
        79, 84, 100
    on the Russian Revolution,
        35
Leningrad (St. Petersburg), 38,
    42-47, 52
    siege of, 55-56, 146-47
Leonard, James, 25-26
Lincoln, Abraham, 69-70

Lincoln, Bruce, 53
Lippmann, Walter, 106
Litvinov, Maxim, 97-98, 102-3
Lloyd George, David, 90-91

MacArthur, General Douglas, 124
McCarthyism, 27, 101, 115
McKinley, William, 74
Madison, James, 66
Manchuria, 75-76, 97
Mao Zedong, 32, 124
Marshall, George, 121-22
Marshall Plan, 119, 122-23
Marx, Karl
  philosophy of, 46
  on religion, 170-71
Marxism-Leninism, 46, 150-52, 180
Massie, Suzanne, 57-58, 142
Meyendorff, John, 162, 193
Mikhoels, Solomon, 188-89
Miller, Wright, 135-36, 138-39, 141-42
MIRVs, 128
Molotov, V. M., 103, 118
Mongols (Tartars), 40-41, 50, 144
Monroe Doctrine, 62-63, 67
Moscow, 38, 41
Muslims, 157

Napoleon, 66
National Conference of Catholic Bishops, 28, 31
National Council of Churches
  attacks on, 28, 201-2, 207
  Orthodox churches in, 203
  and U.S.S.R. churches, 199-202
NATO, 31, 123-24
Nead, Don, 200
Nechayev, Sergei, 46, 146
Nevsky, Alexander, 40
Nicholas I, 43, 145
Nicholas II, 44, 48, 75-78, 80
Niebuhr, Reinhold, 30, 103, 148

Nikodim, Metropolitan, 205
Nikon, Patriarch, 51, 144
Nitze, Paul, 126
Nixon, Richard
  and anti-communism, 115
  and China, 130
  election of (1968), 197
  SALT Talks, 127-29, 197-98
Novgorod, 37-38, 50

Open Door Policy, 74-75, 76

Palme Commission, 214
Pamyat, 189
Paris Peace Conference, 84, 89-93
Perestroika, 16, 77, 139, 151, 181
Perle, Richard, 132
Peter the Great, 42, 51, 73, 144, 170
Philippines, 73-74
Pierce, Franklin, 68-69
Pimen, Patriarch, 177-78, 183, 184, 187
Pius XI, Pope, 31
Pius XII, Pope, 101-2, 109-10
Podhoretz, Norman, 32
Poland, 103, 116, 117, 154
Potsdam Conference, 109
Pugachev, Emelian, 51

Rapallo Treaty, 95-96
Rasputin, Valentin, 24, 152
Reagan, Ronald
  administration of, 16-17, 26, 132-33
  and churches, 17, 184
  and SALT II, 129
Revolution, Soviet, 44-48, 79-81, 83-85
Revolution, U.S., 65
Rigdon, V. Bruce, 200
Robb, Edmund, 30-31
Rodzianko, Bishop Basil, 184
Roman Catholic Church
  and National Council of Churches, 200-201

in U.S., 28, 31
in U.S.S.R., 156, 164-65, 186
Romanov Dynasty, 42-49
Roosevelt, Franklin Delano
and William C. Bullitt, 92, 98
last months, 115-18
Lend-Lease Aid to U.S.S.R., 109-10
recognition of U.S.S.R., 97-98
and religious freedom in U.S.S.R., 97-98
and Stalin, 109-12, 114-18
unconditional surrender policy, 111-13
Roosevelt, Theodore, 76
Roshak, Michael, 203
Rublev, Andrei, 41, 184
Rurik, 37, 42
Russian Orthodox Church
churches in Alaska, 23, 63, 73
and East-West schism, 160-61
membership, 156
Millennium of, 16, 17, 38, 39, 158, 181-88, 203
origins of, 158-59
and Russian culture, 38-39, 148, 155
Soviet policy toward, 172-80, 181-88
and World Council of Churches, 196, 198-99
and worship, 142, 155, 161-64
Russo-Japanese War, 75-76

Sakharov, Andrei, 135, 140
Salisbury, Harrison, 55-56
SALT I, 127-28
SALT II Treaty, 23, 129-32, 199
Sergei, Metropolitan (later Patriarch), 175, 183
Sergius IV, Pope, 160-61
Sergius of Radonezh, Saint, 40-41
Seward, William, 72-73
Shevardnadze, Eduard, 16

Shultz, George, 15-16
Solzhenitsyn, Alexander, 178
Spanish-American War, 73-74
Spanish Civil War, 100-102
Stalin, Joseph
and anti-Semitism, 188-89
and churches, 174-76
collectivization of agriculture, 54, 142
on Constitution (1936), 83
and Korean War, 124
and Marshall Plan, 122-23
and Nazism, 99-104
personality cult of, 150
purges by, 54, 55-56
and Franklin Roosevelt, 109-12, 114-18
Stalingrad (Volgograd), 55, 137, 149
Steffens, Lincoln, 91
Stevenson, Adlai E., 105
Stoeckl, Baron Edouard de, 72
Strategic Defense Initiative, 132

Talbott, Strobe, 132
Taylor, Myron C., 109-10
Tchaadayev, Peter, 145
Tikhon, Patriarch, 73, 169, 172-74
Tocqueville, Alexis de, 64, 107
Tolstoy, Leo, 52
Toth, Karoly, 205-6
Trifonov, Yuri, 24, 35-36
Trotsky, Leon, 47, 79, 84
Truman, Harry
aid to U.S.S.R., 118
atomic bomb, 119-20
Cold War policies, 32, 108-9, 118-20, 125
Japan policy, 125
and Korean War, 124-25

Ugolnik, Anthony, 164
Ukrainian Catholics, 164-65
Ulyanov, Alexander, 45
Unconditional surrender, 111-14

Unification Church, 31
United Methodist Church, 29
    Council of Bishops of, 31,
        162-63, 211, 215
U-2 incident, 126

Varangians, 37
Vietnam War, 125, 127, 153
Vladimir, Prince, 38, 158, 181

War of 1812, 62, 66
Warsaw Pact, 127
Weimar Republic, 98-100, 104
Whitman, Walt, 135
Wiesel, Elie, 189
Wilson, Woodrow
    Fourteen Points, 90
    and League of Nations, 93
    at Paris Peace Conference,
        90-93

on recognition on Soviet
    Union, 96
and Russian Civil War, 86-88
and Russian Revolution, 80
World Council of Churches
    attacks on, 28, 31
    and Soviet churches, 194-99,
        211
World Disarmament Confer-
    ence, 77-78
World War I, 47, 52-54, 77,
    80-81, 84-88
World War II, 54-56, 106, 109-20

Yakunin, Gleb, 176-77, 198
Yalta Conference, 109, 115-17
Yaroslav the Wise, 39
Yevtushenko, Yevgeny, 140

Zernov, Nicholas, 35, 56, 155